INDIAN RIVER JUNIOR COLLEGE LIBRARY
FORT PIERCE, FI

D0982380

PR
4753

7813

Weber
    Hardy of Wessex.

HARDY OF WESSEX

Thomas Hardy.

7813

By CARL J. WEBER

HARDY

OF WESSEX

His Life and Literary Career

PK
473

ARCHON BOOKS

Hamden Connecticut

INDIAN RIVER JUNIOR COLLEGE LIBRARY
FORT PIERCE, FLORIDA

COPYRIGHT, 1940, BY COLUMBIA UNIVERSITY PRESS, NEW YORK
MANUFACTURED IN THE UNITED STATES OF AMERICA
REPRINTED 1962 WITH PERMISSION

THIS EDITION INCLUDES A LIST
OF ADDENDA AND CORRI-
GENDA FOLLOWING THE INDEX.

PREFACE

THE BIRTH of Thomas Hardy on June 2, 1840, is easily the most significant event calling for centennial commemoration in the year 1940. No author born within the last hundred years has made so deep an impression upon the minds and hearts of his readers. Hardy has been the most voluminously discussed writer of modern times, and a memorial publication might easily be justified if it did no more than offer a synthesis of the thousands of books, articles, dissertations, studies, critiques, and annotations which testify to the important position he holds in the modern world. The present volume, however, while offering such a synthesis, attempts something more, for it has been written with the conviction that no account of Hardy's career has yet been published which adequately recognizes the specific problem confronting the biographer of a man of letters.

This problem is not the same as that which faces one writing a life of a man of affairs. In order to explain and illuminate works of the imagination a different kind of treatment is needed from that used to explain the characteristic deeds of a statesman, a soldier, or a manufacturer. In dealing with an author emphasis must be placed upon those facts which determine his emotional personality, for from them emerge his writings. Above all, the biographer must remain keenly alert to detect those radical discords which result in literary activity. His task is to unravel the psychological complexity and unrest that find release in a work of art. In every author's heart there is, as in Hamlet's, a kind of fighting that will not let him sleep. It is the duty of his biographer to discover the causes and effects of the author's adjustment or maladjustment to his world. These causes cannot be discovered in a record of the houses the author lived in, in an account of his travels, in a chronicle of how he danced with Lady This or dined with Lord That, or in the merely external features of an outwardly quiet life. One must penetrate into the inner life of the man, learn what he read and what he thought, inspect his secret desires and ambitions, and study his rebuffs and disappointments. The literary biographer's task is not so much to appraise the pearl as to explain why the oyster grew it. This is often hard to do.

Until recently it has been impossible to penetrate far into the inner life of Thomas Hardy, but the time has now come when the attempt can be made. Access to hundreds of his unpublished letters has facilitated the present study and has often permitted the turning of surmise into dogmatic statement or denial. Hardy, his first wife, and his second wife are no longer living, and there are no children or immediate family to embarrass the wholly objective treatment that an author of his stature deserves. On this centennial occasion, therefore, it is possible for the first time to trace the literary career of the man with intimacy and assurance. The pages that follow attempt to tell why Thomas Hardy wrote, why he wrote on the subjects he chose, and how his books grew from ideas and emotions and experiences to printed volumes. This is the genetic method. For an intimate and thorough understanding of the masterpieces of literature there is no better.

Grateful acknowledgment is here made of my indebtedness to Mrs. Hardy's two-volume biography of her husband, and to the Hardy studies of A. S. McDowall, H. C. Duffin, H. Lea, S. C. Chew, and W. R. Rutland. I regret that space does not permit me to name the many others whose work has made my own the easier. For inquiries patiently answered, for information generously supplied, for numerous and varied services and courtesies I am deeply grateful to dozens of individuals here unnamed, to whom, like Shakespeare's Sebastian,

> I can no other answer make but thanks,
> And thanks, and ever thanks.

There are a few, however, to whom my obligations are of such magnitude or of such long-continued duration that their names must be given: Mr. Frederick B. Adams, Jr., of New York City; Mr. R. Borregaard, barrister of the Inner Temple, London; Dr. Edward Hodnett, of Columbia University; Professor Richard L. Purdy, of Yale University; Mr. E. N. Sanders, of Parkstone, Dorset; Mr. Carroll A. Wilson, of New York City; and my wife, Clara Carter Weber. To the second Mrs. Hardy I am indebted for the copy of the manuscript reproduced on pages 209-10, and I acknowledge with thanks the kind permission of the Trustees of the Hardy copyrights (Lloyds Bank, London, and Miss Irene Cooper Willis) to quote from Hardy's *Collected Poems* and from Mrs. Hardy's *Early Life* and *Later Years of Thomas Hardy*. To the President and Trustees of Colby College I am gratefully indebted for a leave of absence from college duties—a welcome relief which made possible the completion of this writing in time for the centenary of Hardy's birth.

CARL J. WEBER

Colby College
Waterville, Maine
January 20, 1940

CONTENTS

ILLUSTRATIONS

HARDY OF WESSEX

"And one was Lord of the Wessex Coast
and all the lands thereby."

KIPLING IN "THE THREE CAPTAINS"

I

BIRTH AND BOYHOOD AT
BOCKHAMPTON

O N JANUARY 10, 1840, that great benefaction, Sir Roland Hill's penny postage, began its ministrations to mankind, and the world's first postage stamps were issued. Every stamp collector is familiar with the girlish portrait of Queen Victoria on that new postal device, which Hill called "a bit of paper just large enough to bear the stamp and covered at the back with a glutinous wash." Queen Victoria herself remembered the year 1840 less for her appearance upon the first postage stamp than for her appearance before the altar on February 10 to marry Albert.

A hundred miles or so from London a humble English household occupied a small but comfortable brick house with a thatched roof in a secluded spot in Dorsetshire. "It was a spot which returned upon the memory of those who loved it with an aspect of peculiar and kindly congruity. The vast tract of unenclosed wild known as Egdon Heath wore the appearance of a thing majestic without severity, impressive without showiness, emphatic in its admonitions, grand in its simplicity. The qualifications which frequently invest the façade of a prison with far more dignity than is found in the façade of a palace double its size lent to this heath a sublimity in which spots renowned for beauty of the accepted kind are utterly wanting. Haggard Egdon was a place perfectly accordant with man's nature—neither ghastly, hateful, nor ugly: neither commonplace, unmeaning, nor tame; but, like man, slighted and enduring; and withal singularly colossal and mysterious in its swarthy monotony. As with some persons who have long lived apart, solitude seemed to look out of its countenance. It had a lonely face, suggesting tragical possibilities."

On the edge of this heath there stood in 1840 a few dwellings known as the hamlet of Upper Bockhampton, in the parish of Stinsford, Dorset. Stinsford lies about a mile east of Dorchester, and Upper Bockhampton is about two miles east of Stinsford. The houses lined either side of a narrow lane shaded by cherry trees, and in the easternmost thatched dwelling lived Mr. and Mrs. Thomas Hardy, 29 and 27 years of age. Thomas Hardy was a master mason, or building contractor, as we would now say. He and his wife Jemima were occupying the house built in 1801 by Thomas's grandfather, John Hardy, of Puddletown— built for his son, the first Thomas Hardy of Upper Bockhampton, upon the occasion of Thomas's marriage. Thomas I had died in 1837, three years before Thomas II handed the name on to the future novelist, Thomas III. Here, then, on the edge of Egdon Heath, with its "lonely face suggesting tragical possibilities," the Hardys went about their humble activities, awaiting, like their Queen, the arrival of their first-born son.

The baby, born on June 2, 1840, was so frail as to be at first supposed to be dead. Rescued, however, by the family nurse, the child survived and lived to make famous a name that eighty-eight years later was carved into a stone in Westminster Abbey. In spite of obscurity of birth, of deficiency of education, of discouragement and misrepresentation, by sheer imaginative genius and by the power of an artist's pen the frail infant born on the edge of Egdon Heath gained for himself a final resting place among England's greatest.

When that baby of June, 1840, was almost six months old, another birth took place in a neighboring part of England—in the historic Devon town of Plymouth.

> Ah, that is the place
> Where chanced, in the hollow of years ago, . . .
> The birth of a little girl of grace—
> The sweetest the house saw, first or last; . . .
> There, there she lay
> In a room by the Hoe, like the bud of a flower.

"The house" stood on York Street. There, on November 24, 1840, a solicitor named John Attersoll Gifford and his wife, Emma Farman, welcomed into the world "a little girl of grace" whom they named Emma Lavinia. Thirty years later she was to see for the first time the baby boy born on the edge of Egdon Heath, and years after that meeting he was to write about her the poem "Places" from which the lines just quoted are taken.

Several points are worth mentioning in connection with the birth of Thomas Hardy in 1840. First of all, "Egdon Heath"—to call it by the name he afterwards gave to Puddletown Heath—became one of the earliest influences upon his mind. He celebrated its austere dignity not only in *The Return of the Native*, from which the description quoted above is taken, but also in book after book. He learned to love "the enormous Egdon Waste"; and when later on he came to write, it never failed to stir in him the emotional glow of early association. The significance of this for Thomas Hardy was grasped by one of his earliest critics, Lionel Johnson.

Most novelists [he wrote in 1894] are not at home among the places of their imagination; from first to last, they describe their woods and fields, not as long familiarity makes them appear, but as they appear to unaccustomed eyes: there is no heart in them. But Mr. Hardy has the art of impressing upon us so strong a sense of familiarity with his scenes, that we read of Wessex and we think of our own homes.

This familiarity dates from his birth in 1840.

Second, we must remember that Hardy's father's business as mason, or builder, placed the future author, in the England of a hundred years ago, in a very different social category from that into which Emma Gifford was born as the daughter of a Plymouth solicitor. In Chapter VIII of *A Pair of Blue Eyes* is a revealing conversation between Stephen Smith and Elfride Swancourt. While it need not be asserted that these two speak for Hardy and Miss Gifford, yet the conversation indicates sensitiveness to class distinctions on Hardy's part, which is rendered unmistakably clear by the frequency with which this sort of thing is found in the Wessex novels:

"Did you ever think what my parents might be, or what society I originally moved in?"

"No, not particularly. I suppose you have moved in the ordinary society of professional people."

"Supposing I have not—that none of my family have a profession except me?"

"I don't mind."

"Where do you think I went to school—I mean, to what kind of school?"

"Doctor Somebody's academy."

"No. To a dame school originally, then to a national school."

"Only to those! Well . . ."

"What do you think my father is—does for his living, that is to say?"

"He practices some profession or calling, I suppose."

"No; he is a mason . . ."

"O, Stephen! . . . I do own that it seems odd to regard you in the light of—of ——"

As Hardy grew older, English society made it impossible for him ever to forget his own position "in the light of what his father did for his living." His first novel was entitled *The Poor Man and the Lady*, in which the emphasis was upon the same social disparity. In *An Indiscretion in the Life of an Heiress* "this perception of their disparity weighed more and more heavily upon him as the days went on."

On the other hand, for at least three generations books had run in the family of Hardy's mother. Maria Childs, his great-grandmother, moved in literary circles and was the sister of a newspaper editor; his grandmother Elizabeth Swetman was known as an omnivorous reader and the possessor of an unusually large library for a yeoman's daughter. Some of her books descended to her daughter Jemima, to be passed on to her son Thomas, who afterward used the titles to indicate the books owned by Bathsheba and Gabriel Oak in *Far from the Madding Crowd*. Elizabeth's daughter Jemima was known, even as a girl, for her possession of exceptional ability and energy, for her fondness for reading and singing, and for judgment and skill shown in many ways. As in the case of Shakespeare, whose gifted mother traced her ancestry back to the Ardens of Park Hall, so Thomas Hardy owed much to his mother, Jemima Hand, who lived to be nearly ninety-one years old, for those abilities and interests which made him one of England's great authors.

HARDY'S BIRTHPLACE AT UPPER BOCKHAMPTON

On both sides of his family, however, the progression had been down ward. From a position regarded by Victorian society as more worthy— that of landed proprietorship—the descent to the low thatched house on the edge of Egdon Heath was one that Hardy found it hard to forget. Before writing his novel of the Durbeyfield family, degenerated from the ancient D'Urbervilles, he made a note in his journal regarding "the decline and fall of the Hardys. . . . So we go down, down, down."

On February 7, 1921, Hardy wrote to John Galsworthy suggesting the addition of a genealogical chart to the *Forsyte Saga,* which Hardy had been reading. He had found it hard to keep all the Forsyte relationships clear in his mind without the help of such a chart. The reader who shares this inability will find the Hardy family tree set down for the sake of similar clarity on page 235.

On the day of his birth one hundred years ago the stage was already set for molding and fashioning the mind of the future author. His Dorset schooling and his life in London are the only major influences not already present at the moment of his appearance, and even these two were implied; for the modest circumstances of the Hardys made almost inevitable the sort of schooling the future novelist received, and the mason's trade led directly to Hardy's apprenticeship to an architect, and that in turn took him to London. Arnold Bennett once remarked to Hugh Walpole: "My dear Hugh, when you're born, you're done for!" Thomas Hardy's birth and all the circumstances attendant upon that second day of June, 1840, are an excellent illustration of the truth of Bennett's jest.

The house in which Hardy was born is still standing; and, although Egdon Heath beyond it is no longer "the untameable Ishmaelitish thing" that it seemed to be in Hardy's boyish eyes, the garden before the birthplace has seen little change. "A little wicket admitted to the garden, and a path led up to the house. It was a long low cottage with a hipped roof of thatch, having dormer windows breaking up into the eaves, a chimney standing in the middle of the ridge and another at the further end." Since these words from *Under the Greenwood Tree* were written in the house where he was born, Hardy was probably describing his own home. A still earlier word picture of the birthplace is given in his poem "Domicilium," written before he was twenty. This poem, consisting of thirty-four lines of Wordsworthian blank verse, is not given in the *Collected Poems*. It was privately printed in 1916 by C. K. Shorter in a seven-page booklet and was reprinted in Mrs. Hardy's *Early Life*. Hardy always objected when his home was called "a humble cottage." It was a low thatched building; but, he urged, it was nevertheless a rambling and spacious house.

Here he spent the first seven years of his life in unhurried idleness. The time was not wasted, however, for the boy's eyes and ears were wide open. He learned to know the birds and the clouds, the snails and the toads, the spiders and the sheep. Once he pretended to be a sheep. Getting down on all fours he crawled out into the field and pretended to eat grass. For the rest of his life he remembered his own surprise when, on looking up, he found himself encircled by real sheep staring at him in perplexed wonder at this new member of the fold. Nor was the animal world the only part of nature to arouse his interest, for from his father the boy learned to look lovingly upon the mysterious countenance of Egdon Heath.

Tom's physical frailty led his parents to lose hope of his ever attaining to maturity, and he was therefore not sent to school at the usual age. When, however, he had become eight years old, he seemed strong enough to walk to the school at Bockhampton, and there he began his studies. Reading, writing, arithmetic, and geography all came to him so easily from the very start that his mother wished for him better instruction than was available in the village school. In 1849 he was accordingly transferred to a day school in Dorchester conducted by Isaac G. Last. For the next seven years, small and delicate though he was, Hardy had a daily walk of three miles each way to "Mr. Last's Academy for Young Gentlemen." After three years he began the study of Latin, and in 1853 he was reading Eutropius and Caesar. He continued to outstrip his classmates in the academy, and won a copy of Beza's Latin Testament as a school prize.

Life was not all study for the boy. One day his father was driving to Weymouth on business and took Tom along as a treat. At this time Edmund Gosse was a boy of four in Weymouth. Years later these two friends enjoyed figuring out how near they had come to seeing each other as boys in Dorset.

Strict and regular attendance at church services at Stinsford on Sunday resulted in Hardy's learning the morning and evening services by heart. Thomas Hardy, Senior, had helped in earlier years to supply the church music, and the son now followed his father in learning to play the violin. From his mother he received copies of Dryden's *Virgil* and two samples of eighteenth-century fiction—Johnson's *Rasselas* and Bernardin de Saint-Pierre's *Paul and Virginia*. When he was fifteen, private lessons in French were added to the ordinary school curriculum, and with his mother's ambitious encouragement he attempted to teach himself German by subscribing to Cassell's *Popular Educator*. He began to read Dumas and Shakespeare and a history of the wars with Napoleon. He also read *Pilgrim's Progress* and was so alarmed by the description of Apollyon that for the next seventy-five years he remembered his dread of the solitary walk back to Bockhampton in the dark because of his fear that Apollyon would spring out at him. One of his favorite books was *The Scottish Cavalier* (1850), by James Grant, the military novelist. Seventy years later Hardy still retained (so he told S. M. Ellis) vivid memories of the scenes and characters in this now-forgotten romance. The Waverley Novels also received careful though unenthusiastic attention. G. P. R. James's *The Ancient Regime* was another book which Hardy read and liked. But the most powerful literary influence upon him in boyhood was William Harrison Ainsworth, and *Old St. Paul's* was his favorite romance. S. M. Ellis has reported that Hardy described to him an Ainsworth Tour of London which he had mapped out at the precocious age of nine. Later he liked Ainsworth's *Windsor Castle*, and at the age of seventy-three he acknowledged the gift of an illustrated copy by saying: "I am carried back to the days of my boyhood." Another of Ainsworth's novels, *Rookwood,* was one of the most popular novels of Hardy's youth. *Windsor Castle* resulted in his falling temporarily in love with a girl from Windsor; and the hero of *Rookwood*, Dick Turpin, reappears in a sensational chapter of *Far from the Madding Crowd*. Saint-Pierre and Dumas, Grant, James, and Ainsworth—all these names are worth keeping in mind, if one is interested in tracing Hardy's predilection for romantic tales of fair ladies and moonlight meetings, mysterious horsemen and secret marriages, Gothic casements and unlucky accidents.

In addition to absorbing these bookish tastes, Hardy was learning directly from people. During those apparently idle years at Bockhampton he came to know and admire the shepherd whose portrait he later painted as Gabriel Oak in *Far from the Madding Crowd*. Mrs. Hardy's sister, whom young Thomas and his mother visited at Puddletown, appears in the same novel as Bathsheba Everdene. Even in these early years he had learned to look understandingly upon Dorset rustics; and their speech, gait, habits, and ideas became as vividly fixed in his retentive memory as did the tunes he learned to play upon his violin.

These tunes he knew only less well than those which the Wessex winds played upon the trees in the woods through which he walked on his daily tramp between Bockhampton and Dorchester. That walk was often taken in the dark, when the uselessness of eyes increased the keenness of ears. He soon learned that "almost every species of tree has its voice as well as its feature. At the passing of the breeze the fir-trees sob and moan no less distinctly than they rock; the holly whistles as it battles with itself; the ash hisses ámid its quaverings; the beech rustles while its flat boughs rise and fall."

When Hardy was fifteen, he began to teach in the Stinsford Sunday School. In this way he not only increased his familiarity with the characters and the phraseology of the Bible and the Prayer Book but also learned to know the vicar, and the vicar's sons, and the dairymaids, and the farmers, and the tranters—all of whom were later to appear in the Wessex Novels. Marian, in *Tess*, was one of the dairymaids in Hardy's Sunday School class; and the numerous clergymen who appear in Hardy's writings, from Mr. Maybold in *Under the Greenwood Tree* down to the Reverend Mr. Clare and his clerical sons in *Tess*, are traceable to actual personalities.

Hardy also learned things from Dorchester. It was no ordinary or average small town but one that possessed unusual features, some of them extremely impressive. There was, for instance, "the Ring."

[This was] the local name of one of the finest Roman Amphitheatres, if not the very finest, remaining in Britain. The Amphitheatre was a huge circular enclosure, with a notch at opposite extremities of its diameter north and south. From its sloping internal form it might have been called the spittoon of the Jötuns. It was to Casterbridge what the ruined Coliseum is to modern Rome, and was nearly of the same magnitude.

There were other marks of age in Dorchester. In one of the little-used alleys of the town was an ancient doorway, the keystone of the arch of which was a mask.

Originally the mask had exhibited a comic leer, but generations of Caster-bridge boys had thrown stones at the mask, aiming at its open mouth; and the blows thereon had chipped off the lips and jaws as if they had been eaten away by disease. The appearance was so ghastly that one could not bear to look at it.

There were other sights in Dorchester to keep the keystone company. During Hardy's schooldays a woman was publicly hanged for murder. The boy from Bockhampton was on hand, along with all the rest of Dorchester, to see the execution. The night before that impressive event Hardy went down to the hangman's cottage, climbed up on the railing, and looked in to see that grim agent of the law placidly eating his supper. These events lodged in his memory to be dug up many years later.

The boy's daily walk between Bockhampton and Dorchester gave him an opportunity to study faces and to read character. As he approached the town he had to cross two bridges. The first one he came to was built of stone. The second, at the end of High Street, was of weatherstained brick. It was not the bridges themselves, however, that attracted his attention, but the people he learned to associate with them.

To this pair of bridges gravitated all the failures of the town. There was a marked difference of quality between the personages who haunted the near bridge of brick, and the personages who haunted the far bridge of stone. Those of lowest character preferred the former, adjoining the town; they did not mind the glare of the public eye. The *misérables* who would pause on the remoter bridge were of a politer stamp. They included the shabby-genteel men. The eyes of this species were mostly over the parapet upon the running water below. While one in straits on the townward bridge did not mind who saw him so, and kept his back to the parapet to survey the passers-by, one in straits on the stone bridge never faced the road, never turned his head at coming footsteps, but watched the current whenever a stranger approached.

They little suspected how much a little boy who passed them every day was taking in.

In later life Hardy remarked that he had remained a child until he was sixteen. While this was true as far as experience and the development of initiative and resourcefulness are concerned, Hardy's mind and sympathies, like his knowledge and insight, were far from being those of a child when his schooling came to an end shortly after his sixteenth birthday. For one who had had only eight years of formal instruction, he had accomplished amazing things. He had read extensively in English, French, and Latin; and in reading the book of nature he had unwittingly become an expert. When he left Mr. Last's academy in June, 1856, he may have been timid and retiring—like Wordsworth he had learned to know perhaps too well the self-sufficing power of solitude—but in mental equipment he was as far along toward maturity as many a modern boy ready to enter an American college.

II

ARCHITECTURE IN TOWN
AND CITY

A T LEAST ONE person besides Hardy's mother had detected the boy's unusual powers. His name was John Hicks. Mr. Hicks was a Dorchester architect whose plans Thomas Hardy, Senior, had often been called on to carry out in his building contracts. Hicks had observed the intelligent skill shown by young Thomas in occasionally helping his father, and he offered to take the boy as an apprentice. This settled a problem that had been facing the Hardy family for some time.

His early physical frailty had unfitted Tom for practical household duties; and the only suggestion regarding his future that had emerged from his observed tendencies and aptitudes was that he might make a parson. As a boy he learned to recite hymns with great fervency; he soon knew all the church responses; and when, as a little fellow, he had been allowed to stay home from church on wet Sunday mornings under the tolerant eye of his grandmother, he would wrap a tablecloth around his little body, to imitate the vicar's surplice; and then, standing on a chair, he would read the morning service and even "preach a sermon" by repeating some of the admonitions of the vicar. He had his favorite passages in the Bible; one of them was: "and after the fire a still small voice." His teaching in the Stinsford Sunday School and his association with the vicar's two sons had likewise contributed to the thought that Tom might enter the Church. But entering the Church meant a university education and leaving home. Altogether, it was a vague and distant goal, which was further obscured from the vision of the Hardys by the amount of money that would be required for going to Oxford or Cambridge and by Tom's physical immaturity. The proposal of John Hicks, therefore, settled the matter. His ambition to become a clergyman Tom kept to himself. Hardy's friend of later years, Sir James M. Barrie, once remarked: "Whatever angel guards the portals of Elysium, he must have had to push Thomas Hardy in!" No angel was on hand to push him into holy orders. Instead, in July, 1856, he entered the office of John Hicks, architect, at 39 South Street, Dorchester.

For the next four years the daily walk back and forth between Bockhampton and Dorchester continued, often in the dark; and the reading of books, both in English and in Latin, also continued. For in the architect's office Hardy found two other boys with bookish interests, and thanks to them architecture was not allowed to monopolize his time. By getting up at five, or in summer even at four o'clock, Hardy accomplished a great deal of reading before having to begin his hour's walk to the office. Virgil, Horace, and Ovid were thus added to the list of authors he knew. Then, as if his day were not already full enough, he began the study of Greek. He progressed enough to read the *Iliad* and thus unlocked the door of another language whose influence on his own writings is easily traced.

One of the boys in Hick's office was named Henry Robert Bastow. In addition to encouraging Hardy's pursuit of classical studies, Bastow provided a stimulating influence upon Hardy's mind by his stout defense of Baptist doctrines. For the first time in his life Thomas Hardy found Church of England dogma questioned. The arguments that ensued, violent and noisy though they were, served to develop the intellectual fiber and independence of Hardy's mind; and when Bastow brought in two supporters, sons of the Dorchester Baptist minister, the Reverend Mr. Perkins, it was as good as a college course in philosophy for Hardy. More than thirty years later, he called those heated controversies to mind when writing *Tess of the D'Urbervilles.*

Another clergyman who exercised an influence upon Hardy's growing mind was the Reverend Henry Moule, for fifty years the Vicar of Fordington (in Dorchester). Hardy often attended services in Mr. Moule's church, and he spent many hours in the company of one or another of the vicar's seven sons. One of them, Charles, who after-

STINSFORD CHURCH

ward became President of Corpus Christi College, Cambridge, served Hardy as a model for Angel Clare in *Tess of the D'Urbervilles*. This use of his boyhood friend nearly a third of a century later is characteristic of the working of Hardy's mind. The boy's memory of the Reverend Henry Moule was even more enduring. Late in June, 1919, Hardy was reading the fourteenth chapter of the Book of Job, and when he came to the fourteenth verse, "All the days of my appointed time will I wait, till my change come," he remarked: "That was the text of the Vicar of Fordington one Sunday evening about 1860. I can hear his voice repeating the text, just as if it were yesterday." In William Hazlitt's famous essay on "My First Acquaintance with Poets" there is an account of how one cold January Sunday in 1798 young Hazlitt went to hear Coleridge preach. "When . . . Mr. Coleridge rose and gave out his text . . . which he pronounced loud, deep, and distinct, it seemed to me, who was then young, as if the sounds had echoed from the bottom of the human heart and . . . might have floated in solemn silence through the universe." In the same way Mr. Moule's text made a lasting impression upon young Hardy. His poem "Waiting Both," published in 1925 in *Human Shows*, is thus traceable to a boyhood experience sixty-five years earlier.

One of the results of the philosophical and theological arguments of the young apprentices in the architect's office was the study of the Greek New Testament. Hardy temporarily dropped Homer, just when he was becoming familiar with the Ionic dialect, and took up Biblical Greek in order the better to discuss infant baptism, vicarious atonement, and immortality. Somerset's defense of infant baptism in *A Laodicean* and Jude's study of theological Greek in *Jude the Obscure* are reminiscences of these days. By the time that the term of Bastow's apprenticeship was over, his fellow student had learned to stand on his own intellectual feet. This growth was signalized by the fact that young Hardy was among the first to read and to acclaim Darwin's *Origin of Species*. The little girl born in Plymouth, Emma Lavinia Gifford, was celebrating her nineteenth birthday on the day this epoch-making green-backed volume appeared, and the date always marked for her a purely personal anniversary.

Hardy would ordinarily have been ready to leave Hicks's instruction by the middle of 1860; but to his father and his mother he still seemed very young, and the term of his service was accordingly extended until the end of 1861. Hardy himself was not finding his apprenticeship arduous. In addition to working on Latin and Greek he interspersed evenings of playing the violin at country dances, Christmas parties, and the like with his architectonic duties. Thus, while his intellect was being whetted, the store of Wessex tradition was being heaped up in his memory—supplies for such future feasts as his account of the Christmas waits in *The Return of the Native*. The knowledge, the insight, and the power were all there; only one thing in this incubation of the writer was still lacking—the desire to write. And that was not long in making its appearance.

Next door to Hicks's draughting office in South Street was a school taught by the Reverend William Barnes. He was known throughout Dorset as the author of poems in the Dorset dialect, a third collection of which was published in 1862. Barnes was in the habit of contributing a poem once a week to the *Dorset County Chronicle*, published in Dorchester, and there Hardy read many of them as they appeared during his days of apprenticeship under John Hicks. One of these poems, "Woak Hill," quoted by Hardy in *Far from the Madding Crowd*, appeared in the *Chronicle* on March 6, 1862, a little more than a month before Hardy left Dorchester for London. Barnes's homely verses touched a responsive chord in the young architect; and when Hardy went up to London, a copy of Barnes went with him. In the city, finding that Barnes was unknown, Hardy played missionary, talked of the Dorset poet, and gave private readings from his poems. Some years later Hardy wrote a review of Barnes's *Poems of Rural Life* (the review appeared, unsigned, in the *New Quarterly Magazine* for October, 1879), and in 1886 he prepared an obituary notice of Barnes for the *Athenaeum*. Years later he edited a selection of the poems of Barnes for the Oxford University Press. Among the poems, he included one entitled "Blaake's House in Blackmwore." From this poem the imitative step is not a great one to the verses descriptive of Hardy's own native dwelling—the poem

"Domicilium" referred to on page 8. This is the earliest extant piece of Hardy's verse. Written before 1860, it shows that Hardy had already caught fire. Of prime importance is the fact, so often over-looked by readers of Hardy and sometimes by his critics too, that his first creative impulse was toward poetry, not fiction. His early delight in music and dancing, his violin playing, and his admiring interest in what William Barnes had accomplished with the Dorset dialect all combined to foster in Hardy's mind an irresistible desire to write. But when he felt thus impelled, it was, not romantic novels, but lyric poems that stirred in him. And whenever people talked to him, later, about literary technique, he was always surprised to discover that they meant his prose technique, not the poetry with which his impulse to write began. Years later he remarked to Hamlin Garland:

Many nice Americans take the trouble to call. Recently, several professors of English literature came down from London. One of the latest of these tourists left a book he had written on *The Technique of Thomas Hardy*. Upon reading it, I found he had made no reference to my technique as a poet. There isn't any technique about prose, is there? It just comes along of itself.

At any rate, before leaving Hicks's office Hardy had tried his hand at descriptive verse. At the end of 1861 or early in the year 1862, when his term of instruction expired, he left the architect's office with a trained draughting hand, a well-stocked mind, a keen intellect, a sympathetic understanding of life in and near Dorset, an eye and ear for the beauties of nature, a wide acquaintance with the literature of four languages, and a desire to write. What did he lack? Knowledge of London and of science. Both of these came after his departure from Dorset.

Talking of Exhibitions, World's Fairs, and what not, I would not go round the corner to see a dozen of them nowadays. The only exhibition that ever made any impression upon my imagination was the first of the series, the parent of them all—the Great Exhibition of 1851, in Hyde Park, London. None of the younger generation can realize the sense of novelty it produced in us who were then in our prime. For South Wessex, the year formed in many ways an extraordinary chronological frontier or transit-line, at which there occurred what one might call a precipice in Time. As in a geological "fault," we had presented to us a sudden bringing of ancient and modern into absolute contact, such as probably in no other single year since the Conquest was ever witnessed in this part of the country.

These words are from the beginning of Hardy's story "The Fiddler of the Reels" (*Scribner's Magazine,* May, 1893). Although they refer to the Great Exhibition of 1851, they express accurately enough the part that the following London Exhibition, in 1862, played in the life of Thomas Hardy. The Great Exhibition of 1851, originating in a suggestion of Prince Albert at a meeting of the Society of Arts, had been a gigantic success. The Crystal Palace built in Hyde Park to house the industrial exhibits survived, on another site, until some years after Hardy's death. In 1861 Albert proposed an international exhibition in London on an even larger scale and was busy with plans for its realization when typhoid fever carried him off. In spite of this loss, the exhibition was held; and on the day of its opening a twenty-one-year-old young man from Bockhampton and Dorchester was there to have presented to him that "sudden bringing of ancient and modern into absolute contact." For the Dorset he left behind was still, in spite of the new railroad, an ancient land. The Roman Ring, the decaying buildings, the "grizzled" Gothic churches, the Tudor manor-houses were not the sole reminders of the links between Wessex and the past. The speech and attire of the agricultural laborers whom Hardy had learned to know, their superstitions and folklore, their county fairs and holiday dances showed so little change since the time of Shakespeare that the young man from Wessex would have been more at home in the Stratford of Queen Elizabeth's day than he was in the London of the widowed Queen Victoria.

Somewhat shabbily dressed, with a ruddy out-door complexion and a dark moustache, Hardy arrived in London on April 17, 1862, carrying a letter from John Hicks to an architect friend of his, John Norton. Norton made a job in his draughting office for Hardy until the latter could find better employment, and before the month was over this turned up unsought. There came to Norton an inquiry from another

London architect, Arthur Blomfield, for a young draughtsman who
could design churches and other Gothic restorations. Norton recommended Hardy for the position, and on May 5, 1862, Hardy became
Blomfield's assistant. For the rest of 1862 he worked at 8 St. Martin's
Place; in the following year he moved with Blomfield to larger offices
on the second floor of 8 Adelphi Terrace. Thus he found himself for
the first time a self-supporting professional man.

Meanwhile he had not neglected the Exhibition. After his first
visit he repeatedly returned, and throughout the summer of 1862 would
"generally run down to the Exhibition for an hour in the evening two
or three times a week." In August he spent half a day there; even that
was not time enough. There was so much to see, so much to store up
for future use. For instance, the automatic substitutes for human limbs,
designed by a clever Swiss mechanician named Jacquet Droz, came to
mind ten years later when Hardy was describing Fanny's painful
walk in *Far from the Madding Crowd*. He "tried the Underground
Railway one day," and wrote home that "everything is excellently
arranged." Everything in London was new to him. After the Exhibition
was all over, he continued his visits to what Londoners called the
"Brompton Boilers"—iron sheds used until the South Kensington
Museum had been built. One of the results of these visits was the essay
with which Hardy won the Royal Institute prize.

No wonder the year 1862 "formed in many ways an extraordinary
chronological frontier." Not only had he exchanged ancient Wessex for
modern London, the sight of manual agricultural employments for
industrial and mechanical "arts," the two old bridges over the Froom
for the new Charing Cross Bridge and the Victoria Embankment,
pupillage under Hicks for employment with Blomfield but also he had
left behind the trees in Yellowham Wood and the grasshoppers on
Egdon Heath, the familiar faces of dairymaids in Sunday School and
of fellow-apprentices in the office, the friendly greetings of folks who
for a dozen years had seen young Hardy pacing the highway between
Dorchester and Bockhampton, and the picturesque dialect of William
Barnes and of the master-mason's workmen. Hardy spoke with a
Dorset accent, and he knew the rural dialect, but as a boy he was not

permitted to speak it. His mother was too conscious of every mark of social inferiority to allow him to label himself by the rustic vocabulary. She herself spoke the dialect, but only to the Bockhampton cottagers. Hardy's father spoke it, but only to his workmen. The dialect was not used in the home. When young Thomas would inadvertently let drop some word picked up from the speech of his father's workmen, he was reprimanded. He had not forgotten these early lessons when, years later, he was writing *The Mayor of Casterbridge*:

> One grievous failing of Elizabeth's was her occasional pretty and picturesque use of dialect words—those terrible marks of the beast to the truly genteel.
> She happened to say, "Bide where you be a minute, father."
> " 'Bide where you be,' " he echoed sharply. "Good God, are you only fit to carry wash to a pig-trough, that ye use such words as those?"
> She reddened with shame and sadness.
> "I meant, 'Stay where you are,' father," she said, in a low, humble voice. "I ought to have been more careful."

In London Hardy had to be "more careful," for he was now on his own, and he found himself in a world where the pace was faster, friendly interest in others less possible, and competition keener if not ruthless. It was easy for a newcomer to feel a hostility in the atmosphere and to react unsympathetically to it.

Only one thing remained the same—Hardy's interest in books. He still found time to read and he still wanted to write. He was encouraged in this desire by the one Dorchester friend of bookish interests whom he was still able to see in London, Horace M. Moule, the fourth son of the Vicar of Fordington. Moule had gone from Dorchester to Queens' College, Cambridge, but his desire to become a reviewer often brought him to London; and in August, 1862, Hardy spoke of the possibility of Moule's coming and settling permanently in the city. The two talked of architecture and religion, of the classics and modern poets, of novelists and periodicals. Hardy read Ruskin's *Modern Painters* and wrote to his sister about Thackeray. "You must read something of his. He is considered to be the greatest novelist of the day. *Vanity Fair* is considered one of his best." *Vanity Fair* was written in

1846, but upon Thackeray's death in 1863 Hardy wrote as if his novel had not penetrated into Wessex—at least not to Bockhampton. The next year he was reading *Childe Harold*, John Stuart Mill's *On Liberty*, and Tom Moore's *Lalla Rookh*. When Newman's *Apologia* appeared, it revived religious discussions like those of Dorchester days. Moule rated the *Apologia* higher than Hardy thought its logic deserved.

In these early years in London, Hardy continued the practice begun with "Domicilium," and he now not only wrote poems but also sent them off to editors. "Oh, yes," he reminisced years later; "I sent much of my verse out; it invariably came back. No editors even touched it for many years." He tried his hand at Spenserian stanzas, but soon gave up this form. He tried Shakespearean sonnets and blank verse and Wordsworthian ballad forms. Even the poems with which he was somewhat satisfied were returned by the editors. It was Hardy's first literary setback. Years later he was to write:

> I sometimes think as here I sit
> Of things I have done,
> Which seemed in doing not unfit
> To face the sun:
> Yet never a soul has paused a whit
> On such—not one.

And in that "not one" may be heard the echo of Hardy's disappointment—his first reason for not finding life in London what he had expected or desired. With Emily Dickinson he might have said:

> I asked no other thing;
> No other was denied.

For in spite of his interest in Greek and theology and architecture the one goal that Hardy's heart was set on was literary success. That was the one thing that mattered. Success in other activities had been easy. He had done well in school and in the draughting office of John Hicks. He could hold his own in theological disputes and in arguments about Latin syntax. Even in the stiffer competition of London he had proved his superiority. He had arrived in the metropolis when he was not yet twenty-two, and within a year he had won two prizes. The first was a medal offered by the Royal Institute of British Architects. On March 16, 1863, this medal was awarded to Thomas Hardy for an essay (no longer extant) on "The Application of Coloured Bricks and Terra Cotta to Modern Architecture." The second prize was offered by the Architectural Association. On February 19, 1863, Hardy wrote to his sister Mary: "I am now very busy getting up a design for a country mansion for which a small prize is offered." Hardy's design won the prize of two or three pounds. But none of these things really mattered. What did matter was what was denied him, and the iron began to enter his soul (the metaphor is his own). He began to think that the fault lay not in himself but in his stars that his poems were unacclaimed, and in the sonnet "Hap" (written in 1866) he lamented that "Crass Casualty obstructs the sun."

This habit of youth to shrink from self-blame was not forgotten a dozen years later, when Hardy wrote of Eustacia: "Instead of blaming herself . . . she laid the fault upon the shoulders of some indistinct colossal Prince of the World, who . . . ruled her lot." The young man from Wessex was perhaps unusually sensitive. Hardy wrote in his notebook: "The world does not despise us; it only neglects us." And as late as 1922 he still recalled (in *Late Lyrics*) those "cold-shouldering results upon an enthusiastic disciple." As a result nothing that he wrote in London in those first three years (1862-64) has survived.

Meanwhile he kept up his interest in the classics. His attachment to architecture was too lukewarm to serve as a rival to his interest in literature. When he won the Architectural Association prize, he promptly bought several volumes of Bohn's Classical Series—English versions of the Greek dramatists made by Theodore A. Buckley. Here in Buckley's *Aeschylus* (1849) Hardy found the "Aeschylean phrase" which he recalled in *Tess of the D'Urbervilles* a quarter of a century later, thereby making it famous and himself notorious.

One event of the year 1865 may be described in Hardy's own words (sent by him to the London *Times* in 1906) not only because they indicate how he spent some of his time in London but also because they provide his comment upon an essay which remained a potent influence in his mind from this day on until the ideas and words of its author reappear in the pages of *Jude the Obscure*. Hardy regarded John Stuart Mill as "one of the profoundest thinkers of the last century" and wrote this account of his appearance "in his actual form and flesh":

It was a day in 1865, about three in the afternoon, during Mill's candidature for Westminster. The hustings had been erected in Covent Garden, near the front of St. Paul's Church; and when I—a young man living in London—drew near the spot, Mill was speaking. The appearance of the author of the treatise *On Liberty* (which we students of that date knew almost by heart) was so different from the look of persons who usually address crowds in the open air that it held the attention of people for whom such a gathering in itself had little interest. Yet it was, primarily, that of a man out of place. The religious sincerity of his speech was jarred on by his environment—a group on the hustings who, with few exceptions, did not care to understand him fully, and a crowd below who could not. He stood bareheaded, and his vast pale brow, so thin-skinned as to show the blue veins, sloped back like a stretching upland, and conveyed to the observer a curious sense of perilous exposure. The picture of him as personified earnestness surrounded for the most part by careless curiosity derived an added piquancy—if it can be called such—from the fact that the cameo clearness of his face chanced to be in relief against the blue shadow of a church which, on its transcendental side, his doctrines antagonized. But it would not be right to say that the throng was absolutely unimpressed by his words; it felt that they were weighty, though it did not quite know why.

Hardy's statement that he knew Mill's treatise *On Liberty* "almost by heart" is not to be taken lightly. The thoughts that came from behind that "vast pale brow" exercised a profound influence upon Hardy's own thoughts and encouraged the young man from Wessex in habits that were destined to make the road rough for him. In his chapter on "Liberty of Thought" Mill had declared: "No one can be a great thinker who does not recognize that as a thinker it is his duty to follow his intellect to whatever conclusions it may lead. Truth gains . . . more by the errors of one who . . . thinks for himself, than by the true opinions of those who . . . do not suffer themselves to think." Thomas Hardy resolved to "follow his intellect to whatever conclusions" it might lead, without knowing that that same intellect was bound to come into violent collision with his tender and sympathetic affection for all those aspects of life which his first twenty-two years in Dorset had brought close to him.

Meanwhile Hardy's duties in the architect's office continued. These came to include the giving of instruction to younger men whom Blomfield had taken as pupils. Hardy managed to include instruction in literature with his lessons in architecture, and this combination of interests resulted in his writing a sketch which he called "How I Built Myself a House." After this had served its purpose in amusing if not instructing his pupils, Hardy sent the article to the editor of *Chambers's Journal*. The contribution was accepted, and *Chambers's* thus gained the distinction of printing Hardy's first published words—in the issue for March 18, 1865. In later years Hardy placed a low estimate upon this composition and turned down a proposal for reprinting it.[1] "That was a trifle," he said, "done for my pupils. A short time ago an American wrote a notice of me for some paper in which he said that I had published an article describing how I built Max Gate. My essay was published twenty years before this house was built."

In declining to reprint "How I Built Myself a House" Hardy wrote, in a characteristically phrased letter: "The idea does not commend itself to me, the sketch being unrepresentative, and having arisen out of an incident that had no connection with my literary pursuits at the time." Hardy's "literary pursuits" in 1865 have left almost no record. The only poem of that year that has come down to us is "Amabel," an uninspired lyric of eight short stanzas in which the poet's success in finding eight rhymes for "Amabel" does not conceal the mediocrity of the performance. It may be no more than an echo of Tennyson's "Oriana"; or its reference to "love like ours" may supply a hint as to one direction Hardy's thoughts at this time were taking. That direction is the same one indicated by the last few sentences in the prose sketch about the house:

The last thing I remember was Sophia jumping up one night and frightening me out of my senses with the exclamation: "O that builder! Not a single bar of any sort is there to the nursery-windows. John, some day

[1] See Appendix 2, p. 236.

those poor children will tumble out and be dashed to pieces." You may be sure that some bars were put up the very next morning.

Thoughts of home and wife and children were still in Hardy's mind three months later when he wrote in his notebook: "June 2: my 25th birthday. Walked about by moonlight in the evening. Wondered what woman, if any, I should be thinking about in five years' time."

That woman, recently released from a girls' school on the Hoe at Plymouth, was now receiving riding lessons from her father, J. Attersoll Gifford, and helping her only sister in preparations for the latter's approaching marriage to the Reverend Caddell Holder, who ministered to a small parish in Cornwall. But "Crass Casualty" hid all this from Hardy's eyes. The chief thought present to his consciousness at this time was that London was a pretty heartless place to live in.

III

STUDIES IN PAINTING
AND POETRY

WHILE WORKING in Blomfield's office at 8 Adelphi Terrace,
Hardy resided at 16 Westbourne Park Villas, where he
was within a few minutes' walk of Swinburne and even
nearer Browning, recently returned as a widower to London. Hardy
was well trained by his daily tramp between Bockhampton and Dorchester, and on Sunday, July 14, 1865, he walked all the way from his
lodgings near Hyde Park to Harrow, a good four-hour trip. He
remembered the day because he called at a house where everyone was
discussing the tragedy on the Matterhorn, where three Englishmen,
two of them from Harrow, lost their lives. There was only one sur-
vivor, the mountaineer Whymper. Thirty years later Hardy met
Whymper at a dinner table, and characteristically asked him for a
sketch-map of the Matterhorn showing the path taken by the climbers
and the exact spot of the accident. The two incidents exemplify Hardy's
zest for walking over the countryside and the extraordinary interest
he took in geography and in topographical exactness.

During lunch hours in London he spent a great deal of time in
another sort of walking—through the corridors of museums and galleries. In fact his interest in art resulted in his going to the National
Gallery almost every day. His desire to succeed as an architect was
too feeble to raise any hesitation in his mind about letting other
interests encroach upon his devotion to architecture. At one time he
thought of becoming an art critic, but found it as hard to confine his
interest to painting as to architecture. His own "inconstancy" was
recalled by him years later in Rome and led to his writing his poem

on "The Vatican." In 1866 he jotted down, as "A Young Man's Epigram on Existence," his belief that

> A dolt is he who memorizes
> Lessons that leave no time for prizes.

Hour after hour he spent in studying the work of painters—English, French, and German; Italian, Flemish, and Dutch; Spanish, too, and Belgian. This study on his part is worth noticing, not only because it led to his own artistic efforts, as shown in the drawings he provided for *Wessex Poems* in 1898 and for *The Famous Tragedy of the Queen of Cornwall* in 1923, but also because it accounts for one of the marked characteristics, sometimes an annoying characteristic, of the Wessex Novels—that of referring to one or another of a list of European painters covering six centuries in the history of art. In his very first published novel the habit appeared, and it remained with him to the end of his career as a writer of fiction. At times this practice helps the reader to gain a more vivid impression of the person or object that Hardy is trying to describe, especially if his reference is to some painter whose work is commonly known—for instance, when we read in *Far from the Madding Crowd* that "fine autumn afternoons and eves intensified into Rembrandt effects the few yellow sunbeams." But when, in the same novel, we come upon a reference to the "effects in the landscapes of Ruysdael and Hobbema," we may well question whether the reader's imagination is cleared or clouded by the allusion.

Whatever the success he made in his use of this wide acquaintance with painting, Hardy's expert and detailed knowledge is unquestioned. The list of artists whose work he knows is an impressive one. Without turning the pages of more than five or six of the novels, we find the names of more than thirty painters, stretching from Giotto in the thirteenth century to Hardy's contemporaries, Wiertz and Van Beers.[1] His allusions to these painters were made, not as a cheap parade of learning, but in a sincere desire to enable the reader to see as clearly as Hardy himself saw. The frequent references to paintings nevertheless often seem intruded.

---

[1] The list is given in Appendix 3, p. 236.

In another way the young architect was making good use of his time in London. Upon the continued rejection of his poems by the editors to whom his manuscripts were sent, Hardy apparently concluded that a wider acquaintance with the English poets might be of help to him. Editorial discouragement had not succeeded in extinguishing the fire within. "I wrote verse for years," Hardy later declared, "long before I thought of writing prose. I wrote it because I had to, because of orders from within." He accordingly gave himself as thorough a course of study of English poetry as he had had of European painting. In 1865 he had known John Stuart Mill "almost by heart," and in October of that year he was sending his sister a copy of Trollope's *Barchester Towers* and telling her it was "considered the best." But when, early in 1866, Swinburne flashed upon the scene, Mill and Trollope and prose were forgotten. "I loved 'Atalanta,'" Hardy declared, years later. "I used to walk from my lodgings near Hyde Park to the draughting office every morning, and never without a copy of the first edition of the *Poems and Ballads* sticking out of my pocket." Swinburne's *Poems* dropped like a bomb into a social order that was as unprepared for them as the poet was unprepared for the storm of censure that his book aroused. Young men were delighted. "It simply swept us off our legs with rapture," recalled one eminent critic, then an undergraduate at Oxford. At Cambridge, so Edmund Gosse reported, young men joined hands and marched along the streets shouting the words of "Dolores" or of "A Song in Time of Revolution." The metaphors and similes of water, light, wind, and fire, which seemed to inspire and animate that wonderful poetry, took the whole lettered youth of England by storm with their melody and audacity.

Thomas Hardy read Swinburne with gusto and then he went back to Byron and Shelley and Keats. For two years he read no prose at all. His standards were raised; his judgment improved. He no longer sent his poems to editors. What he wrote he kept by him and worked over, and eighteen poems of 1866 have thus survived.[2] Thus, day after day the English poets insisted upon intruding upon the architect's time and attention.

[2] See Appendix 4, p. 237.

The man who is destined to write poetry begins by reading poetry. The power to delight others with thoughts and feelings expressed in verse has always appeared in conjunction with a lively interest in the thoughts and feelings of others as expressed in their verse. Hardy was never without a book. To Edmund Blunden years later Hardy "acknowledged himself a book-hunter. In the pre-Kingsway days he had haunted Booksellers' Row." Like Wordsworth he might have written a "Prelude" and said:

> Thus far a scanty record is deduced
> Of what I owed to Books in early life . . .
> But let me add at once that . . . *many* books
> Were read in process of this time, devoured,
> Tasted or skimmed, or studiously perused.

Wordsworth's record may be "scanty"; fortunately for those who are interested in following Thomas Hardy's development, his record is by no means scanty. Hardy liked to quote. He filled his pages with fragments from Shakespeare and Milton, from Wordsworth and Shelley; and when not quoting he was alluding even more frequently to authors than to painters. For some readers Hardy's novels are too "literary," but for those who desire to follow the formative influences upon him, his habit of citation and allusion, of quotation and paraphrase is extremely helpful.

It is important to linger a few minutes on this phase of his work in order to correct erroneous statements that have tended to spread into popular misconceptions. One recent writer, for instance, declares:

Hardy is a great and lonely figure in our literature. It is possible to trace the descent of almost every other writer, to name the artistic influence that went to his making, but Hardy is without literary ancestry. We know what porridge John Keats had, but we do not know that of Hardy.

This statement is strangely naïve. It reminds one of a similar remark once made about another genius: "How knoweth this man letters, having never learned?" No major English author has ever been so careful to record in his own writings his relationship to previous writers. A few years ago a critic in an American educational journal lamented the fact that schoolbooks are made by teachers with no creative fire within, that "poets are not makers of textbooks." Most of them are not, but Thomas Hardy was an exception. It is easy to construct the table of contents of his literary textbook. His habits of exactness and accuracy, learned in the draughting office, resulted in his rarely thinking of an idea merely as an idea, but usually as Somebody's idea; and when a phrase or a sentence came to his mind, it was not as the words of some indefinite one or other, but as "Coleridge's proof," or "as Comte argued," or "in Matthew Arnold's familiar phrase," or "to use Wordsworth's observation," or "if one may quote Tennyson"—all of these taken from one piece of Hardy's writing, the "Apology" of February, 1922 (*Late Lyrics*). We are thus greatly helped in naming the books and the authors that left their imprint upon him. Readers who are interested in what might be called Thomas Hardy's "Anthology of English Literature" will find its table of contents given in Appendix 5 (page 240).

In this tabulation of writers who influenced Hardy the name of William Shakespeare must stand first. As a boy at Bockhampton, Hardy had already made the acquaintance of Shakespeare's plays, and upon his arrival in London he was delighted to find Charles Kean and his wife acting in them at the Princess's Theatre. When the actor Samuel Phelps began his series of Shakespearean plays at the Drury Lane Theatre, Hardy went to every one. He went, not as an idle spectator seeking amusement, but carrying a copy of the play with him, and he was among the first in the pit crowd, night after night. Most of the early sonnets written by Hardy follow the Shakespearean form in rhyme scheme and approach the Shakespearean phraseology and structure closely enough to show that Hardy had not confined his study of Shakespeare to the dramatic works alone. Shakespeare's important formative influence was exerted with particular strength upon Hardy in these early years in the London of Charles Kean and Samuel Phelps, but for sixty years thereafter Hardy continued to keep alive within him an enthusiasm for Shakespeare, with results of surprising extent in the Wessex Novels.[3]

[3] See Appendix 6, p. 246.

Thus, by 1867 Hardy, who had had only eight years of formal schooling, had covered an immense amount of literary ground. Before his twenty-seventh birthday he was better acquainted with the chief English authors, especially the poets, than are most American college graduates.

IV

THE POOR MAN AND
THE CRITIC

HARDY HAD NOW been in London five years. He had worked hard—mornings in the office, noons in the art gallery, afternoons in making drawings and giving instructions to pupils, evenings at the Museum or the theater, then reading and studying and writing poetry until late at night. He gave up outdoor exercise, and his health began to suffer. Just when Blomfield finally suggested that Hardy take a vacation in the country, an inquiry from John Hicks arrived pat from Dorchester, asking whether Hardy could recommend a good assistant to help him with some church restoration. Hardy told Hicks he would come himself, and before the end of July, 1867, he found himself back in his father's home at Upper Bockhampton, once more making a daily trip on foot to Hicks's Dorchester office.

But this young man of twenty-seven was not the youth who had completed his course of instruction under Hicks and gone off to the big city. Those years in London had been years of rapid maturing. Ten years later, when he was describing another native who returned to Dorset, one whom he called Clym Yeobright, he wrote:

Mentally he was in a provincial future, that is, he was in many points abreast with the central town thinkers of his date. Much of this development he may have owed to his studious life in Paris, where he had become acquainted with ethical systems popular at the time. In consequence of this relatively advanced position, Yeobright might have been called unfortunate. The rural world was not ripe for him.

Substitute "London" for "Paris" and one may easily read "Hardy" for

"Yeobright" in the above quotation. When Hardy returned to Dorset in 1867 he brought with him not only a youthful beard but also a mind that had already settled its goal, its philosophy, its tone, and its mood. The next sixty years were to bring about surprisingly little further development and practically no change in intellectual attitude. What he had yet to acquire was literary skill.

Hardy has supplied an interesting portrait of himself at this point in his life.

He's a very worthy fellow. There's no nonsense in him. Though he is not a public-school man, he has read widely and has a sharp appreciation of what's good in books and art. His knowledge isn't nearly so exclusive as most professional men's. That's a great deal to say of an architect. This man is rather of a melancholy turn of mind. Of course he isn't married. He is a thorough artist, but a man of very humble origin, the son of a farmer, or something of the kind. He's about six-and-twenty. He is rather untidy in his waistcoat. He's a thorough bookworm—despises the pap-and-daisy school of verse—knows Shakespeare to the very dregs of the footnotes. Indeed, he's a poet himself in a small way. Architecture is a bewitching profession, but he won't advance in it. Worldly advantage from an art doesn't depend upon mastering it. He used to think it did; but it doesn't. Those who get rich need have no skill at all as artists. They need a certain kind of energy which men with any fondness for art possess very seldom indeed—an earnestness in making acquaintances, and a love for using them. They give their whole attention to the art of dining out, after mastering a few rudimentary facts to serve up in conversation. When he found all this out, from having already loved verse passionately he went on to read it continually; then he went rhyming himself. If anything on earth ruins a man for useful occupation, and for content with reasonable success in a profession or trade, it is a habit of writing verses on emotional subjects. Poetical days are getting past with him, according to the usual rule. Writing rhymes is a stage people of his sort pass through, as they pass through the stage of shaving for a beard, or thinking they are ill-used, or saying there's nothing in the world worth living for.

Hardy applied these words to Edward Springrove (in *Desperate Remedies*), a character he has explicitly stated he patterned after a young architect's assistant whom he met in Weymouth. This may be true enough as far as appearance and experiences are concerned; but it is obvious that Hardy also transferred to the creation of his pen many of the attitudes, ideas, and interests which he himself held.

The "habit of writing verses on emotional subjects" had stayed with him down to the time of his leaving London. Among his possessions which he temporarily left behind in the lodgings near Hyde Park were the eighteen poems of 1866, together with nine others. These are the product of the year 1867, though they were published later at intervals extending over more than a quarter of a century.[1]

But with Hardy as with Springrove "poetical days were getting past with him." He turned from verse to fiction; not because he wanted to write novels, but because he was determined to become a published author. "I never wanted to write prose novels at all. I was forced to manufacture my novels; circumstances compelled me to turn them out." These statements (made by Hardy in 1923) and others like them have led to a misunderstanding of his interest in the novel as a type, to an ignorance of the care he expended upon his prose, and to a blindness for the persistence with which desire for literary success fired his mind. Readers who have come across Hardy's declarations made late in life should balance them against the known facts about those years before he was thirty. Only a few weeks before his death Hardy remarked to his wife that he had done all that he meant to do. His only ambition, he said, had been to get some poem or poems of his into a good anthology, like Palgrave's *Golden Treasury*. With the eventual attainment of this ambition he naturally lost interest in, or even forgot, the tedious steps by which the goal had been reached.

Such disparagement of one's early work is an old story. Certainly few young men in the history of English poetry have been more ambitious for the success of their verses than was young William Wordsworth. No reader acquainted with the determined persistence with which he put every other interest aside will need any proof of the statement. Yet on December 23, 1839, this same William Wordsworth, then sixty-nine years old, wrote in a letter:

I am standing on the brink of that vast ocean I must sail so soon—I must speedily lose sight of the shore and I could not once have conceived how

[1] See Appendix 4, p. 238.

little I now am troubled by the thought of how long or short a time they who remain upon that shore may have sight of me. I feel justified in attaching comparatively small importance to any literary monument that I may be enabled to leave behind. It is well, however, I am convinced, that men think otherwise in the earlier part of their lives.

Thomas Hardy thought otherwise in the earlier part of his life. Disappointed in his attempt to appear before the world as a poet and restored to health by the quiet routine of life lived in Dorchester and Bockhampton he promptly set about the pursuit of literary fame by a different approach. Back in the home where he had read the novels of Grant and James, of Ainsworth and Scott, he did not forget the stir caused in London four years earlier by the death of another novelist, Thackeray, or forget the talk about still another, Anthony Trollope, which had two years before led him to buy a copy of *Barchester Towers* and send it to his sister. Nor had he forgotten that back in London he had written: "Looking at novel writing of the highest kind as a perfect and truthful representation of actual life is no doubt the proper view to take." Why not put poetry aside, at least for the time being? His poems had invariably been returned to him by the editors to whom he had sent them, but he had had two indications that his prose might receive a kinder welcome. The judge of the competition in which he had entered a technical article had called his essay "a very fair one" and awarded it the medal. And *Chambers's Journal* had accepted the only words of his that had as yet appeared in print. Why not make further attempts in prose? Why not write a novel?

The work with John Hicks was not very pressing. When the older architect went off one day to Cornwall to visit a dilapidated church at St. Juliot, near Tintagel, which he had been asked to restore, Hardy found time enough to drop pencil and square and take up his pen. What he thus began was his first attempt at fiction. In view of the conflicting stories that have been told about it, in order to be helpful rather than confusing, any account of that first attempt must be particularly explicit. Here may be mentioned some of the causes of difficulty. Hardy entitled his first novel *The Poor Man and the Lady*. No book with this title has ever appeared. On October 29, 1921, Hardy was visited by Vere H. Collins, who asked about the manuscript of the first novel. Hardy's reply was: "When I was moving, I got rid of it." Early in 1925 Ernest Brennecke, Jr., published the statement that "the manuscript is at present in the possession of Mrs. Hardy." When Hardy's own volume, *Human Shows,* appeared in this same year, it contained a reference to "the story of *The Poor Man and the Lady,* written in 1868, but never printed and ultimately destroyed." Three years later Mrs. Hardy stated that the story was written in 1867, but that "what he did with the manuscript is uncertain and he could not precisely remember in after years." To complicate matters, ten days after Hardy's death his friend Sir Edmund Gosse announced that back in 1921 Hardy had told him that he had "destroyed, as he thought, the whole manuscript but lately he had come upon four or five pages of it." Gosse also stated that Hardy wrote the story at Weymouth, to which town he did not move until 1869. Hardy's literary executor, Sir Sydney Cockerell, reported that in 1916 Hardy found the pages from the manuscript—not "four or five pages" as Gosse reported, but "a good portion of the manuscript." Hardy allowed Cockerell to have the pages bound in blue morocco; but shortly before his death he came to the conclusion that he did not wish to preserve this manuscript, and he thereupon burned it in his study fire.

These confusing and mutually contradictory stories indicate that the hunter of the truth must walk charily through these bibliographical woods. Some will think the prey not worth the effort, and that was Hardy's own view. "It is hunting very small deer!" he remarked to Edmund Gosse. But Gosse was certainly correct in thinking that "the student of Hardy's mind in its early development will hardly agree with him." Quite apart from its value as a work of art, the author's first faltering attempt at fiction is interesting as evidence of his method of teaching himself how to write a novel. With almost no previous experience in the writing of English prose, with no formal rhetorical training of any kind, with little previous interest in the novel as a literary type, with no tutor, adviser, or critic to help, Hardy set out to try to join the ranks of Dickens, Thackeray, George Eliot, and Trollope.

Before beginning to write *The Poor Man and the Lady* Hardy, like a good architect, took account of the materials he had to work with and the sort of structure he wished to build. His own experience as a "poor man" and one "of very humble origin" supplied him with a point of view. Not that he would tell the private story of his own life; he would invent incidents, but he would associate these with a young architect who went from a school such as that at Bockhampton and a church such as that at Stinsford up to London in order to make his fortune. Nor would he find it necessary to invent all the incidents. He remembered that in awarding him the Royal Institute of British Architects' medal for his essay on the modern use of colored bricks and terra cotta the judge had withheld the ten-pound prize that was sometimes given with the medal because Hardy had "scarcely gone sufficiently into the subject proposed." That decision had naturally enough seemed niggardly to the disappointed young architect; but the young would-be novelist could now make use of the incident. He also remembered having gone with Arthur Blomfield to New Windsor, where the memorial stone of a church was laid by the Princess Royal. When Blomfield handed her the trowel, the Princess got her glove soiled with mortar and handed the trowel back to the architect, whispering impatiently, "Take it! Take it!" That incident too could be used. As for "the Lady," a suggestion came from memories of the Bockhampton school. The building where Hardy had begun his studies in 1848 had been erected by the mistress of Kingston Maurward House at Stinsford. She had often visited the school, had provided two teachers for it, and had taken an interest in young "Tom." When in the following year he was transferred to the academy in Dorchester, "the lady of the manor" was offended. Building work on the Kingston Maurward estate, which had been in the hands of Thomas Hardy, Sr., was taken away from him. That event could be used in a novel. How should he provide for the meeting of the poor man and the lady? Well, Hardy remembered how his own father and mother had met. Later he was to record their meeting in his poem "A Church Romance." That incident, too, might be utilized in a novel. So much for Dorset.

Then, by drawing on his observations in London—in the theater, in Hyde Park, in Covent Garden, in the art galleries and the dance halls at Willis's or at the Argyle, and in the conversation of fellow architects in Blomfield's office—he could certainly fill out enough of a contrast with the worthy poor man of Bockhampton to provide the skeleton of a novel. Having heard Wilkie Collins spoken of as a successful contemporary novelist, Hardy bought a copy of *The Woman in White* (1860) to supply himself with models of dramatic incidents. By close study of Collins, Hardy thought he could learn the tricks of enlivening a plot. To add a literary polish he could call on the poets for help—Shakespeare and Browning, Shelley and Byron; Waller and Homer, and Virgil, too (by quoting from the copy his mother had given him). Both atmosphere and originality could be obtained by descriptions of architecture and by allusions to Turner and Romney, to Raphael and Rubens and others. The plan was complete; the materials were available; and in July, 1867, Thomas Hardy set to work.

In five months the first draft of the novel was finished. On January 16, 1868, he began to make the fair copy which he completed on June 9. His first attempt at fiction had thus occupied about ten months—five in making the original draft, five in copying and revising. On July 25 he mailed the manuscript to Alexander Macmillan, the publisher, and there followed three weeks of impatient waiting. At last he received a letter from Macmillan, dated August 10, 1868:

I have read through the novel you were so good as to send me with care and with much interest and admiration, but feeling at the same time that it has what seem to me fatal drawbacks to its success, and what, I think, judging the writer from the book itself, you would feel even more strongly —its truthfulness and justice.

Your description of country life among working men is admirable, and, though I can only judge of it from the corresponding life in Scotland, which I knew well when young, palpably truthful. Your pictures of character among Londoners, and especially the upper classes, are sharp, clear, incisive, and in many respects true, but they are wholly dark—not a ray of light visible to relieve the darkness, and therefore exaggerated and untrue in their result. Their frivolity, heartlessness, selfishness are great and terrible, but there are other sides, and I can hardly conceive that they would do otherwise than what they seek to avoid, "throw down the book in disgust."

Even the worst of them would hardly, I think, do things that you describe them as doing. For instance, is it conceivable that any man, however base and soul-corrupted, would do as you make the Hon. Fay Allamont do at the close, accept an estimate for his daughter's tomb—*because it cost him nothing?* He had already so far broken through the prejudices of his class as to send for Strong in the hope of saving his daughter's life. Then is it at all possible that a public body would *in public* retract their award on the grounds you make them avow in the case of the Palace of Hobbies Company?

The utter heedlessness of *all* the conversation you give in drawing-rooms and ball-rooms about the working-classes, has some ground of truth, I fear, and might justly be scourged, as you aim at doing, but your chastisement would fall harmless from its very excess. Will's speech to the working men is full of wisdom—(though, by the way, would he have told his own story in public, being, as you describe him, a man of substantially good taste?)— and you there yourself give grounds for condemning very much that is in other parts of the book. Indeed, nothing could justify such a wholesale blackening of a class but large and intimate knowledge of it. Thackeray makes them not greatly better in many respects, but he gave many redeem- ing traits and characters; besides, he did it all in a light, chaffy way that gave no offence—and, I fear, did little good—and he soothed them by de- scribing the lower class, which he knew nothing of and did not care to know, as equally bad when he touched them at all. He meant fair, you *"mean mischief."* "Dukes and duchesses and all the kit are humbugs, society is based on humbug, but it's rather pleasant and amusing, when you can get pleasant dinners and nice wines, and everybody is the same—it's all natural. When we can't pay our tailor and he duns us, and won't give us another coat, or when we have to dine off cold mutton, and perhaps not enough of that, we don't like it, but let us wait our turn." That was his tone; but then, he added, and with truth, "there are many of us who wouldn't grudge giving a poor fellow a dinner, or even a five pound note, when it did not greatly inconvenience us—and even when it did some of us." I don't think Thackeray's satire did much good; indeed, I fear it did harm. He was in many respects a really good man, but he wrote in a mocking tone that has culminated in the *Saturday Review* tone, paralysing noble effort and generous emotion. You seem in grim earnest, and, as I said, "mean mischief," and I like your tone infinitely better. But it seems to me that your black wash will not be recognized as anything more than ignorant misrepresentation. Of course, I don't know what opportunities you have had of seeing the class you deal with. My own experience of fashion- ables is very small, and probably the nature of my business brings me into contact with the best of the class when I do meet them. But it is inconceivable to me that any considerable number of human beings—God's creatures—should be so bad without going to utter wreck in a week.

Of the story itself I hardly know what to say. I should fear it is very improbable, and would be looked on as a sort of Reynolds' Miscellany affair, though your really admirable handling often gives a certain dignity and power that greatly redeems it. Much of the detail struck me as strained and unnatural. The scene in the church at midnight has poetical qualities—but could it happen? Then is it within the range of likelihood that *any* gentleman would pursue his wife at midnight and *strike* her? Though you give a good deal about the family life afterwards, there is nothing to justify that very exceptional scene. It is too palpably done to bring about the meeting of the lovers.

Much of the writing seems to me admirable. The scene in Rotten Row—seen as it is and described by an outsider—is full of real power and insight. And the characters, on the whole, seem to me finely conceived and presented. The fault of the book, as it seems to me, is that it lacks the *modesty of nature* of fact. "Romeo and Juliet" and "Hamlet" have many unnatural scenes, but Shakespeare puts them in foreign countries, and took the scenes from old books. When he was nearer home and his own time you don't find such things in his writing. King Cophetua and the beggar-maid made a pretty tale in an old ballad; but will a story in which the Duke of Edinburgh takes in lawful wedlock even a private gentleman's daughter? One sees in the papers accounts of gentlemen's daughters running away with their father's grooms, but you are not in that region. Given your characters, could it happen in the present day? The "modesty of nature" takes into account all the conditions.

You see I am writing to you as to a writer who seems to me, at least potentially, of considerable mark, of power and purpose. If this is your first book I think you ought to go on. May I ask if it is, and—you are not a lady, so perhaps you will forgive the question—are you young?

I have shown your MS. to one friend, whose judgment coincides with my own—I wish to show it to another man of a different stamp of mind, who knows more of the upper class than either, and is yet a very noble fellow, that I may get his view as to whether it would do with modifications. Would you be willing to consider any suggestions?

P.S.—I have just got my friend to write his opinion in his own words, and I enclose it. I mean the one who has already had the MS.

The friend was John Morley, whose opinion of the manuscript throws further light upon it. He wrote that the story was "a very curious and original performance: the opening pictures of the Christmas-eve in the tranter's house are really of good quality: much of the writing is strong and fresh." But he added that there were faults, that "the thing hangs too loosely together," and that some of the scenes are wildly extravagant, "so that they read like some clever lad's dream." He wound up by saying, "If the man is young he has stuff and purpose in him."

Hardy's answer to Macmillan's question: "Would you be willing to consider any suggestions" as to modifications in the story was a trip to London in December and a call on Macmillan. On this occasion the publisher assured Hardy he could not publish the story, but gave him a letter of introduction to Frederick Chapman of the publishing firm of Chapman & Hall. On December 8 Hardy called on Chapman and left his manuscript with him. A month later, on Chapman's invitation, Hardy again called and was told that the publisher was not prepared to purchase the story of *The Poor Man and the Lady* outright, but that Chapman & Hall would be willing to publish it, if Hardy would guarantee twenty pounds against possible loss. Hardy agreed to this proposal, but two months went by without his hearing any more about it. Then he received a request from Chapman to come and meet "the gentleman who read your manuscript," who turned out to be the novelist George Meredith. Hardy went in March, met Meredith, and was by him advised not to publish his novel. Meredith assured him that if Chapman & Hall proceeded with the publication as agreed the book was certain to raise a storm of censure and that Hardy would find himself on the same sort of stormy sea that Swinburne had had to sail only three years earlier. Meredith thought that it might be possible to rework the story, softening the satire on London society; better still, put it aside and write another novel, one with a more complicated plot. Though he was somewhat surprised to hear that his manuscript contained so much high explosive, Hardy was enough impressed with Meredith's advice to carry the manuscript away with him and to release Chapman & Hall from their agreement.

Although it has been frequently stated that Hardy made no further attempt to get *The Poor Man and the Lady* into print, the statement is not true. After thinking it all over for several months, Hardy decided to make one more attempt; if it would not get his novel into print, it would at least secure further critical opinion as to its value. Tinsley Brothers (William and Edward) had published novels by Trollope and by Hardy's boyhood favorite, James Grant. And in 1868 the Tinsleys published *The Moonstone*, by Wilkie Collins. This firm might not agree with Macmillan and Meredith. Although they are not named, it was probably to Tinsley Brothers that on June 8, 1869, Hardy wrote the following extant letter:

> Gentlemen: I beg leave to call your attention to a novel "The Poor Man and the Lady" which has been submitted to you.
> Should it be the custom of your house to be indifferent to the perusal of MSS. without some kind of introduction to the writers of them, be good enough to send a line and I will obtain one—a step not taken at first to avoid troubling acquaintances for what might be unnecessary.
>
> Faithfully yours
Thomas Hardy.

This third firm read the manuscript; the reader scrawled a big "Return" across the face of Hardy's note; and for the third time *The Poor Man and the Lady* came back into the hands of its author. This time it stayed there.

If there are any readers who after hearing Macmillan's detailed criticism of the first novel would like a glance at the manuscript themselves, they should read *Desperate Remedies*, Chapter V; *Under the Greenwood Tree*, Chapters I-VIII; *A Pair of Blue Eyes*, Chapter XIV; and "An Indiscretion in the Life of an Heiress." The reasons for this statement will appear in the pages that follow.

During the months when the manuscript of *The Poor Man and the Lady* was in the hands of Chapman & Hall, Hardy stayed in London, reading and pondering, and there he heard that his old teacher, John Hicks, had died. G. R. Crickmay, a Weymouth architect, purchased Hicks's practice, and in April he wrote to Hardy to invite him to assist in carrying out the work of church restoration that Hicks had agreed to do. The result of this invitation was that after the third rejection of *The Poor Man and the Lady* Hardy migrated to Weymouth and there spent the rest of 1869 as Crickmay's assistant. His full beard made him look much older than twenty-nine.

He was, however, still under "orders from within." The work in Crickmay's office was no more able to monopolize Hardy's time than had been the work in the offices of Hicks or of Blomfield. It was not long before another novel was under way—one planned to meet Meredith's desire for a more complicated plot. Life in Weymouth, too, gave Hardy fresh material to work with. The pleasant bay on which he rowed and in which he often went swimming and the Weymouth dancing class which a fellow assistant architect persuaded him to join extended his knowledge of places and of people.

The new novel he called *Desperate Remedies*. The assistant was put into it under the name Edward Springrove, but to him Hardy transferred much of himself, as has already been suggested. For the purposes of this new novel "with a plot," Hardy needed an old manor house; and since Kingston Maurward House, which he had chosen as a setting in *The Poor Man and the Lady*, had not appeared in print, he could make use of it again. He called it Knapwater House, and he may have used the same description written for *The Poor Man and the Lady*. So, with two young architects and two places where he had himself lived as starting points, Hardy mapped out an elaborate and gruesome murder story. When he found that the social life and the frivolities of Weymouth were likely to interfere with his progress with his novel, he returned to Bockhampton and once more wrote under his father's roof.

By the end of February, 1870, he had the manuscript of *Desperate Remedies* ready, and on March 5 he mailed the second offspring of his brain to Alexander Macmillan. One month later it was returned to him. Doggedly he rewrapped the manuscript and sent it to Tinsley Brothers. When the manuscript reached William Tinsley, he was just going out to lunch. He took the sheets with him to the Gaiety Bar. There he met an old friend, William Faux, known to his intimates as "Old Faux," who asked about the manuscript. Tinsley replied that it was apparently a story by a writer unknown to him and that he had not yet read it. "Give it to me!" said Faux; "I'll take it home and read it for you." Faux read it and advised Tinsley to publish it. Tinsley, however, was a cautious fellow, and on May 6 he wrote Hardy that he would be willing to publish his novel if Hardy would guarantee the costs. Determined now to see the venture through, Hardy agreed to put up seventy-five pounds. During the latter part of 1870 a fair copy of the story was written; in January, 1871, the money was paid; and on March 25, 1871, *Desperate Remedies* appeared. Hardy had become an author. The three anonymous volumes were bound in a dull red cloth, appropriate to the gory narrative.

" 'Pon my soul, Mr. Hardy," Tinsley exclaimed later, " 'twas a blood-curdling story! You wouldn't have got another man in London to print it! Be hanged if you would!"

A reviewer in the *Spectator* thought that Tinsley too ought to have refused to print such a wild tale. "This is an absolutely anonymous story," said the reviewer. "By all means let the novelist bury the secret of his name in the profoundest depths of his own heart. The law is hardly just which prevents Tinsley Brothers from concealing their participation also." Years later, Hardy referred to his first published novel and with a smile said: "It was nearly snuffed out, mainly by an article in the *Spectator*." Tinsley had printed 500 copies; of these 370 were sold at 31/6 ($7.50) each.

Critical views of this early work have shown surprising disparity. On the one side is the statement that *Desperate Remedies* is of interest only in the same painful sense as are Shelley's *juvenilia*. "Perhaps the most interesting thing about it is that it offers a remarkably good parallel to *Titus Andronicus*." On the other side is the judgment that this first work offers adumbrations of some of the characteristic virtues of later novels by the same author.

In a preface to *Desperate Remedies* written in January, 1889, Hardy frankly admitted that "the principles observed in its composition are, no doubt, too exclusively those in which entanglement, surprise, and moral obliquity are depended on for exciting interest." He had followed Wilkie Collins all too closely. Hardy's modest statement has led some readers to dismiss the novel as an immature work, of interest only because it illustrates what crude pages a genius may produce in his early years. But to regard *Desperate Remedies* as crude and immature is to ignore certain aspects of it which are far from crude and is to fail to profit by Hardy's own remark (in his February, 1896, preface) that "certain characteristics in my latest story were present in my first." Although "mystery, entanglement, and surprise" make up a great deal of the story, Hardy handles the complication efficiently and clearly. In his attempt to enable the reader to follow the intricate plot which dealt with a slain wife, a feigned wife, and a forsaken one, Hardy charted for himself a rigorously followed time scheme. From the events of Chapter I, on October 12, 1863, down to Chapter XXI, at ten minutes past four on March 30, 1866, every hour, almost every minute, is accounted for. The experience gained in writing this novel, when he was, as he said in the 1889 preface, "feeling his way to a method," stayed with him; and in planning subsequent novels, even though they were never again exclusively devoted to mystery and entanglement, he began with the preparation of a time chart. In order to try to attain the reality that had apparently been lacking in *The Poor Man and the Lady*, he confined himself to the actual locality where he was living: the Weymouth ("Budmouth") scenes were written at Weymouth and the later "Knapwater" scenes at Bockhampton. Similarly he confined himself to the "present" time: the events of the novel, written in 1869, end on Midsummer Night in 1867. Subsequently in all his most successful novels Hardy followed both these practices. There are no other English novels of any age or by any author so minutely specific with regard to geography and topography as are the Wessex novels. Years later, visitors to Hardy's study noticed the road map pinned on the wall, with distances between the places that figure in the novels indicated in pencil.

These attempts to achieve reality did not prevent the manufacture of more of those wildly extravagant scenes such as John Morley had noted in *The Poor Man and the Lady*. *Desperate Remedies* includes a scene in which three spectators, unknown to each other and each with a different purpose, spy in the dark on the guilty Manston. Also, a murder and a suicide in jail aid in bringing about a happy marriage. Hardy's novel of intrigue, however, is not to be classed with much modern frenzied detective fiction. While it is easy to dismiss the char-

acters as "story-book" people, it should be recognized that the women
are more convincingly drawn than the men and that Cytherea Graye is
the first of Hardy's gallery of fresh, charming, and unstable heroines.
In Manston, Hardy showed the result of his recent study of Shakespeare
by producing a portrait of a selfish man in the grip of an overmastering
passion. The contest between a sensual Edmund and a devoted, self-
sacrificing Kent for the possession of a fascinating Ophelia (Hardy
never drew a Cordelia) is a theme which, used here for the first time,
Hardy was to return to again and again. Like Shakespeare, he never
objected to repetition.

Not all the characteristics of *Desperate Remedies* are of interest merely
because they are the harbingers of something better to come. Two may
be mentioned as good in themselves—neither crude nor immature. The
rustic scenes of the sort that Morley had praised in *The Poor Man and
the Lady* include the railway porter, the postman, Clerk Crickett, and
others equally well done. Their humorous dialogue shows how atten-
tively Hardy had listened to the talk of the Dorset natives and how
skillful he was in recording it. Second, his descriptions are fresh and
delicate without losing precision. Cytherea "glowed amid the dulness
like a single bright-red poppy in a field of brown stubble." The masons,
working at a distance, "appeared little larger than pigeons, and made
their tiny movements with a soft, spirit-like silentness." Hardy's years
of quiet observation of nature were now ready to pay dividends. There
was no immaturity here. "The water gurgled down from the old mill
pond to a lower level, under the cloak of rank broad leaves—the sensu-
ous natures of the vegetable world." "He halted to listen to the intensely
melancholy yet musical wail of the fir-tops, and as the wind passed on,
the prompt moan of an adjacent plantation in reply."

Horace Moule was certainly correct in urging Hardy to pay no attention to *The Spectator's* scornful review. *Desperate Remedies* was a beginning the author need not be ashamed of.

V

EXCURSION INTO LYONNESSE

I
N THE INTERVAL between the completion of the manuscript of *Desperate Remedies* and the publication of the book Hardy received an answer to the question with which he had amused himself on the evening of his twenty-fifth birthday: "Wondered what woman, if any, I should be thinking about in five years' time."

While Hardy was bringing his mystery tale to its sensational conclusion, Crickmay wrote asking him whether he could make a trip to Cornwall. Crickmay wished him to inspect the St. Juliot church, the restoration of which John Hicks had undertaken before his death, but about which nothing had since been done. Hardy was at this moment unwilling to put his writing aside; but when *Desperate Remedies* was finished, Crickmay happened to renew his offer, and this time Hardy accepted.

In 1870 Cornwall was farther away from Dorset than it is now. In order to make the trip in one day from Bockhampton to St. Juliot, Hardy set out by starlight on Monday, March 7.

> When I set out for Lyonnesse
> A hundred miles away
> The rime was on the spray,
> And starlight lit my lonesomeness
> When I set out for Lyonnesse
> A hundred miles away.

It was a sixteen-hour trip, on foot, by train, and by horse, to the St. Juliot rectory, where lived the Reverend Caddell Holder, who had married the sister of Emma Lavinia Gifford.

Miss Gifford was now twenty-nine and had come to live with her sister and her brother-in-law. The riding lessons her father had given her had made her an expert horsewoman, and she loved to gallop a mare she called Fanny over the wind-swept hills and up and down the narrow lanes in the neighborhood of St. Juliot. She could sing and paint, too. Some of her water-color sketches had been sold to help raise money for the restoration of the old church. Among other things, she had painted a picture of the nave of the church at Tintagel. King Arthur's ruined castle was not far away, on the rocky, black, northern coast of Cornwall—a coast quite different from the red cliffs and sandy beaches of south Dorset. Hardy had never seen Cornwall before and had of course never heard of Miss Gifford.

> What would bechance at Lyonnesse
> While I should sojourn there
> No prophet durst declare,
> Nor did the wisest wizard guess
> What would bechance at Lyonnesse
> While I should sojourn there.

Hardy reached St. Juliot by seven P.M. His rather shabby overcoat and his beard made him seem much older than he really was. Actually, he had not yet reached his thirtieth birthday and was only five months older than Emma Gifford. Since the Reverend Caddell Holder was confined to his bed by gout (he was much older than Mrs. Holder), Hardy was received on his arrival at the rectory by Miss Gifford. Her thoughts on this occasion Hardy afterward recorded in a poem, "A Man Was Drawing Near to Me." After the evening meal this "young lady in brown" played and sang and thus got herself into Hardy's notebook. Before the week of his stay was over she was in his heart. In his records "Miss Gifford" soon became "E.L.G." Tuesday, March 8, he spent in drawing and measuring at the church; on Wednesday the ninth he visited nearby quarries. Then, instead of returning to Dorset he stayed on. The whole of Thursday the tenth he spent with Miss Gifford. In the morning they visited Beeny Cliff on the Cornish coast. She rode her mare; Hardy walked.

O the opal and the sapphire of that wandering western sea,
And the woman riding high above with bright hair flapping free—
The woman whom I loved so, and who loyally loved me.

The pale mews plained below us, and the waves seemed far away,
As we laughed light-heartedly aloft on that clear-sunned March day.[1]

As they talked Miss Gifford forgot about his beard. She noticed his
Dorset accent, but soon forgot that. She liked his soft voice. She discovered that he wrote poetry. In the afternoon they visited Boscastle.

> Myself and a girlish form benighted
>   In dry March weather, we climbed the road . . .
> What we did as we climbed, and what we talked of
>   Matters not much . . . But was there ever
> A time of such quality, since or before,
>   In that hill's story? To one mind, never.[2]

It was a perfect day; too perfect, Hardy thought, ever to return. "The
tender grace of a day that is dead will never come back to me." Tennyson's lines occurred to him. He was sorry to have to announce his return
to Dorset the next day.

In order to reach home by night he had to make another early start,
but "E.L.G." was up to see him off. They had breakfast together and
talked of the cold weather. It had been a severe winter.

> "There was a frost
>   Last night!" she said,
> "And the stove was forgot
>   When we went to bed,
> And the greenhouse plants
>   Are frozen dead!"
>
> By the breakfast blaze
>   Blank-faced spoke she,
> Her scared young look
>   Seeming to be
> The very symbol
>   Of tragedy.[3]

[1] "Beeny Cliff."
[2] "At Castle Boterel."
[3] "The Frozen Greenhouse."

Without waiting for her to cover her head, they went outdoors together to look at the frozen plants.

> She looked like a bird from a cloud
>   On the clammy lawn,
> Moving alone, bare-browed
>   In the dim of dawn.
> The candles alight in the room
>   For my parting meal
> Made all things withoutdoors loom
>   Strange, ghostly, unreal . . .
>
> "I am leaving you . . . Farewell!" I said,
>   As I followed her on
> By an alley bare boughs overspread;
>   "I soon must be gone!"
> Even then the scale might have been turned
>   Against love by a feather,
> But crimson one cheek of hers burned
>   When we came in to-gether.[4]

Hardy had acted promptly. He didn't believe in conduct like that of
Browning's duke, who allowed the next day to pass and the next day
yet, till weeks grew months, years. Nor is this allusion to "The Statue
and the Bust" an irrelevant one. Hardy had quoted from this poem
twice in *The Poor Man and the Lady*, and again in *Desperate Remedies*. Over and over again in future novels he was to quote from this
same poem. No words of Browning were more familiar to him than
those of this narrative with the advice to "stake your counter boldly,
whether winning or losing." Hardy staked his on Miss Gifford's cheek
and won. By nighttime on Friday the eleventh he was back in his
father's house. His mother noticed that something had happened, but
said nothing.

> When I came back from Lyonnesse
>   With magic in my eyes,
> All marked with mute surmise
> My radiance rare and fathomless,

[4] "At the Word 'Farewell.' "

When I came back from Lyonnesse
With magic in my eyes![5]

Letters began to go back and forth between St. Juliot and Bockhampton, or Weymouth, or London. In August, 1870, Hardy was again in Cornwall. He and "E.L.G." made another visit to Beeny Cliff, where she remarked, "It never looks like summer here." Years later he recorded the words in a poem. Miss Gifford lost an earring in a crevice between the rocks. That episode, too, was remembered, to be resurrected in *A Pair of Blue Eyes*. In May, 1871, there was another visit. Two or three times a year thereafter Hardy "set out for Lyonnesse," and at the St. Juliot rectory discussed with Miss Gifford his hopes and chances of literary success. On one of these visits (in 1872) they walked to Lanivet. On the way back Miss Gifford stopped to rest at a crossroads, propping herself up against the signpost. To Hardy's imaginative eyes she suddenly appeared "as one crucified," and he was further startled to discover that the very same thought had occurred to her. The incident was recorded years later in the poem "Near Lanivet."

The course of this true love ran smooth, and eventually, on September 17, 1874, Emma Lavinia Gifford became Mrs. Thomas Hardy. On their honeymoon they went to the ancient town of William the Conqueror and of Joan of Arc—Rouen—and later they made a brief stay in Paris. It was Hardy's first visit to the French capital, but his years in London had made him much more at home in a big city than was his wife. Visiting the Louvre was a logical continuation of the National Gallery habit begun years before in London. Emma kept a little diary, in pencil, on her honeymoon, and in it recorded her opinion that "the Louvre is very French." Upon their return to England, they settled for the winter of 1874-75 at Surbiton, a suburb of Kingston. During the progress of his Cornish romance toward this suburban goal, Hardy had not been neglecting his literary interests, and the story of their progress must now be told.

[5] "When I Set Out for Lyonnesse."

VI

THE YOUNG NOVELIST

TINSLEY BROTHERS, who with Hardy's money had published *Desperate Remedies*, had their office at 18 Catherine Street, in the Strand. One day, about a year after this publication, William Tinsley met Hardy in the Strand and asked him when he would let him have another novel. Hardy replied that he had already written a short one. "Let me see it," said Tinsley; and that invitation was the beginning of a great improvement in the history of Hardy's literary ambitions. He never again had to seek out a publisher or advance money for the publication of what he had written.

In May, 1872, Tinsley Brothers published *Under the Greenwood Tree* and paid Hardy thirty pounds for the copyright. The story appeared in two volumes, bound (again appropriately in keeping with the title) in green cloth. Like *Desperate Remedies* it appeared anonymously. Hardy was not yet willing to risk the danger of having to pursue an architect's career with a name already advertised on an unsuccessful novel. Reviewers handled *Under the Greenwood Tree* very gently. Tinsley selected for quotation in his own magazine the statement of a reviewer in the *Standard* that "for light, happy touches of life and humor we know of no rustic dialogues to be compared with these but in the earlier and best pages of George Eliot."

Hardy had begun this story, as he afterward told his wife, by salvaging eight chapters from the beginning of *The Poor Man and the Lady*. These John Morley had praised, and it would be too bad to lose them. Just as Knapwater House and its mistress were probably lifted from the manuscript of *The Poor Man and the Lady* into *Desperate Remedies*, so the tranter and his family, the Stinsford musicians, and the woods at Bockhampton were transferred to this third story, whose idyllic character is suggested by its Shakespearean title. Hardy's experience with the intricacies of the plot of his first published novel taught him to make no such mistake again. Here he went almost to the other extreme. If this third novel (the second published) was not what he had at first intended to make *The Poor Man and the Lady*, "a story with no plot," it was at least only very lightly loaded with entanglements. The heroine, who has been pointed out as the only one of Hardy's charming creatures who has nothing to suffer, proves fascinating to two men and conceals from one her promise to the other. That is the only structural device—a plot so simple as to give the effect of complete artlessness. In *Desperate Remedies* Manston's last words record his "having found man's life to be a wretchedly conceived scheme." Hardy's poems show that he had come to the same conclusion, though he didn't tell Miss Gifford so. But in *Under the Greenwood Tree* all bitterness is left out. This story only hints at seriousness. It is full of country tunes and birds' notes. The absence of the undertone of bitterness which some readers have come to associate with Hardy's most characteristic work has been sometimes explained as due to his having learned that it takes, as one of his characters puts it, "a judicious omission of your real thoughts to make a novel popular." More likely Hardy was for the moment under the full spell of his Cornish romance.

Another cause contributing to the blithe rural atmosphere of the novel was Hardy's return to the land of William Barnes and his poems. Once again he was where "Blackmwore" and "Trees Be Company" originated; and when Barnes gave Hardy a copy of the 1868 edition of *Poems of Rural Life*, the young man found many an old friend in its pages. Parts of *Under the Greenwood Tree* seem to have been written with one eye upon Barnes's volume. The chapter "Driving Out of Budmouth" recalls Barnes's "A Bit o' Sly Coorten'"; the chapter "A Confession" suggests the poem "Meaken Up a Miff"; the chapter on "Yalbury Wood and the Keeper's House" recalls the poem "The Settle an' the Gret Wood Vire." And when (in 1908) Hardy came to edit the poems of William Barnes for the Oxford University Press, every one of the poems just named went into the selection. Similarly Barnes's young lady, Fanny, may have suggested the name of Hardy's surprising heroine. Fancy Day, though not one of Hardy's great portraits, is yet vividly portrayed; and, like Cytherea before her and many more to come after her, she is as unstable as she is fascinating. It is already apparent that in his observation of women during the first thirty years of his life Hardy had been charmed by their rich emotional natures, but he had also been impressed by their instability of purpose and their weakness of will. He was convinced that women as pictured in the novels of Scott and of Dickens, as in most Victorian novels, are misrepresented. In his own portraits of the other sex he would strive to be more truthful, if less flattering.

The most original portraits in *Under the Greenwood Tree* are the musicians. In the days before the manufacture of small, inexpensive church organs such men provided the music for the church services in many Dorset parishes. The amusing attempts of Hardy's musicians to maintain their accustomed place in the west gallery of the church, their comical determination not to yield to the harmonium without a fight, their pathetic resolve not to "dwindle away at some nameless paltry second-Sunday-after or Sunday-next-before-something" are described with a sympathy and a skill that quite justified Miss Gifford's expectations for Thomas Hardy. Among others, Leslie Stephen, editor of the *Cornhill Magazine*, read the novel with pleasure.

Because of the vividness with which he describes the church musicians it has sometimes been supposed that Hardy was drawing on his own experiences in *Under the Greenwood Tree*. The Stinsford ("Mellstock") instrumentalists were organized by Hardy's grandfather, the first Thomas Hardy to settle at Bockhampton. But he died before Hardy was born. Hardy himself never saw the church band, and in 1904 he wrote: "So far as I am aware, there are no church string-bands left in Wessex at the present date." A similar disappearance has removed another ancient link between the novel and the past. A fine old beech tree, at least 150 years old, stood near the old Bockhampton schoolhouse and was pointed out to visitors as "Hardy's Greenwood Tree." In 1934 it fell a victim to the woodman's axe.

KING'S ARMS HOTEL, DORCHESTER

In spite of the delightful spontaneity of the story Tinsley was disappointed in its sale.

In that book [he afterward related] I felt sure I had got hold of the best
little prose idyll I had ever read. I almost raved about the book, and I gave
it away wholesale to press-men and anyone I knew interested in good fiction.
But, strange to say, it would not sell. Finding it hung on hand in the
original two-volume form, I printed it in a very pretty illustrated one-
volume form. That edition was a failure. Then I published it in a two-
shilling form, with paper covers, and that edition had a very poor sale
indeed; and yet it was one of the best press-noticed books I ever published.
But even though it is as pure and sweet as new-mown hay, it just lacks the
touch of sentiment that lady novel-readers most admire.

These remarks by Tinsley are worth keeping in mind in following
Hardy's next move. Unless his books sold well, he could never abandon
architecture; and his desire to marry Emma Gifford only sharpened
his realization that the domestic wheel would turn much more easily
on a well-greased axle. Tinsley was disappointed by the apathy of the
book-buying public,[1] but his judgment told him that the fault was not
the young author's. "Mr. Hardy, I do like your writings," he exclaimed
on the occasion of another chance meeting in the Strand, and then he
made a proposal that was to have far-reaching effects upon Hardy's
career—upon his methods, plots, characters, and fame. Tinsley proposed that Hardy do a novel to appear serially in *Tinsley's Magazine*.
This would mean that his potential audience would be made up, not
of those who patronized the London or other metropolitan circulating
libraries, but of provincial and rural subscribers to the magazine, who
would follow the story month after month throughout a year. No doubt,
in making the proposal, Tinsley called attention to the need for "the
touch of sentiment that lady novel-readers most admire." He failed to
call attention to Mrs. Grundy. Tinsley also said that he would hire an
artist to illustrate the story. Hardy agreed to the proposal, and thus
entered upon the practice of writing for magazines which was to continue to the very end of his career. J. A. Pasquier drew for the novel
eleven illustrations, which Edward Evans engraved.

[1] For further information about the publication of *Under the Greenwood Tree* see
Appendix 7, p. 257.

Hardy at once set about writing a story he had already thought of. Equipped with a few notes and a general outline, he began work before the end of July, 1872, little knowing what was involved in serial publication. Tinsley apparently had complete confidence in Hardy's industry and began the publication of "A Pair of Blue Eyes" in the September number of his magazine, before Hardy had written out more than a few chapters. The fact that copies of this magazine are not now easily available accounts for some of the inaccurate statements that have been made about Hardy's first serial. One recent book about Hardy, for instance, states that *"Tinsley's Magazine* ran a serial story called 'A Winning Tongue Had He.' This narrative . . . was the first book that Hardy acknowledged as his own from the start." Neither of these statements is correct. The title "A Pair of Blue Eyes" was used from the very start in *Tinsley's Magazine*, and in none of the eleven installments from September, 1872, to July, 1873, did Hardy's name appear. Not until the end of May, 1873, after the June number of the magazine had been issued and when there was only one final installment yet to come did Tinsley publish the novel in book form. It was then issued in three volumes, bound in green cloth, and the price asked for the three was again 31/6 ($7.50). Then for the first time English readers saw the words "By Thomas Hardy." The young architect was at last ready to give up pencil and square and to devote himself entirely to writing. In this exchange of professions he was encouraged by the press notices his book received. The *Saturday Review*, which had been gentler in its treatment of Hardy's earlier anonymous work than the *Spectator* had been, declared *A Pair of Blue Eyes* to be "the most artistically constructed of the novels of its time." The friendly reception the book received in London was promptly followed by publication in America; Henry Holt issued it in one volume in July, 1873.[2] In later years Hardy liked to recall that *A Pair of Blue Eyes* was the favorite novel of Tennyson and of Coventry Patmore.

Working under pressure, in his attempt to keep ahead of the monthly appearances of *Tinsley's Magazine*, Hardy had found it helpful to make use of many recent experiences of his own. The plot of the story he

[2] See Appendix 7, p. 258.

had already thought of before Tinsley had proposed a serial, but into this plot Hardy had inserted a heroine who looked very much like Miss Gifford. Elfride Swancourt, the heroine with the blue eyes, lived in Cornwall. Endelstow vicarage was patterned after St. Juliot rectory, Castle Boterel after Boscastle, and the Cliff-without-a-Name after Beeny Cliff. Apart from fictitious names, Hardy did not hesitate to make generous use of his Cornish experiences. The novel, like his own romance, began with the arrival of a young architect at a Cornish hamlet where resided a young pony-riding heroine with freely flapping hair. Miss Gifford was twenty-nine, while Elfride is described as being only nineteen; but the heroine of the novel is equipped with many of the capacities and interests which Hardy had observed in "E.L.G." He used her in sketching Elfride, exactly as he had used himself in describing Springrove's literary and professional interests in *Desperate Remedies*. Elfride, like E.L.G., played the organ at church. Like her, too, she lost an earring between the cliff rocks. Knight read the Bible for Mr. Swancourt at the evening service, as Hardy had done for Mr. Holder. In order to supply what Tinsley had felt was lacking in *Under the Greenwood Tree*, "the touch of sentiment that lady novel-readers most admire," Elfride was provided with four lovers—one who had died, one who was jilted, one who succeeded only to resign his prize, and one who married her only to be called upon to supply her with a grave.

The startling surprises, the coincidences which at times carry credulity to the extreme, and the amazing conjunction of circumstances in the last chapter, may be explained as due partly to Hardy's natural bent toward the sensational, partly to the unconscious influence of his first published novel, the murder story, and partly to a justifiable feeling that every installment in *Tinsley's Magazine* ought to contain some episode or event striking enough to make readers notice the narrative and wish for more. However, there has been a tendency on the part of critics to overemphasize the great number of coincidences in the novel. Mr. Swancourt happens to choose for his secret marriage the same day that his daughter selected for hers. On Elfride's return from London she happens to meet the one person in all Cornwall she wished to avoid. The missing earring happens to turn up at the most embarrassing moment possible. Knight and Smith, each attempting to elude the other, happen to take the same train; and that train happens to carry the coffin of Elfride. Some readers are more disturbed by such chance events than are others. It is more important to notice the psychological insight which Hardy shows in portraying his characters, particularly his heroine. Elfride's chess game with Knight is described with remarkable understanding of the girl's mind, and the unhappy maiden's thoughts and feelings after capturing and reading Knight's notebook, in which she found observations suggested by her own conduct, are subtly revealed. Accident and coincidence are never allowed to distort the naturalness of characters whom Hardy really knew.

As the months slipped by and the novelist found himself hard pressed to keep the publisher supplied with copy, Hardy turned to two special sources of material—the rejected manuscript of his first novel and the Dorset peasants. Mrs. Swancourt, who while riding in Hyde Park discussed "the language of artificiality" and "the members of a Fashionable World whose professed zero is far above the highest degree of the humble," is certainly a sister of the Mrs. Allenville, who, according to Sir Edmund Gosse,[3] appeared in *The Poor Man and the Lady*; and it is quite possible that much of the satire on London society (in Chapter XIV) was lifted from the unpublished first novel. The humor of the Cornish workmen is cast in a familiar Dorset mold. The driver of the dogcart, Martin Cannister, John Smith the mason, patterned after one of the workmen employed by Thomas Hardy, Sr., are all in the style which Hardy had used in *Under the Greenwood Tree*. The dialogue is easy and natural, and the humor fresh and piquant. Special mention must be made of the scene in which Martin Cannister and William Worm prepare the tomb of Lady Luxellian. Their dialogue is as amusing as that of the gravediggers who prepare for Ophelia's burial, and to twentieth-century ears more natural than that famous Elizabethan scene.

One thing appears here for the first time in Hardy's writings. The scene in which Knight slips over the edge of the cliff and is saved from

[3] "Thomas Hardy's Lost Novel," *Sunday Times*, London, January 22, 1928.

7813

a horrible death only by Elfride's resourcefulness and energy is the first indication of Hardy's ability to sustain interest in a tense situation by the sheer power of vivid description. It is not easy to forget the torture of that scene with Knight, when "Time closed up like a fan before him." That gripping episode is of interest not only because of the sensational event itself but also because of the psychological results— results which are presented by Hardy with the artlessness of real life.

These virtues won enthusiastic readers for the novel and gained permanent admirers for Hardy. William Dean Howells serves as an illustration: "Thomas Hardy I first knew in *A Pair of Blue Eyes*. After I had read this book, I wished to read the books of no other author, and to read his books over and over. I could not get enough of them." Coventry Patmore felt the same way. After reading this novel for the first time in 1875, he continued to have his wife read it aloud to him over and over again throughout the next twenty-one years. Each time he felt the same shock of surprise in its pathos and of pleasure in its art. Hardy had demonstrated conclusively that he had the makings of a novelist in him, and any writer who could produce a story like *A Pair of Blue Eyes* was certain to have every editor in London seeking contributions from his pen.

INDIAN RIVER JUNIOR COLLEGE LIBRARY
FORT PIERCE, FLORIDA

VII

WESSEX REVIVED

LESLIE STEPHEN, editor of the *Cornhill Magazine*, wrote asking Hardy for a serial, and as a result the young author began work on a new novel almost as soon as *A Pair of Blue Eyes* had been finished. He spent the summer of 1873 at Bockhampton in his father's house. Gray's *Elegy* supplied a title for the new work; and by September 30 *Far from the Madding Crowd* had progressed far enough for Hardy to send part of the manuscript to the *Cornhill* editor. Publication began in the January, 1874, issue of the magazine—before Hardy had completed the story. His timidity probably accounts for the fact that it made its appearance anonymously for a few months; but the chorus of praise that greeted it soon led to disclosure of the author's identity, and after the spring of 1874 Hardy never wrote anonymously. Even *The Spectator*, which had damned *Desperate Remedies*, was enthusiastic about this new novel. Before Hardy's authorship was disclosed it said: "If *Far from the Madding Crowd* is not written by George Eliot, then there is a new light among novelists." There was, indeed; and readers were not slow to discover it. *Far from the Madding Crowd* marked the beginning of Hardy's ascent to fame. Before the year was over the novel had been published seven times,[1] and its success enabled Hardy to marry Miss Gifford, as already recorded, and to take her to France for their honeymoon.

Stephen engaged Helen Paterson to illustrate the novel. Her twelve drawings pleased Hardy greatly and later led him to call her the best illustrator he had ever had. Her drawings are not as vigorous or as dramatic as those that Hubert Herkomer later drew for *Tess of the*

[1] See Appendix 7, p. 258.

D'Urbervilles, or as impressive and poignant as W. Hatherell's drawings for *Jude the Obscure*; but Miss Paterson had an eye for detail
that pleased the Wessex author. Her illustration of the use of Bible
and key tells more about this old method of divination than can be
learned from the text of the novel. Notice (in the picture facing page
62) the way the key is tied inside the Bible and supported on the
wedding-ring fingers of the two women. In the spring of 1874 Hardy
came up to London and met Miss Paterson. He also made Leslie
Stephen's acquaintance, and through Stephen he came to know George
Murray Smith, head of the firm of Smith, Elder & Co. The fact that
the books which Tinsley had published for Hardy had not made money
for him contributed to his willingness to form a connection with another publishing house. Accordingly it was Smith, Elder & Co. who,
in November, 1874, issued *Far from the Madding Crowd* in two volumes, each volume reproducing as full-page illustrations six of the
Cornhill drawings by Helen Paterson. The price was twenty-one
shillings. This ended Hardy's three-year association with Tinsley
Brothers and began a business relationship with Smith, Elder & Co. that
was to continue (with a two-year intermission) through the year 1886.
Ten or eleven days before the appearance of the two volumes in
London, the novel was issued in one volume by Henry Holt in New
York. With a potential audience in America much larger than Hardy's
British audience, Holt was able to offer the novel for $1.25. This low
price greatly encouraged the building up of an immense following for
Hardy in America.[2]

While praise of the new novel was arising on all sides, Hardy had
two experiences which cast new and unexpected light upon what a life
of authorship might turn out to be. Leslie Stephen wrote him to say that
the seduction of Fanny Robin would have to be treated in a gingerly
fashion, because *Cornhill* subscribers were already beginning to write
to the editor, voicing their Grundian objections to certain passages in
the story. Hardy was astounded and did not know what to reply, but

[2] Bibliographical details regarding Hardy's numerous American publishers are given
in "Thomas Hardy in America" by Carl J. Weber, in *The Colophon* (ns III, 383-405),
New York, September, 1938.

he accepted Stephen's dictation; and accordingly "Liddy came close to her mistress and whispered into her ear" the "wicked story" that readers of the *Cornhill* could guess at but must not read. The second experience was even more of a surprise to Hardy. A deputation of six "humanitarians" from America one day turned up at Hardy's door and remonstrated against the "cruel incident" that occurs after Fanny's being assisted from the Dorchester bridge to the Workhouse by a stray dog on whom she leans for support. The deputation objected to the passage in which, upon Fanny's asking later for her friend the dog, she is told that it had been stoned away. The American "humanitarians" wanted this scene changed.

"Far from the Madding Crowd is a great novel," declared James M. Barrie. Although in it Hardy makes more use of coincidence than some readers like, there is less of it than in *A Pair of Blue Eyes,* and in every way the design of the novel shows a marked advance over the three novels that had preceded it. Hardy had at last learned how to construct a plot; and once learned, the lesson was never forgotten. For the next twenty years he was to use the same device over and over again. The overcomplicated intricacy of *Desperate Remedies* and the unduly simple placidity of *Under the Greenwood Tree* had taught him to steer a middle course. This he had attempted in *A Pair of Blue Eyes,* but there the complication caused by the series of lovers who were attracted by Elfride's blue eyes was somewhat tinged with artificiality, because accident played a larger part in the story than human motivation. In *Far from the Madding Crowd* Hardy shows that he has learned how to correct this defect. His formula is humorously described by Christopher Julian in *The Hand of Ethelberta*: "I have heard of one-sided love, and reciprocal love, and all sorts, but this is my first experience of a concatenated affection. You follow me, I follow Ethelberta, and she follows—Heaven knows who!" Beginning with a single love story, that of Bathsheba and Oak, the situation is complicated by the natural introduction of Boldwood. Then Troy and Fanny are brought in, with further involvement of cross purposes and wills. When the various threads have been well tangled up, one after another is singled out and eliminated—first Fanny, then Troy, and then Bold-

HELEN PATERSON'S BIBLE-AND-KEY ILLUSTRATION

wood, leaving at the end the original pair, Bathsheba and Oak. This plan of evolving one story into two, into three, or into four; then resolving it again into two, and eventually into one, is a simple procedure which Hardy found it convenient to use as often as Shakespeare did his device of dressing a girl up in boy's clothing.

Hardy made careful use of the calendar. Professional habits of mind had built up in him a characteristic that he was later to ascribe to Egbert Mayne in "An Indiscretion":

He could recall at a moment's notice that he saw her at eleven o'clock on the third of April, a Sunday; at four on Tuesday, the twelfth; at a quarter to six on Thursday the twenty-eighth; that on the ninth it rained at a quarter past two; that on the seventeenth the grass was wet; and other calendrical and meteorological facts of no value whatever.

The story *Far from the Madding Crowd* begins on December 20, 1869, and ends in January, 1873—the same year in which Hardy began to write it. The habit of the architect is seen in the patient charting that enabled the novelist to know that Valentine's Day came on Monday in 1870. The events of a little more than three years are followed with the same chronological precision that Hardy had learned to use in writing his early murder story. Such little matters as the fact that J. B. Dykes's musical setting for "Lead Kindly Light" was new in 1868 are brought in with as much scientific accuracy as artistic skill.

The characters are easily the best portraits so far painted in words by Hardy. Bathsheba is a sister of Cytherea, Fancy Day, and Elfride, but there are more striking contrasts in her character than in theirs. She is more convincingly drawn, more appealingly alive; and her progress through the novel involves a development, a maturing, that if not wholly lacking was merely suggested in the preceding stories. Hardy's aunt who lived at Puddletown ("Weatherbury") was used as a basis for Bathsheba's character, which was not flattering enough to be wholly satisfactory to many readers of the same sex. After his loss of the protection afforded by anonymous writing Hardy began to receive letters from readers, and from this time on till the end of his life he was as much annoyed by violent denunciations of his writing as he was pleased with occasional letters of genuine appreciation. To one correspondent Hardy wrote shortly after *Far from the Madding Crowd* had appeared in book form:

> I myself, I must confess, have no great liking for the perfect woman of fiction . . . The majority of women are quite worthy enough in nature to satisfy any reasonable being, but I venture to think that they too frequently do not exhibit that nature truly and simply, and thus the nature is condemned by their critics when the form of its manifestation only is at fault.
> I had an idea that Bathsheba, with all her errors, was not devoid of honesty of this kind; it is however a point for readers to decide. I must add that no satire on the sex is intended in any case by the imperfections of my heroines, those qualities being merely portrayed in the regular course of an art which depends rather on picturesqueness than perfect symmetry for its effects.

Gabriel Oak was suggested by a shepherd whom Hardy had known and admired as a boy. Nothing in the novel is finer than the way Hardy presents this estimable shepherd without making him either an impossible prig or a sentimental weakling. In each of the novels that preceded *Far from the Madding Crowd* Hardy had shown superior skill in drawing women. Now Hardy shows for the first time that his insight into masculine character is just as great. It has been remarked that Troy is not a very villainous villain; nor is he. Hardy did not intend him to be an Iago. He is plausibly sketched, however, from officers attached to regiments of soldiers stationed at Dorchester when Hardy was a boy. Better still is the company of comedians, the rustic frequenters of Warren's Malthouse, whose "chat" matches that of Dogberry and Verges or of Bottom and his Athenian companions. To those who have not made the acquaintance of Henery Fray, Jan Coggan, Joseph Poorgrass (that "fearfullest man" who said "sir" to an owl), and Billy Smallbury, it may sound like unwarranted exaggeration to compare this group of Hardy characters to Shakespeare's immortal rustics, but no other comparison will serve. Whether chatting in the malthouse at Weatherbury or stopping for a "tipple" at the Buck's Head in Roy-town, these characters talk with an unconscious humor and an untutored wisdom that is little short of inspired. Critics have sometimes maintained that no such amusing rustics ever lived, but Hardy vouched for them. There were half a dozen of them on the Hardy farm, he declared, and he once offered to show a visitor where two were buried. Henery Fray's real name was Isaac West, and Joseph Poorgrass was drawn from John Amey.

Hardy handled the Dorset dialect with the ease born of long familiarity. The native's pronunciation of "Dorset" as "Darset" recalled to Hardy's mind Trollope's name for the same county, "Barset," in the Barchester novels. "Barchester" was Trollope's name for Salisbury. Hardy's "Melchester" refers to the same cathedral city, and in *Far from the Madding Crowd* he uses for the first time a geographical term which he lifted from the poems of William Barnes. "Wessex" as a vague designation for the country southwest of Oxford has now come into such common use that readers often learn with surprise that Hardy's employment of the term in this novel was the beginning of this general practice. Trollope's successful invention of Barsetshire may have suggested to Hardy the making of his own similar map. At any rate, from the date of the publication of *Far from the Madding Crowd* Hardy gave as precise care to geographical accuracy as he had given to the study of the calendar. Later he revised the place names used in earlier writings to make them conform to the terminology he set up for "Wessex."

Other characteristic marks of Hardy's authorship may be briefly noted. All the humble persons who live "far from the madding crowd" know the Bible. There are more than three dozen Biblical quotations or allusions, the Old Testament appearing more than twice as often as the New. Shakespeare is represented by a dozen quotations, from eight different plays; and other poets are similarly used, among them Milton, Scott, and Wordsworth; Shelley, Keats, and Browning. Nine or ten painters are cited.

Caught in the glow of successful creation and with the prospect of marriage coloring his thoughts, Hardy wrote *Far from the Madding Crowd* with an almost total absence of the bitter thoughts that are found in his early poems and are to reappear in later work. Here Henery Fray is allowed to wail: "Your lot is your lot, and Scripture is nothing; for if you do good, you don't get rewarded according to your works, but be cheated in some mean way out of your recompense." And the author speaks of "the impersonator of Heaven's persistent irony." But apart from these two suggestive sentences, Hardy was here content to postpone judgment of heaven and censure of God.

Far from the Madding Crowd is supremely successful in the excellence and the variety of its descriptions of nature. Hardy has an eye and an ear for everything. Dry leaves "simmering and boiling in the breeze," the wailing of trees and murmuring of hedges, the pool that "glittered like a dead man's eye," the pink flush which arose and overspread the neck and shoulders of a sheep where they were left bare by the clicking shears, a poplar that stood out "like an ink-stroke on burnished tin," the note of the sheep bell, that "chronic sound that only makes itself noticed by ceasing or altering in some unusual manner from the well-known idle tinkle which signifies to the accustomed ear that all is well in the fold," the "toad humbly travelling across the path," the "huge brown garden-slug which had come indoors to-night for reasons of its own"—all are noticed with the eye of a lover and touched into the picture of Wessex life with the hand of an artist. Most wonderful of all is the description of the coming of the storm and the play of thunder and lightning. There is nothing equal to it anywhere in the whole range of English literature. Those chapters (XXXVI-XXXVIII) were written by a master.

Henry James (who had by an interesting coincidence made his first appearance as an anonymous writer in the *Atlantic Monthly* in March, 1865, the same month and year in which Hardy first appeared in print) was writing reviews for the New York *Nation* in 1874. His unsigned comment on *Far from the Madding Crowd* indicated a basic lack of sympathy with Hardy's work; but in spite of this disqualification as a critic, James recognized the genuine merit of the descriptive passages. His grudging tribute is worth resurrecting from a forgotten page: "Hardy describes nature with a great deal of felicity, and is evidently very much at home among rural phenomena. The most genuine thing in his book is a certain aroma of the meadows and lanes,—a natural relish for harvestings and sheep-washings." By the publication of this work and its enthusiastic reception by the public, Hardy felt himself at last definitely launched upon a career as an author. At the age of thirty-four he turned his back permanently upon the architect's office.

VIII

TRAGEDY IN ART

HARDY WAS NEVER WILLING to allow his life to settle into a complacent groove. Just as the apprentice read Greek and the young architect frequented the art galleries, so the young novelist read philosophy, and the would-be poet drew pictures. But the passion for writing remained constant. At home or abroad, in Dorset or in London, in good spirits or "in tenebris," he wrote. During the years of constant application to prose fiction he had continued to compose verse from time to time, and a year after the publication of *Far from the Madding Crowd* he had the satisfaction of seeing his first poem in print. In November, 1875, the *Gentleman's Magazine* printed "The Fire at Tranter Sweatley's" (reprinted in America in *Appleton's Journal*, November 6, 1875, and collected in *Wessex Poems* in 1898 under the title "The Bride-Night Fire").

At this time Hardy was frequently shifting his residence. In the search for a house that would satisfy the demands of health, comfort, economy, and literary craftsmanship he moved from London to Swanage; from Swanage to Yeovil; from Yeovil to Sturminster Newton; from there back to London; thence after a period of ill health to Wimborne; and from Wimborne to Dorchester. There he settled soon after his forty-third birthday. Two years later he built himself a house on the outskirts of this town, and there he remained for the next forty-three years of his life.

Meanwhile Leslie Stephen, pleased with the public reception of *Far from the Madding Crowd*, asked Hardy to supply the *Cornhill* with another novel. The author felt unable to carry out his resolve to avoid the predicament of having to rush the composition of a story while it was appearing serially. He therefore accepted the *Cornhill* offer, but he surprised its editor with what Hardy afterward called a "somewhat frivolous narrative." Critics have hazarded various guesses in attempting to explain this startling departure from Hardy's normal path, but his wife left no doubt about the real cause. It was his extreme sensitiveness to criticism. When the *Spectator* had conjectured that *Far from the Madding Crowd* might be by George Eliot, Hardy had read into the remark a charge of imitation; and this (so Mrs. Hardy told Rebekah Owen) "discouraged him greatly, and he went off at a tangent and wrote *The Hand of Ethelberta* by way of contrast while at Swanage." Mrs. Hardy never liked it; there was "too much about servants in it."

The Hand of Ethelberta began its appearance in July, 1875, but the writing of the novel was not completed until half a year later. Written in the intervals of house hunting, it reveals in many respects Hardy's lack of inspiration. George du Maurier provided eleven illustrations, which were used again in April, 1876, when Smith, Elder & Co. published the novel in two volumes, bound in brown (or terra cotta) cloth.[1] The price was twenty-one shillings.

The public shared Leslie Stephen's feeling that *Ethelberta* was a long way from being up to the standard of *Far from the Madding Crowd*. Hardy consoled himself with the belief that "the novel suffered for its quality of unexpectedness—that unforgivable sin in the critic's sight." He thought that they had looked for another pastoral novel and were therefore unprepared for this story of leisurely society, of dinner parties, of the Royal Academy, Hotel Beau Sejour, and Enckworth Court. The critics, however, were right. In spite of Hardy's attempt at sprightliness, a good deal of the novel is slow and some of it is dull. Ethelberta's father, the butler, is drawn with natural sympathy and quiet dignity. Once in the company, however, of the lords and ladies, Hardy lost this reality of characterization. Although he never liked to hear it said, the truth is that he was unable to make his people of "gentility" come alive. The reader is uncertain whether he is expected to admire or despise. Ethelberta is an adventuress, but perhaps (as with Bathsheba) "no satire on the sex is intended," not even when she marries the dissipated old Lord Mountclere. None of these characters

---

[1] See Appendix 7, pp. 258-59.

have the interest or the vitality that Meredith or Thackeray might have given them, and it is clear that Hardy did not know them in the intimate and affectionate way that he knew the simple Dorset countrymen. He observed them as an outsider. His description of the drawing-room audience while it is listening to Mrs. Petherwin's singing is vividly done, and suggests that Hardy might have made an excellent cartoonist for *Punch*; but he is not at home in that drawing-room company.

Among her many accomplishments Ethelberta "is very clever at verses." Remembering Hardy's own poetic ambitions, the reader will find some of Ethelberta's remarks of more than passing interest.

"Then you own you do not feel so ardent as you seem in your book?"
"I do own it."
"And you think the verses may tend to misrepresent your character as a gay and rapturous one, when it is not?"
"I do fear it."
"Then, of course, you will suppress the poems."
"I will not. I don't wish them to be suppressed. I am not ashamed of them; there is nothing to be ashamed of in them."

Hardy was here anticipating those critics who later predicated an unhappy life for him because he wrote poems on gloomy subjects. "One of Hardy's ancestors must have married a weeping-willow tree," a recent reviewer observed; as if Mark Twain's writings were proof of his having led an uproariously funny life instead of an increasingly cynical one. Another passage in *Ethelberta* discusses the value of tragedy in art.

Enough misery is known to us by our experiences without having gratuitous grief inflicted upon us. [As for Shakespeare's tragedies] I am sure that thousands of people who have seen those plays would have driven home more cheerfully afterwards, if by some contrivance all could have ended happily. Well, it is an old and worn argument—that about the inexpedience of tragedy—and much may be said on both sides.

Passages like these show that Hardy was not only writing but was thinking about the art of the writer as well. He had learned to create plots. He knew how to portray those characters with whom he could sympathize. He knew how to describe nature, how to hold a reader with rapid and vivid narrative, how to develop tense and dramatic situations. As far as any of these aspects of novel writing are concerned, *Far from the Madding Crowd* represented an eminently satisfactory achievement. But it lacked one thing—and that one lack, to a man of Hardy's mind, was a serious one. He wanted a theme, a philosophical motif. The more he thought about the matter, the clearer his own bent and his opportunity became to him. In June, 1877, he wrote in his notebook: "There is enough poetry in what is left after all the false romance has been abstracted, to make a sweet pattern." Thus shortly after he became thirty-seven years old, he had found the text for all of his greatest work yet to come. "If Nature's defects must be looked in the face and transcribed," he wrote down, "whence arises the *art* in poetry and novel-writing? I think the art lies in making these defects the basis of a hitherto unperceived beauty, by irradiating them with 'the light that never was' on their surface, but is seen to be latent in them by the spiritual eye." The day he recorded this thought in his journal is an important one in the history of Hardy's development, and the quietness of its entry in a notebook should not conceal the significance of the event for Hardy and for his readers. Thenceforth "a hitherto unperceived beauty," to be sought in the defects of a sorry universe, was to be his lodestar.

His artistic formula when put into concrete action is well illustrated by Mrs. Yeobright in *The Return of the Native*. In her journey across the heath,

she came to a spot where independent worlds of ephemerons were passing their time in mad carousal, some in the air, some on the hot ground and vegetation, some in the tepid and stringy water of a nearly dried pool. All the shallower ponds had decreased to a vaporous mud amid which the maggoty shapes of innumerable obscure creatures could be indistinctly seen, heaving and wallowing with enjoyment. Being a woman not disinclined to philosophize she sometimes sat down under her umbrella to rest and to watch their happiness, for a certain hopefulness gave ease to her mind.

That inclination to philosophize on maggots in a mud-puddle is Hardy's own. Years were to elapse before he would describe "the spot called 'Cross-in-Hand,' " but the view-point of 1877 was steadily held when he wrote: "Of all the spots on the bleached and desolate upland this was the most forlorn. It was so far removed from the charm which is sought in landscape by artists and view-lovers as to reach a new kind of beauty, a negative beauty of tragic tone."

Having once settled in his mind this basis for further artistic activity, Hardy was ready to proceed. Most of the year 1877 was spent in applying the motif to the composition of a new novel. For the first time since he had begun to write for serial publication he was not pushed by having to keep up with the printer. He had time for careful planning and for thoughtful writing. And for the first time he decided not to use the locality where he was living—he was then at Sturminster Newton—but to use a part of Dorset that lay between the country of *Far from the Madding Crowd* and that of *The Hand of Ethelberta*, namely, the vast heath on the edges of which he had been born. His imagination was thus called into freer play, and memories of irresponsible boyhood days brought an emotional warmth to his writing that had been entirely lacking in *Ethelberta*. In one respect Hardy clearly resembled Clym Yeobright.

If any one knew the heath well it was Clym. He was permeated with its scenes, with its substance, and with its odors. He might be said to be its product. His eyes had first opened thereon; with its appearance all the first images of his memory were mingled; his estimate of life had been colored by it; his toys had been the flint knives and arrow-heads which he found there, wondering why stones should "grow" to such odd shapes; his flowers, the purple bells and yellow furze; his animal kingdom, the snakes and croppers; his society, its human haunters. Take all the varying hates felt by Eustacia Vye towards the heath, and translate them into loves, and you have the heart of Clym.

And you have the heart of Thomas Hardy. He found it pleasant to dream that "the extensive tract here described may be the heath of that traditionary King of Wessex—Lear." He made a sketch map of the region, in order to guide himself in describing the movements of his characters. "Unity of place is so seldom preserved in novels," he remarked, "that a map of the scene of action is as a rule quite impracticable." His map was afterward reproduced in the book edition of the story, and it thus became the first of the maps which have become a common feature in all modern editions of the Wessex Novels.

The decision to use the heath and his memories of it naturally led to another decision not to write about "the present." His novel would deal with the eighteen-forties, not the eighteen-seventies. Following his usual practice he prepared a careful time chart. Describing himself as "old-fashioned enough to think there is a virtue" in strict observance of the unities, he gave particular attention to the calendar. The action of the heath story was to begin on November 6, 1842, and end just one year later, on the night of November 6-7, 1843. The plot was to be a slight modification of the one that had proved so successful in *Far from the Madding Crowd*: three men and two women, unhappily associated in "concatenated affection." With the framework in time and place settled, the characters and plot determined, the guiding motif clearly held in mind, Hardy gave himself over enthusiastically to the writing. Like Browning's Andrea del Sarto he could afterward refer to "that long festal year."

> I surely then could sometimes leave the ground.
> A good time, was it not, my kingly days?

The "negative beauty of tragic tone" about which he was writing did not interfere with the positive happiness of the author's life, and in after years Hardy remembered those days of working on his first great tragedy as "our happiest time."

He was somewhat puzzled as to what to call the new novel. While still debating the matter he made a visit to London and kept an engagement to meet J. Henry Harper, the American publisher. Harper not only wanted a story for his New York periodical but also was considering the publication of a European edition of *Harper's Magazine*. If the project were carried out, he would be eager to have a novel from Hardy to use in the new venture. Hardy called at Mr. Harper's hotel, and the two men strolled out into the Green Park and sat on a bench. According to the publisher, the following conversation took place:

Hardy pulled out a roll of paper from his pocket, covered with titles, and asked me to look them over and express my opinion as to which one I thought would be most appropriate for his new serial.

"You can hardly expect a suggestion from me," I protested, "when you have always been so happy in your titles. For instance *Far from the Madding Crowd, A Pair of Blue Eyes,* and so on." I asked him which one of his tentative titles he himself preferred.

"Well," he reflected, "I like 'The Return of the Native.' "

This title was chosen.

The active publishing house of Chatto & Windus in London had offered to buy Hardy's next novel for use in their magazine *Belgravia,* and before the end of 1877 *The Return of the Native* was ready. It began its appearance in January of the next year and ran for twelve months. In New York Harper ran it in his magazine just one month after it appeared in *Belgravia.* For the English magazine Arthur Hopkins drew twelve illustrations, four of which were copied in *Harper's.*

Hardy again had the experience of meeting editorial interference with his own plans. The original conception of his story did not call for a marriage between Venn and Thomasin. Venn was to have retained his isolated character consistently to the end and to have disappeared mysteriously from the heath. Thomasin was to have remained a widow. But, as Hardy later put it, "certain circumstances of serial publication led to a change of intent." He extended the time of the action and provided for Venn's marriage. Then he added: "Readers can choose between the endings, and those with an austere artistic code can assume the more consistent conclusion to be the true one."

Toward the end of 1878 the novel was published by Smith, Elder & Co., in three volumes, bound in brown cloth. The world did not acknowledge it, but a masterpiece of English literature had appeared. It is Hardy's most nearly perfect work of art. There is no reason to think that this was his own opinion at the time; but, in view of the care he had lavished upon his novel, he cannot have been other than shocked and discouraged at the reception the reading public gave the book. It was called "distinctly inferior" to anything he had written. One reviewer was content to remark that in it the reader would find himself taken farther from the madding crowd than ever. Sir James M. Barrie afterward related: "In an old library copy of *The Return of the Native* I have been shown, in the handwriting of different ladies, 'What a horrid book!'—'Eustacia is a libel on noble womankind,' and 'Oh, how I *hate* Thomas Hardy!'" The author was rapidly discovering that the rose of literary fame carries many a thorn with it, and it took only a slight scratch to cause pain to his sensitive nature. He came to feel that he "was living in a world where nothing bears out in practice what it promises incipiently." Clym's view that life is "a thing to be put up with, replacing that zest for existence which was so intense in early civilizations," settled more permanently than ever upon Hardy. Nobody told him that his hymn in praise of Egdon Heath was one of the most magnificent pieces of prose writing in the whole range of English literature. He didn't live long enough to hear it called "in the sweep of its prose a superb poem." No one remarked on the mastery of design, on the structural unity of the novel. Readers were ready to complain that Hardy rarely rewards the truly deserving in his world of ironic thwartings, but they failed to observe that in their treatment of him, the author, they were demonstrating the very truthfulness of his reading of life. So rare was praise or appreciation of the new novel that Mandell Creighton, bishop of London, scandalized a company at his own dinner table by praising it. In America *Harper's Magazine* called it one of the two best serial novels of the year 1878, and Henry Holt published the story in book form (one volume, December, 1878), but readers failed to respond. It was nearly fifteen years before *The Return of the Native* was heard of again.

The reader's attention must not be directed solely to structure, to style or to philosophical tone. *The Return of the Native* contains some of Hardy's greatest characters, notably Eustacia and Clym. Eustacia shares with Bathsheba and Elfride many of those qualities which led "lady novel-readers" to dislike Hardy's heroines. But Eustacia is easily distinguished in the company. The fire of her rebellion against her isolation on Egdon Heath, the sensuousness of her nature, her force of will and independence of character, combine to make her just what Hardy called her, "the raw material of a divinity," whose whole being is analyzed in a famous chapter exclusively devoted to that "Queen of Night." She is the most powerfully drawn woman in Hardy's portrait gallery. Her selfishness, her unbridled passions, and the low level on which her aspirations are pitched cannot blind one to her "celestial imperiousness," her beauty, and her charm. She is a fit partner for Clym, but it is one of the ironies of "hap" that she hated what he loved —the heath.

Clym's reflection of Hardy's own experience of the heath has already been mentioned. Later Hardy remarked: "I think Clym is the nicest of all my heroes, and *not a bit* like me." Were it not for this cautionary declaration one would be tempted to think it quite probable that the author shared his character's attitude and purpose in life.

Yeobright loved his kind. He had a conviction that the want of most men was knowledge of a sort which brings wisdom rather than affluence. In striving at high thinking he still cleaved to plain living—nay, meagre living in many respects, and brotherliness with clowns. "I want to do some worthy thing before I die. As a schoolmaster to the poor and ignorant, I think to do it," said Clym. "Can any man deserving the name waste his time in flashy business, when he sees half the world going to ruin for want of somebody to buckle to and teach them how to breast the misery they are born to?"

Clym had one great gift—the gift of content, which Eustacia lacked.

The heath brought these two together, but it could not reconcile their divergent interests. From the moment of their marriage things began to go wrong. Instead of blaming herself, Eustacia "laid the fault upon the shoulders of some indistinct, colossal Prince of the World, who had framed her situation and ruled her lot"; and in such a moment of Aeschylean self-exculpation, there was no Cassius by to remind her that the fault, dear Brutus, is not in our stars. "How destiny has been against me!" she cried. "I do not deserve my lot! O, the cruelty of putting me into this ill-conceived world! I have been injured and blighted and crushed by things beyond my control! O, how hard it is!" With the utmost naturalness Hardy follows the tragic history of this ill-mated pair up to the most powerful climax he ever drew. When Clym charges Eustacia to tell him "who was with you on the afternoon of the thirty-first of August," that fateful Thursday when Mrs. Yeobright found the door barred against her, there follows a scene that inevitably reminds the reader of a similar one between Othello and Desdemona. It is praise enough to say that Hardy's scene does not greatly suffer by comparison with Shakespeare's. Clym is not master of Othello's poetry, and Eustacia lacks the pathos associated with Desdemona's innocence. But for success in recording in rapid, intense dialogue the anguish of two human hearts caught in mutual misunderstanding, suspicion, and jealousy, Hardy can claim a place not much lower than that which the world has assigned to Shakespeare.

Other characters in the book are equally alive, if not equally important—Wildeve and Mrs. Yeobright particularly, and even those two who have learned to find their happiness in renunciation, Thomasin and Diggory Venn. The critic is tempted to linger, too, over further illustrations of Hardy's eye for nature, of his use of the poets and painters, of his delight in songs and music; over the vividness of his account of the tragedy that ends the life of Eustacia and the quiet restraint of the artistic concluding paragraph of the novel. *The Return of the Native* has completely recovered from early neglect and has received more adequate treatment in modern annotated editions than any other book that Hardy wrote.[2] But even the briefest account must include two observations. First, *The Return of the Native* is a rich storehouse of Wessex traditions and customs. The fires that commemorate the Gunpowder Plot, the Village Picnic, or dance, at East Egdon, with its musicians "sitting in a blue wagon with red wheels scrubbed as bright as new," and above all the Christmas play of Saint George as presented by the "mummers," whom Hardy had known as a boy, all these are part of that historical richness which makes the Wessex Novels a delight to readers interested in the past and its ways. The picture of humpbacked Father Christmas, swinging his huge club, is one that Hardy obviously enjoyed recalling from his own boyhood.

> Make room, make room, my gallant boys,
> And give us space to rhyme;
> We've come to show Saint George's play,
> Upon this Christmas time.

[2] See Appendix 7, p. 259.

Hardy's service as an antiquarian and historian was recognized by James M. Barrie. In 1889 the latter contributed to the *Contemporary Review* an article on "The Historian of Wessex," in which this aspect of Hardy's literary work received warm praise.

Closely allied with these memories of Wessex customs and festivals is the record of superstitions and folklore in which *The Return of the Native* is likewise rich. Johnny Nunsuch's "crooked sixpence" was prized by him because it would keep witches away. Susan Nunsuch pricked Eustacia in church with a long stocking needle, "so as to draw her blood and put an end to the bewitching of Susan's children." A wax effigy of Eustacia was stuck full of pins and then held in the fire while it melted slowly away, to the accompaniment of the Lord's Prayer said backwards—all "to counteract the malign spell" which Eustacia was supposed to be working upon a sick child. Hardy's memory of stories told him by his grandmother rushed back into consciousness while he was engaged in recounting the experiences of dwellers on the heath, and *The Return of the Native* is merely one of many books in which he records this wealth of folklore.[3]

The manifold points of interest that this Egdon tragedy possesses have in the course of sixty years and more become generally appreciated. The novel has long outlived the blind criticism of 1878 and has become one of the classics of English fiction.

[3] See Appendix 7, p. 259.

IX

LITTLE IRONIES AND BIG
ENDEAVORS

WHATEVER HARDY'S OWN FEELINGS were when *The Return of the Native* dropped into an unappreciative world, Chatto & Windus were convinced that they had found an important author. Before the novel had run half its course in *Belgravia* they were issuing a fourth edition of *Under the Greenwood Tree*—Tinsley having consented to sell (at a good profit) the copyright of this prose idyl. Chatto & Windus were also the publishers of the *New Quarterly Magazine*, and for this periodical they solicited a contribution from Hardy. If he had no full-length novel ready or in mind, could he provide a shorter piece of fiction? Since contributing a short story to the New York *Times* in 1874, Hardy had given little thought to the writing of short stories, but the chance inquiry of his publishers turned his attention to a field in which his pen was subsequently active for twenty years.

When the request for a contribution to the *New Quarterly Magazine* came, Hardy had nothing suitable ready or even in mind. It so happened, however, that at this time he and Mrs. Hardy were packing up to leave Sturminster Newton, where *The Return of the Native* was written, to return to London. In collecting his papers he came upon the remains of the manuscript of his first and unpublished novel, *The Poor Man and the Lady*. More than once he had used these rejected pages in writing subsequent books. It seems likely that a short descriptive passage had gone into *Desperate Remedies*. The first eight chapters had provided a beginning for *Under the Greenwood Tree*. Mrs. Allamont and her "society" talk had probably been lifted into the pages of

A Pair of Blue Eyes, leaving Miss Allamont without a mother. There were, however, fifteen chapters or so left, and if the *New Quarterly* could use them, Hardy would welcome the addition to his income. It would not take long to cover up the scars left by the successive extractions from the early manuscript. In the rewriting the names of the characters were changed, and the first person of the original story was exchanged for the third person which Hardy had used in all six of his published books. Slight though the revision was, it called for a new title, and Hardy accordingly named it "An Indiscretion in the Life of an Heiress." The story appeared in the *New Quarterly* for July, 1878. Hardy was not proud of it. The hasty revision of this less mature piece of early writing came so closely upon the heels of the carefully composed chapters of *The Return of the Native* that the contrast in quality was painfully obvious. The author's willingness to send out a thing like "An Indiscretion" can be explained only on two grounds: the meagerness of his income, which made it desirable for him to take advantage of every opportunity that came his way, and the current comments on a work of genius like *The Return of the Native,* which made him somewhat indifferent to, if not absolutely scornful of, public opinion. "An Indiscretion" would be good enough for readers who could call *The Return of the Native* inferior. According to his own austere artistic code "An Indiscretion" was a trifle which was only of commercial value. He never reprinted it, never referred to it.[1]

"An Indiscretion in the Life of an Heiress" will, however, always be of genuine interest because it is the nearest approach now possible to *The Poor Man and the Lady.* It alone can tell the world what sort of prose Hardy was able to write ten years before he came to describe Egdon Heath. It alone can show what progress in character portrayal he had made in a decade. The ascent from Geraldine to Eustacia is amazing. And even in this slight performance there are marks of the genuine Hardy. There are interesting bits of nature description, characteristic marks of desire for topographical accuracy, the same tendency to delight in secret marriages, accidental meetings, and melancholy deaths, that the six published novels show. And even in these compara-

[1] See Appendix 7, pp. 259-60.

tively insignificant pages the reader can feel the beating of Hardy's tender and sympathetic heart. When Miss Allenville watched the school children going off in the pelting rain and noticed "the rain spots thickening upon the faded frocks, worn-out tippets, yellow straw hats and bonnets, and coarse pinafores of the little flock," she exclaimed, "Poor little wretches!" Egbert's reply is Hardy's own: "Say 'poor little *children*,' madam."

Just as sympathy with the lowly and the unfortunate makes itself apparent in this early fragment, so the reflective habit of Hardy's mind is easily discernible. Hardy knew from his own experience what it was like for Egbert Mayne to make an early start on a new venture.

On the morning of departure he rose at half-past three, for Tollamore was a remote nook of a remote district, and it was necessary to start early. The candle-flame had a sad and yellow look when it was brought into his bedroom. Few things will take away a man's confidence in an impulsive scheme more than being called up by candlelight upon a chilly morning to commence working it out.

"An Indiscretion in the Life of an Heiress" inevitably suffers by its chronological juxtaposition with *The Return of the Native*. Read alone, however, it can entertain in spite of the stiltedness of much of the dialogue and the unreality of the pictures of "high society." And that is, perhaps, all that was wanted for the readers of the *New Quarterly Magazine*. At any rate the editor of the magazine was satisfied. Less than a year later he came back to Hardy for more, and a year after that made still another appeal. In the April, 1879, number of the magazine appeared "The Distracted Preacher," and in April, 1880, "Fellow-Townsmen." Hardy thus embarked upon the business of supplying short stories to magazine editors, and before the end of the century he had written more than forty. It will be convenient to deal with all of them at once and thus avoid having to interrupt the account yet to be given of the full-length novels of the next twenty years.

Hardy's skill as a writer of short stories was immediately recognized by the editors, and with his increasing fame as a novelist the requests for short pieces of fiction multiplied. Quite apart from the periodicals which printed the novels as serials, no less than twenty magazines and reviews printed Hardy stories in the twenty-two years that he devoted to this type of writing. His success in London was quickly followed by reprinting in America. The absence of copyright protection led to more frequent publication in the United States than in England, and Hardy's American audience soon greatly outnumbered his British readers, in spite of the difficulties at times presented to Americans by the Dorset dialect. When the London *Graphic* printed "The Romantic Adventures of a Milkmaid" in its summer issue of 1883, this comparatively insignificant story was promptly snapped up and issued at least ten times in America,[2] whereas at home it was thirty years before Hardy tucked it into a corner of his last volume of collected tales. The spread in time and the unavailability of the magazines may have had something to do in earlier days with the common ignorance regarding Hardy's extensive work as a short-story writer; but after he had gathered his stories into four volumes, there was less excuse for allowing the greater novels to overshadow these minor works so completely. Since many of them are still not widely known—not even by title—the reader may find it convenient to have them listed.[3]

Hardy's short stories have sometimes fallen unannounced into the hands of readers who have been surprised by their high quality. Not all the short stories are excellent or even good. Like the novels, some are very good; some are very poor. In general they show the same characteristics and record the same interests as the novels. They come from the same Wessex environment and through the mind of the same thinker and observer. Some deal with old traditions, some are founded on historical facts, some treat of folk superstitions, and some are Hardy's own inventions. No short story offers an opportunity for the gradual building up of interest in a powerfully drawn character like Eustacia or room for the slow approach of a gathering storm that finally breaks in a scene of dramatic climax and of tragedy. But in their own class and judged by their own proper standards, Hardy's short stories are often excellently done. Among the best are "The Three Strangers,"

[2] See Appendix 7, p. 261.
[3] See Appendix 8, pp. 265-68.

"On the Western Circuit," "The Withered Arm," "A Tragedy of Two Ambitions," and "The Waiting Supper."

"The Three Strangers" deals with the sort of freak of coincidence that Hardy delighted in. A hangman, his intended victim, and the victim's brother all chance, plausibly enough, to meet on a rainy night at Shepherd Fennel's cottage. The situation is boldly sketched. The suppressed terror of the escaped but unrecognized thief, drying himself in the chimney-corner while the hangman expresses his delight at the prospect of professional employment on the morrow, and the embarrassed terror of the thief's brother, who stumbles upon the scene and darts out into the rain again, are excellently contrasted. The brother's impulsive flight leads to an amusing Dogberrian climax, which, in spite of the sensational nature of the preceding events, has been so naturally prepared for that the whole acquires the semblance of truth rather than of fiction. Sir James M. Barrie saw the stage possibilities in "The Three Strangers" and suggested dramatization. Hardy acted on the suggestion, and "The Three Wayfarers" of 1893 was the result.

"On the Western Circuit" deals with a young lawyer who "played the disturbing part in two quiet feminine lives," those of Mrs. Harnham and her maid Anna. That instability of character which has been noticed in the heroines of all of Hardy's novels is here again observed, with the result that another instance of "concatenated affection," though on a smaller scale, occurs. Charles Raye falls in love with the writer of letters he receives; but, because of Mrs. Harnham's deception in allowing him to think that Anna wrote the letters, he marries the maid and learns the truth only when it is too late. He faces an unhappy future "with dreary resignation." The irony of blighted hopes following close upon honorable purposes and sincere intentions is traced with poignant restraint.

In "The Withered Arm" Hardy is back in the company of Susan Nunsuch, dealing with hallucinations and dreams, superstitious fears and conjuror's charms. Coincidence again plays a large part in the action, but the subtle analysis of the normal human motives and feelings of the deformed bride and her alienated husband makes the story seem natural enough and leads the unsuspecting reader up to the powerful climax with which Hardy concludes this little drama. It is an impressive Hallowe'en tale.

"A Tragedy of Two Ambitions" deals with two aspiring sons of a drunken father. With motives of the highest sort they attempt to provide a suitable marriage for their sister, and in a moment of hesitation allow the disreputable father to drown. That act so weighs upon their consciences that their ambitions turn to ashes, and only too late do they come to realize that true greatness of character would have required them "to have endured the cross." It is not a pleasant story, but it is a striking one, and one that gains force from the simplicity and directness with which it is told.

"The Waiting Supper" is not up to the standard of the three stories already described. The first half of it is reminiscent of *The Poor Man and the Lady* and is marred by the same stiltedness of dialogue and artificiality of situation that have been noted in Hardy's earliest work. But after the story has got well under way and Christine has become Mrs. Bellston, it develops into a very characteristic piece of Hardyan irony. For seventeen years Mrs. Bellston and Nicholas Long dutifully await the return of a husband who all that time lies drowned under a waterfall on the estate. The story is told without comment other than to quote with ironic significance Browning's "Statue and the Bust": "Better wait."

While Hardy was engaged upon these "little ironies," a young Russian author (twenty years Hardy's junior) was inventing a new formula for the production of short stories. Most of the Wessex tales, however, were in print before Chekhov's resounding footsteps echoed in England, and Hardy was still content to follow the pattern used by Poe and Maupassant. Not that he consciously imitated the American or the French writer, but his short stories, like theirs, are based on anecdotes. They are, of course, usually more than mere anecdotes, but each relates an unusual and striking incident. Hardy, who was well acquainted with the poetry of Edgar Allan Poe (see pages 245-46), has left no evidence of acquaintance with Poe's critical writings; but whether he knew Poe's formula or not, Hardy's genius for story-telling led him to write in complete agreement with the directions given by Poe:

A skilful literary artist . . . having conceived . . . a certain unique or single effect to be brought out . . . then invents such incidents . . . as may best aid him in establishing this preconceived effect. . . . A picture is at length painted which leaves in the mind of him who contemplates it . . . a sense of the fullest satisfaction.

Only a few of Hardy's short stories measure up to Poe's or to Maupassant's in quality, but Hardy did not, like them, concentrate his efforts upon this type of fiction. It was congenial to him, for it gave him an opportunity to satisfy his taste for the curious and the unusual; but novel writing left him time for only a few really excellent tales.

During the year in which he contributed "The Distracted Preacher" to the *New Quarterly Magazine* he was at work upon a new novel. Its general theme had been in his mind for many years. As a young boy at Bockhampton he had sometimes seen parts of military uniforms and had been told that they were the remains of volunteer-service days, when the Wessex natives had hourly feared invasion by Napoleon. Later, while riding about the country with his father he saw a heap of bricks and clods on a hilltop and was told that they were the remains of the hut which had been occupied by a beacon keeper stationed on the hill in order to light the fire that was to warn the countryside that Napoleon had landed. When he was a young architect at Weymouth he saw outhouse doors riddled with bullet holes and heard that they had been used as targets in firing practice in the days when Napoleon's arrival was hourly expected. For years, therefore, Hardy had kept in mind that time of tense excitement. While he was living at Sturminster Newton he wrote a poem on the siege of Valenciennes and composed the rollicking "Sergeant's Song,"

> When Boney he'll come pouncing down,
> And march his men on London town!

His decision, therefore, to write a novel about the Napoleonic era came about most naturally.

Upon turning his thoughts back, however, to the period of 1800-1815 he found an unexpected difficulty. The new novel must necessarily be based on testimony rather than on observation and experience. He could to some extent trust the recollections of old persons whom he had known in childhood, but these recollections did not easily guide him to the coherent sort of narrative that he liked to write—one event leading logically to another. He became aware, as he said later, "of the difficulty of ascertaining the true sequence of events indiscriminately recalled." To overcome this difficulty Hardy gave himself a careful course of reading. He hunted up the Army Regulations for 1801. He copied down an "Address to All Ranks and Descriptions of Englishmen," found in a museum. He read all the newspapers of the period, as far as he could get hold of them. He bought the two massive volumes of C. H. Gifford's *History of the Wars Occasioned by the French Revolution*, published in London by W. Lewis in 1817. In this work he came upon an amusing description of a drill by local militia; and, thinking it would help him to get a clear picture of what went on in those days of excitement near Weymouth, he copied it out. He little knew what that act was to lead to.

Writing in London about "Overcombe" and "Oxwell Hall," where he had never lived, and about people he had never seen but only heard about, and dealing with events that not only fell outside his own life but also concerned a national crisis such as he himself had never witnessed, Hardy found *The Trumpet-Major* a much more difficult novel to write than *The Return of the Native*. He found it impossible to force historical events into the sort of organically balanced plot that he liked to construct. He discovered that his characters refused to take on the reality of those whose voices he had heard and whose faces he had seen. He finished *The Trumpet-Major* before the end of 1879, but it was not one of his great achievements. "Napoleon" and "Waterloo" were names that still stirred him deeply; but this novel has never aroused readers in the same way. It never will. The lack of sympathy with the spirit of historical romance which had made it impossible for the boy Hardy to enjoy the novels of Sir Walter Scott now made it impossible for the man to accomplish all that he set out to do.

The new story was accepted by a magazine called *Good Words*.

Publication was begun in January and continued throughout 1880. John Collier designed two or three rather crude illustrations for each number. Late in October, just after the November number of the magazine was issued, the novel was published in book form by Smith, Elder & Co. The three volumes, bound in red cloth, sold for 31/6. On the cover of this first edition there was a stiff and rather amateurish drawing of the mill at Overcombe; although it was unacknowledged, this drawing was made by Hardy himself.

The name of the trumpet-major is John Loveday. He and his brother Robert fall in love with pretty Anne Garland, who is graceful and slender and, like many Hardy heroines, uncertain of her own mind. Her shuttle-cock shiftings from one brother to the other leave the reader bewildered; and when she finally chooses Bob and allows John to go off to lose his life "upon one of the bloody battle-fields of Spain," there is no feeling of inevitability, of "rightness," about the conclusion. Festus Derriman is an amusing poltroon who probably owes more than a little to Parolles in *All's Well That Ends Well*. His bravery after learning that the report of Napoleon's landing was a false alarm provides an entertaining chapter. One of the most amusing scenes is that in which the volunteers drill, dressed in their workaday clothes, but eager to do their duty in repelling the invader.

"As every man was anxious to see how the rest stood, those at the end of the line pressed forward for that purpose, till the line assumed the form of a bow. 'Look at ye now! Why, you are all a-crooking in! Dress, dress!' "

The hilarious scene that follows was based closely upon the one that Hardy had copied out of Gifford's *History*. The matter of about three pages is thus adapted, and about 275 of Gifford's exact words reappear. No mention of this borrowing was made in the edition of 1880. The omission was to have unforeseen results.[4]

Before *The Trumpet-Major* had ceased running in *Good Words* Hardy had engaged himself to supply a novel for the European edition of *Harper's Magazine*, and *A Laodicean* began its appearance in December, 1880. Thus one periodical was printing the first installment

[4] See Appendix 7, p. 260.

of a new novel at the same time that another magazine was printing the last installment of an old one. It was doubly unfortunate that Hardy had not already completed the writing of the new story. He had learned by experience the dangers of having to complete a narrative that had already begun to appear in print, but he could not have foreseen the cruel blow that the "colossal Prince of the World" now had in store for him. Upon the eve of the first appearance of *A Laodicean* Hardy was taken seriously ill. He was ordered to bed by the doctor and told to stay there. An internal hemorrhage made it necessary for him to lie with his feet higher than his head, and for nearly six months he lay unable to move. A man of less determination and will would have dropped all thought of completing *A Laodicean*, but Hardy would not listen to such a proposal. Unable to write he dictated the novel to his wife. The completion of the story in the December, 1881, number of *Harper's* and its publication the same year in book form stand as memorials to Hardy's courage and devotion to what he regarded as his duty. These facts make one wish to forget that *A Laodicean* is the poorest novel Hardy ever wrote. George du Maurier's illustrations gave readers something to look at, but it was fifteen years before *Harper's* asked for another novel from Hardy. Even after the revision which he was able to give the work before it appeared in book form, it remained a failure. Not even *Ethelberta* is so jejune. Sampson Low, Marston, Searle, and Rivington—Fleet Street publishers —issued *A Laodicean* in three volumes, bound in slate-green cloth; but even their ponderous name was not enough to make this novel other than light and insignificant.

In the emergency of dictating during a painful sickness Hardy had fallen back upon his own experiences. No novel of his is as full of autobiography as is this one. He recalled a garden party of the preceding year, when a thunderstorm had sent all the guests scampering for shelter. He used that episode. He called up the Rev. Mr. Perkins from memories of Dorchester days, and used him. He plunged his hero Somerset into the technicalities of architecture and filled pages with "shop-talk." He described an architect's interest in poetry and brought in the old themes of social position, belief in one's own future, High

Church arguments, and old families. When these subjects failed, the author turned to his diaries of travels on the continent in the summers of 1876 (the Rhine, Holland, and Belgium) and 1880 (France). Unfortunately Hardy had not been greatly interested in foreign manners and had little to write about in his notes except the appearance of the places he named. So through chapter after chapter his characters wandered in idle and dull uncertainty.

When he had exhausted his own experiences he drew upon his wife's memories. She told him of a man in Cornwall who asked for a drink of wine, calling it "that that isn't gin." That story went into the novel. Then, just as he had used Gifford's *History* while writing *The Trumpet-Major*, he now turned to an article in the *Quarterly Review* for 1833 and copied out a passage by Charles Apperly. This he used in describing Sir William De Stancy.[5] When it was time to bring the villains into the novel, Hardy again slipped into sensationalism. Every reader will wish to draw the curtain upon the scene in the church vestry, in which Dare and Abner Power, each with a revolver in hand, face each other across a table. It is not surprising that Hardy afterward destroyed the manuscript of this novel. When by the middle of 1881 he was able to get up and go about again, he had no heart for further labor over this tedious story. He turned his attention in another direction—to the theater.

Charles Reade (with whom Hardy had called on Prime Minister Disraeli only a few years earlier representing the Association to Protect the Rights of Authors) had written novels and successful plays as well. If Hardy could write dramatic dialogue for Eustacia and Clym in a novel, why not in a play? If Troy and Bathsheba could hold the attention of novel readers by the power of their words, why could they not hold theatergoers in the same way? And since the story of Troy and Bathsheba had already proved successful—in fact their story was the one great success of Hardy's life so far—why not rework that novel into a play?

Hardy set about doing this, but soon discovered that dramatic technique is a different thing from the technique of novel writing. He

---

[5] See Appendix 7, p. 260.

worked away, however, and eventually completed a play based upon *Far from the Madding Crowd*. He then sent his manuscript to a London critic named Comyns Carr, inviting his assistance in making the play better suited for a London theater and in bringing it to the attention of some theater manager. Carr made certain improvements in the text and shortly reported to Hardy that the St. James Theatre had taken the play and that he might look forward to its production.

Hardy had meanwhile moved from London to Wimborne in Dorset. In his exultation over newly regained health, he made rapid progress on a new novel, and he had high hopes for cheering reports on the new venture in London. But on December 27, 1881, the *Times* announced that a new play called "The Squire," by A. W. Pinero, would be opened the following day, and on the twenty-ninth the first performance of that play was reported. Friends immediately rushed letters off to Hardy in Wimborne; and as the year 1881 died out, he was experiencing the same sort of disappointment regarding his dramatic hopes that he had earlier suffered with regard to his poetic aspirations. On the first day of 1882 he wrote the following letter:

To the Editor of The Times:
Sir,
My attention has been drawn to the play entitled *The Squire*, now just produced at the St. James Theatre, by a somewhat general declaration on the part of the daily Press that the play is an unacknowledged adaptation of my novel *Far from the Madding Crowd*. I should have read this announcement with no strong feelings had my labours in connexion with the subject been limited to writing the novel; but the aspect of the matter is changed by the fact, of which the spectators were ignorant, that the managers of the St. James Theatre have had in their hands, not only the novel accessible to everybody, but a manuscript play of my own based on the novel. I had long been impressed with the notion that the central idea of the story—a woman ruling a farm and marrying a soldier secretly, while unselfishly beloved through evil and through good report by her shepherd or bailiff— afforded a promising theme for the stage. I accordingly dramatized the story, sent the play to Mr. Comyns Carr, the art critic, who kindly improved it, and offered the play to the theatre above mentioned. I suggested to him that the rank of the personages should be raised, particularly that Sergeant Troy should appear as a lieutenant, and that in this case the names should

be changed, and he told me that the suggestion was duly reported to the theatre. Moreover, a gipsy who does not exist in the novel, was introduced into our play, and I see that a gipsy figures in *The Squire*. I then learnt that the play was verbally accepted and would soon appear; then that it was rejected. Silence ensued till *The Squire* is proclaimed by many observers as in substance mine. My drama is now rendered useless, for it is obviously not worth while for a manager to risk producing a piece if the whole gist of it is already to be seen by the public at another theatre.

I am, yours faithfully

THOMAS HARDY.

Wimborne, Dorset, Jan. 1.

London readers who preferred the *Daily News* to the *Times* were on January 2, 1882, greeted by a similar letter from Hardy. It began: "The critics who have so unanimously traced the 'new and original' play at the St. James Theatre to my novel *Far from the Madding Crowd* are probably unaware of a fact more singular than that of mere adaptation," and he then went on to tell about the Hardy-Carr play much as he had told it in the letter to the *Times*.

Pinero replied immediately, stating that he was not acquainted with Hardy's work. The theater managers wrote to say that Pinero had assured them that his play was original. Comyns Carr replied; others joined the discussion; and for months the argument was continued. The *Daily News* contained letters on the subject on January 2, 3, 4, 5, 6, 7. The *Times* duplicated this list and added further correspondence on January 9, 10, and 11. On March 3, 1882, the *Times* stated that "the controversy over the coincidences between Mr. Pinero's play and Mr. Hardy's novel is not yet at an end." Hardy himself had contributed nothing after his New Year's Day letters; but others kept the dispute alive, and on March 13, 1882, the *Times* printed a letter from Pinero, lamenting that "now-a-days, on the production of a successful play, the writer of any novel dealing with the same theme, however common the theme, and permeated with the same atmosphere, however common the atmosphere, may start up and claim the sole title to a common subject, and charge the playwright with theft."

In reviewing the history of this controversy, several points must be made clear. First of all, there is no basis for such statements as that published in the New York *Critic* (April, 1906): "Mr. Hardy and Mr. J. W. Comyns Carr dramatized *Far from the Madding Crowd*, which had the same plot as Mr. Pinero's *The Squire*, and this fact led to tiresome litigation." There was no litigation whatever. Not only has no record of any legal action ever been found, but no contemporary reference to the controversy mentions litigation. It was merely a heated newspaper discussion.

In the second place, there is no evidence whatever to support a further statement in *The Critic*, unfortunately repeated elsewhere as if reliable, that "some woman had sold the same plot to Mr. Pinero and to Mr. Hardy without letting either know what she had done." In no contemporary record of the dispute is there any reference to "some woman." At the time of creating the plot of *Far from the Madding Crowd* Hardy was an anonymous writer, and if the story had not been his own he certainly would not have rushed to defend it as his. Pinero, it is true, also declared that the play was his. But Pinero often talked plays and plots over with Kendal, one of the managers of the St. James Theatre, and Kendal had heard about the Hardy-Carr play from his partner Hare, to whom Comyns Carr had submitted the Hardy manuscript. Thus Pinero, without reading Hardy's play or even knowing about its existence, may have gained some knowledge of its plot and then proceeded to write his own play thereon.

In any event the newspaper records of 1882 show that Pinero's *Squire* ran on successfully until July 15, and that in October it was being given at Daly's Theatre in New York. But contrary to his expectation, Hardy's play got onto the stage after all. It was produced at Liverpool on February 27, and on April 29 it opened at the Globe Theatre in London, where it ran less than a month. On May 22 the *Daily News* reported that the Hardy-Carr play was to be given at the Court Theatre, and on the twenty-ninth the same paper reported two performances at the Crystal Palace. In spite of having appeared in four different theaters, the play made no money for Thomas Hardy, and it was hard for him not to agree with his own Henery Fray that "if you do good, you don't get rewarded according to your works, but be cheated in some mean way out of your recompense." It was easy to think of Arthur Wing Pinero as "the impersonator of Heaven's persistent irony."

While he was having this bitter disappointment to swallow, another public attack stung his sensitive nature. On February 18 *The Academy* printed charges (quoted from American magazines) that in both of his last-published novels Hardy had without acknowledgment lifted passages from the work of other authors. In both cases the borrowing was slight. In neither novel had it affected the originality of Hardy's plot or characters. He had done little more than he had been doing with Shakespeare for the last fourteen years. He had made frequent and obvious unacknowledged raids upon the Shakespearean plays; and phrases, lines, and whole passages had been moved from Stratford to serve anew in Wessex. A few words taken from lesser authors were certainly too unimportant to make a fuss over. To Hardy it seemed wisest just to ignore the charges printed by *The Academy*. "This is the chief thing," he learned to quote from Marcus Aurelius: "Be not perturbed."

There was, however, a mystery connected with the episode in *The Trumpet-Major*. *The Critic* charged Hardy with lifting a passage from an American author named A. B. Longstreet, author of *Georgia Scenes*, first published in 1835 and reprinted with illustrations in New York in 1840. Now Hardy had never heard of this book or of its author. He did not say so in 1882; but fourteen years later, when a collected edition of his novels gave *The Critic* an occasion for repeating its charge of plagiarism from *Georgia Scenes*, Hardy then declared. "I know nothing of the latter work. Some of the details of this drill were suggested by a similar description in Gifford's *History*." And that was his final word on the subject. The charge and denial have continued to mystify students ever since, for the simple reason that no one can read "The Militia Company Drill" in Longstreet's book without seeing at once that it *is* the original of Hardy's drilling episode. Since no previous biography of Hardy has given any explanation of this curious bibliographical dilemma, it may be well to state the facts here.

Hardy had taken his drill scene from Gifford's *History*, as he afterward acknowledged in the preface of his novel. But in making his transcription from Gifford he had failed, even though he owned the book, to notice that Gifford was not the author of the passage. Gifford had quoted from John Lambert's *Travels through Lower Canada and the United States in the Years 1806, 1807, and 1808.* This book of *Travels* was in its day a very successful publication. The first edition appeared in London in 1810 (published in three volumes by Richard Phillips). A second edition in 1813 (reprinted in 1814) was issued by C. Cradock & W. Joy in two volumes, and a third edition was published by Baldwin, Cradock & Joy in 1816. But the passage which Gifford took from Lambert had not been written by Lambert. He, too, was quoting. In the second volume of the *Travels* Lambert declared that at New York he had gone on board one of the regular packets for Charleston on January 9, 1808, and found himself again on shore in South Carolina on the twenty-third. Then he said: "While I was at Charleston I met with an excellent satire. As it may afford my readers some amusement, I have taken the liberty to lay it before them."

What John Lambert found in Charleston was a pamphlet (or a reprint of it) entitled *The Ghost of Baron Steuben.* It must have been written and printed as early as 1807. No author's name appeared upon it, but everyone in Georgia (where the author lived) knew it to be the work of an amusing lawyer by the name of Oliver H. Prince. At least one copy of Prince's comical pamphlet has survived. Its physical appearance—without date, name of author, or name of publisher— leads to the conjecture that it may have been reprinted (perhaps using the same type) from the *Washington* [Georgia] *Monitor,* a newspaper edited by Prince's uncle, David P. Hillhouse. In the years following the first publication of *The Ghost of Baron Steuben* it was frequently reprinted in other newspapers (for example, in the *Augusta* [Georgia] *Chronicle,* the *Louisville* [Kentucky] *Public Advertiser,* and the *States Rights Sentinel,* Augusta, Georgia), and in the course of these reprintings it came to be known under various titles: "Captain Clodpole"; "The Oglethorpe Muster"; and "The Militia Company Drill." In the year 1835 A. B. Longstreet published a book of descriptive sketches which he called *Georgia Scenes.* Among his own work he included Prince's "Drill," stating in a footnote that this one sketch was "from the pen of a friend." Longstreet's book became famous at the time, and it was reprinted in New York in 1840 and frequently thereafter. Thus the "Militia Company Drill" had come to be widely known in America before Hardy's *Trumpet-Major* appeared in 1880 with its similar passage. American readers did not know Gifford; English readers, including Hardy, did not know Longstreet; and Lambert, who had provided the transatlantic transportation for Prince's sketch, had been long forgotten. The bibliographical mystery disappears in noting this sequence of events: O. H. Prince wrote his sketch in or before 1807. Lambert picked it up in Charleston in 1808 and printed it in London in 1810. Gifford copied it from Lambert in 1817. Longstreet copied the same sketch directly from Prince in 1835 and reprinted it frequently thereafter. In 1880 Hardy adapted it out of Gifford. And Hardy's American readers, knowing nothing of Gifford or of Lambert or of Prince, accused the Wessex author of stealing from Judge Longstreet, of Georgia.

During the weary half-year that Hardy spent lying upon his back he had plenty of opportunity to meditate on the smallness of his own life in contrast with the bigness of the universe represented by the sky which he could see through the window—the sun and clouds by day and the stars at night. The poetical thought occurred to him that he might write a novel in which he would "set the emotional history of two infinitesimal lives against the stupendous background of the stellar universe." Wimborne, where he had settled after his illness, was a town not much more than twenty miles from Dorchester and even nearer to Sturminster Newton, where *The Return of the Native* had been written. At Wimborne he found an interesting old minster and a curious churchyard, his study of which resulted, in the following year, in his writing an amusing poem, "The Levelled Churchyard." Two unexpected things connected with this move to Wimborne recalled his previous thoughts "of the stellar universe." He arrived in Wimborne on June 25, 1881, and that evening noticed a comet in the sky. Shortly afterward he made the discovery that in Charborough Park, an estate near the town, there was an old tower which suggested astronomical studies. Hardy's father had owned a seaman's telescope, and boyhood memories of seeing his father peer through it, sometimes for half an hour at a time, came back to him. Hardy made a special trip to the Greenwich Observatory, and he then felt ready to proceed with his story.

The novel was rapidly written. Hardy even dispensed with the usual frills of chapter titles or mottoes. In spite of an August excursion into Scotland, he had the manuscript of *Two on a Tower* ready to mail across the ocean before the end of 1881, and in the January number of the *Atlantic Monthly* this astronomical story began its year's run. It was the first of Hardy's novels to make its first appearance in a foreign magazine. In November, 1882, *Two on a Tower* was issued, in three volumes, bound in green cloth, by Sampson Low, Marston, Searle & Rivington. The publication price was 31/6 ($7.50).[6]

Hardy's own words tell what happened next.

On the publication of the book people seemed to be less struck with the high aims of the author than with their own opinion, first, that the novel was an "improper" one in its morals, and, secondly, that it was intended to be a satire on the Established Church of this country. I was made to suffer in consequence from several eminent pens,—such warm epithets as "hazardous," "repulsive," "little short of revolting," "a studied and gratuitous insult," being flung at the precarious volumes. It is sufficient to draw attention to the fact that the Bishop is every inch a gentleman, and that the parish priest who figures in the narrative is one of its most estimable characters.

Victorian readers of the novel were upset by Viviette's deception of the Bishop of Melchester regarding the parentage of her son. Modern readers will be more disturbed by that old defect of Hardy's—the woodenness of the people in polite society. *Two on a Tower* is classed among Hardy's second-rate novels simply because it is deficient in the two things he knew best, rural characters and natural phenomena. Amos Fry appears all too little, and the "shade-loving insects who had engraved patterns of no human style or meaning" around the base of the astronomer's tower are not pertinent in this study of stellar space. Stars seen through the telescope cannot take the place of slugs and toads and maggots fondly watched on Egdon Heath. When the bishop

---

[6] See Appendix 7, p. 261.

and Lady Constantine discuss the bowling scene of *Richard II*, one wishes he could slip away to a different talk of bowling and listen to Joseph Poorgrass (in *Far from the Madding Crowd*) telling how he had served as "errand-man at the Women's Skittle Alley at the back of the Tailor's Arms in Casterbridge." Occasionally Hardy falls back upon his own experiences. Mr. Torkingham's amusing efforts in training the choir to sing "Honwerd, Christen sojers," are reminiscent of Hardy's own observations as a boy at the Stinsford church.

Swithin's remarks to Viviette are less like those of a zealous young astronomer than like those of a sick author gazing in melancholy impotence at the sky: "Until a person has thought out the stars and their interspaces, he has hardly learnt that there are things much more terrible than monsters of shape, namely, monsters of magnitude without known shape. Such monsters are the voids and waste places of the sky." When he wrote that "events mocked her [Viviette] on all sides," Hardy thought back over the past five years of his own life; but in his bitterest moment he could not have foreseen the irony of his making another astronomer "forestall by a period of about six weeks" Swithin's discovery with regard to variable stars, only a short time before Pinero was to forestall by a similar period Hardy's experiment with the London theater. Viviette's unselfish and half-maternal devotion to a young lover is tenderly portrayed, and readers ought to have been grateful to Hardy for a heroine with qualities that he usually reserved for his men. But Viviette never achieves the reality of Bathsheba or of Eustacia, and her brother comes and goes with mechanical artificiality.

Hardy's melancholy view of a universe indifferent to mankind and possibly without guidance of any kind was deepened by the announcement of the death of Charles Darwin. On April 26, 1882, Hardy attended the funeral of the man whose *Origin of Species* he had been one of the first to read and appreciate in all its epochal significance. And as the eighteen-eighties wore on, his reading and interest in science led to an interest in philosophy. English writers led him back to German philosophers, particularly to Eduard von Hartmann, whose influence can be detected in the novels that Hardy wrote next.

X

PORTRAIT OF A MAN OF
CHARACTER

IN VIEW OF the chorus of disapproval that followed the publication
of *Two on a Tower*, Hardy felt little inclined to begin work at once
upon another novel. He was particularly grateful, therefore, for the
genuine appreciation that he found in an article on "The Novels of
Thomas Hardy" in the *Westminster Review* for April, 1883. It was
written by Havelock Ellis. Here was a critic who seemed able to meet
the author more than half way. On April 29 Hardy wrote from
Wimborne to Ellis:

I have read with great interest your article in the *Westminster*, and can in-
adequately express by letter my sense of your generous treatment of the
subject. I consider the essay a remarkable paper in many ways. If novelists
were a little less in the dark about the appearance of their own works, what
productions they might bring forth! But they are much in the position of
the man inside the hobby-horse at a Christmas masque, and have no consciousness of the absurdity of its trot, at times, in the spectator's eyes.

A few years before this Hardy had, through his membership in the
Savile Club in London, become acquainted with another man, whose
friendship was to continue and gladden his heart for the next fifty
years. Edmund Gosse, like Havelock Ellis, saw the real merit in
Hardy's work and poured a warmth of friendship out upon the Wessex
author that Hardy was much in need of. Letters and visits were exchanged. In June, 1883, Hardy dined with Gosse in London. Shortly
afterward, while Hardy was looking for a house to which to move on
leaving Wimborne, Gosse visited him in Dorset. Later the two traveled
together as far west as Bridport, where, having lost their way in the

leafy mazes of that borough, they asked a grave young countryman the way to the railroad station. Gosse long remembered that "not content with misdirecting us, the scoundrel must needs officiously conduct us up terraced paths until he had seen us fairly started on the highway that led out of the *opposite* end of the town!" Gosse asked Hardy if this was the vaunted courtesy of the Wessex yokel; and Hardy could only suggest that the young man had acted in good faith, but that he had probably never traveled as far as the railroad station.

Hardy eventually settled upon Dorchester as the town to which he would move when his two-year lease at Wimborne expired. Not being able to find the sort of house he wanted, he decided with some hesitation to build one. Meanwhile he found temporary quarters in Shire Hall Lane, Dorchester, to which he moved in June, 1883. About one mile from town, on the north side of the road to Wareham, he acquired a one- or two-acre plot of ground, and for two years he resumed the architect's profession for which he had studied in Hicks's office. Work was begun on the property in October and was continued throughout 1884. On June 29, 1885, he moved into his own home, which he called Max Gate. According to Vere H. Collins the second Mrs. Hardy supplied the following explanation of the name:

The little cottage a few yards further up the road used to be a toll-gate kept by a man called Mack. In the scene in *The Dynasts*, where the beacon is lit on the Ridgeway, one of the characters is made to say that from up there the light at "Mack's Gate" can be seen. When my husband bought the plot of ground on which to build, Mack had been dead some time, but this point on the road was still known locally as Mack's Gate. My husband felt he could not call his house "Mack's Gate," but he wished to preserve the old association, and so he called it Max Gate.

Here he lived until his death. This does not mean that he became the hermit that some people imagine him to have been. In the next twenty years he spent months at a time in London, usually in the spring. But except for seasonal visits to the city his days of house hunting were over. The native had returned to stay.

During the twenty months during which he supervised the construction of his house Hardy did little writing, especially in the first part of this period. He rushed through the "Milkmaid" story already referred to and wrote a tale[1] requested by the *Youth's Companion*. The story of the "Interlopers" is one of two published in 1884.[1] Shortly before moving into Max Gate, he wrote a short story ("A Tryst") suggested by the ancient earthworks near Dorchester and afterward dealt with these same curious prehistoric remains in a descriptive article. Ancient landmarks had always interested him. Shortly before leaving Wimborne he had joined the Society for the Protection of Ancient Buildings, and he remained a member until his death. After settling in Dorchester, he made at the request of this society several visits of inspection to old buildings in Dorset and made reports on them. In this gratuitous labor he wrote descriptions of the old tower of the East Lulworth Church and the White Horse Inn at Maiden Newton. Nor was he interested merely in mounds and buildings. Farm laborers and stonemasons, country vicars and corn merchants— all came under his eye and found their way at one time or another into prose writing that was quite independent of his fiction. In the July, 1883, number of *Longman's Magazine* he wrote on "The Dorsetshire Labourer," objecting to his being regarded as "Hodge." From this time on he was frequently engaged in minor literary activities, which are easily overlooked among his major achievements.[2]

One of the reasons for the immense superiority of *The Return of the Native* over the novels written immediately before and immediately after it is the leisurely pace that Hardy was able to set during his residence at Sturminster Newton. Hasty work never brought good results with him. He was a writer to whom time for careful revision was important. That is one reason why London never appealed to him as a permanent residence. He could endure the city for a season, but the quiet and the leisure of the country were necessary for his best work. During the latter part of the months spent in daily supervision of the construction of his new house Hardy enjoyed this quiet and this leisure. Accepting no contracts that demanded immediate fulfillment,

---

[1] See Appendix 8, p. 266.
[2] For a list of these articles and essays see Appendix 2, p. 236.

resolutely declining to let any periodical begin a story of his until he had the manuscript entirely completed, he provided himself with the conditions necessary for the incubation of another work of art. For an entire year he worked off and on at a new manuscript; and when, on April 17, 1885, he wrote the last words, recording his discovery that happiness is not merely an "occasional episode in a general drama of pain," even then he allowed himself time for those last touches and afterthoughts which often account for the distinction of his style. This conscientious care is one reason why *The Mayor of Casterbridge* is a great novel.

Another reason is that in writing about Dorchester ("Casterbridge") he was dealing with material with which he had been acquainted for thirty-five years. No need here to consult histories of Napoleonic wars or to visit astronomical observatories. He had known the brick bridge and its loafers and the stone bridge with its shabby-genteel ever since boyhood. He remembered the iron railing on which as a boy he had climbed up to peer in on the hangman placidly eating his supper the night before a public execution. The grizzled church of St. Peter's, the dark walk along the Froom River, the old Roman Ring, the King's Arms Hotel, and the workhouse were all as well known to him as Egdon Heath. No wonder Robert Louis Stevenson could declare: "Dorchester is touched in with the hand of a master."

In planning this new novel Hardy decided to do several things that he had never done before. The more closely a reader examines *The Mayor of Casterbridge* the more he will be impressed with the fresh marks of originality that it shows. With the exception of those stories that deal with polite society, all of Hardy's novels had been set in an agricultural background. The characters are farmers and shepherds, tranters and dairymen. He now planned to turn to town life and to deal with merchants and innkeepers and other townsmen. In his previous stories Dorset rustics had been used chiefly to provide comic interludes. He now planned to give them a serious, even though minor, part in the plot. And as for that plot, he decided to write for the first time a novel that was not in any important respect a love story, but one in which he would center the drama in one person. Although the formula of "concatenated affections" need not be entirely forgotten, it was to be definitely placed in the background. Susan and Lucetta are never allowed to assume a major role, and Elizabeth-Jane's self-effacement is partly Hardy's artistic effacement of her. Of the men, Newson hardly appears upon the stage at all, and Farfrae comes on just enough to annoy native Scots with his accent (picked up by Hardy in 1881 from a young Edinburgh cab driver) and to annoy some envious readers by his unbroken good luck. But Henchard is a full-length portrait, and the novel is truly subtitled "A Story of a Man of Character."

In deciding to present "The Life and Death" of Michael Henchard Hardy was again breaking with his former practice. Most of his stories had emphasized the unpredictability of human fate, the inscrutability of the workings of the colossal Prince of the World. Character after character had echoed Henery Fray's opinion that "your lot is your lot, and Scripture is nothing." While lying in bed for six months in London, Hardy had had excellent opportunity for sounding the shallowness of this myopic sort of determinism; and in the novel dictated to Mrs. Hardy there is a revealing observation placed in the mouth of Sir William De Stancy: "With a disposition to be happy, it is neither this place nor the other that can render us the reverse. In short, each man's happiness depends upon himself." Hardy now decided to write an entire novel upon this theme, that "Character is Fate."

The genesis of Henchard's character is worth lingering over for a moment, since he is the most forceful and one of the most original characters that Hardy ever drew. The author began by calling him "James Henchard," and not until the story was completed to the last page of the manuscript was the mayor's name changed to the now familiar Michael. The name did not greatly matter, at least in the early conception of the story. What was settled from the start was that he was to be a colossal figure—no puny nonentity, but a heroic man cast in Shakespearean mold. That was the starting point; and, as Hardy once remarked, "it is easy for an author to take a person, and see the potentialities in his temperament for the events he creates." The naturalness of Henchard's make-up has inevitably aroused questions as to where his original was found, for Hardy often repeated the statement he made to Henry Arthur Jones, that he had never put a character into one of his books that he had not had warranty for in real life. Readers who have been told that "*The Mayor of Casterbridge* may be rightly described as owing its origin to both Biblical and classical influences" may succeed in discovering traces of *Samson Agonistes,* Aeschylus, and *King Lear.* But what makes Michael Henchard a man of such marked individuality is the fact that his conduct throughout the story has about it the genuine surprise of real life.

In September, 1883—at the time when Hardy was planning Max Gate—Trollope's *Autobiography* appeared. Hardy had long been interested in the older novelist. He had bought a copy of *Barchester Towers* to send to his sister, for Trollope's "Barsetshire" was the talk of London when young Hardy arrived there. Later in the seventies Hardy bought a copy of Trollope's *The Eustace Diamonds,* and he afterward admitted that he admired its construction. Trollope's "Barchester" and Hardy's "Melchester" refer to the same city. Late in life Hardy remarked to a caller:

"I like Trollope. You know, at one time it was thought he was going to be recognized as the greatest of the Victorian novelists. Dickens was said to be too much of a caricaturist; Thackeray too much of a satirist. Trollope was put forward as the happy mean."

Anthony Trollope died on November 3, 1882, and a year later everyone was reading the famous *Autobiography,* which he had left in the hands of his son. Referring to the year 1833 Trollope had written:

Just before Christmas my brother died, and was buried at Bruges. In the following February my father died, and was buried alongside of him. I sometimes look back, meditating for hours together, on his adverse fate. He was a man of great parts, with immense capacity for work, physically strong very much beyond the average of men, addicted to no vices, carried off by no pleasures, affectionate by nature, most anxious for the welfare of his children, born to fair fortunes,—who, when he started in the world, may be said to have had everything at his feet. But everything went wrong with him. The touch of his hand seemed to create failure. He embarked in one hopeless enterprise after another, spending on each all the money he could at the time command. But the worst curse to him of all was a temper so irritable that even those whom he loved the best could not endure it. We were all estranged from him, and yet I believe that he would have given his heart's blood for any of us. His life as I knew it was one long tragedy.

There you have the catalogue of Michael Henchard's character. The "great parts," the "immense capacity for work," the physical strength, the affectionate nature, the irritable temper, the estrangement from his family, the business folly, the death in a foreign land, all are his. His life, like that of Trollope's father, was one long tragedy. If the suggestion that there is a relationship between the two makes it seem to some as if the delicate gossamer of literary hypothesis were being spun too thin, it will at least serve to correct any tendency to condemn Hardy for an overdrawn picture. Those who regard the sad fortunes of the mayor of Casterbridge as due chiefly to a bad case of cynicism on the part of the novelist will do well to read over again Trollope's account of his own father. Hardy began his novel six months after the *Autobiography* appeared.

In creating the events with which to show Michael Henchard in action Hardy was somewhat influenced by his knowledge that the novel was to appear in the weekly magazine *The Graphic*. The tone of this publication invited an emphasis on the sensational, and in later years Hardy was inclined to believe that he had yielded somewhat to the temptation to get some striking episode into every installment. Certain it is that the story is unusually crowded with happenings. This provided less opportunity for the gradual, carefully-prepared working up to a crashing climax. An over-supply of incident, however, does not mean the loss of reality. There is a much smaller amount of coincidence in this novel; one episode is merged so logically into the next that the gradual decline of Henchard's fortunes seems inevitable. And the novel is rich in vivid and memorable scenes. From the striking opening episode when Henchard sells his wife to the tragic discovery of his penciled will, Hardy's invention never flags. The fight in the granary-loft between Farfrae and Henchard, with one arm of the latter tied against his side so that his superior strength might be no unfair advantage to him; Henchard on the brink of Ten Hatches

Weir, planning suicide and horrified to see his own effigy floating as
if dead in the water before him; Henchard on the ramparts of Mai
Dun Castle, telescope in hand, spying on Elizabeth-Jane's meetings
with Farfrae; the fatal skimmington ride of the "two images on a
donkey, back to back, their elbows tied to one another's"; the startling
announcement that "Michael Henchard have busted out drinking
after taking nothing for twenty-one years":—these are only a few of
the incidents which are hard to forget. So neatly is the entire action
knit together that the passage of twenty-one years hardly destroys the
unity of time. *The Return of the Native* has achieved greater distinction for structural unity only because it takes place within a single year.

On the last page of his manuscript Hardy noted: "Written 1884-85."
Publication of *The Mayor of Casterbridge* began in *The Graphic* on
January 2, 1886, and ended on May 15. Robert Barnes drew twenty
illustrations. In America the novel was issued simultaneously in
Harper's Weekly. In May it was published by Smith, Elder & Co. in
two volumes, the first of Hardy's books to appear bound in blue
cloth. Its success was immediate. "Henchard is a great fellow," wrote
Robert Louis Stevenson, and George Gissing pleased Hardy by con-
fessing: "In your books I have constantly found refreshment and
onward help." "Michael Henchard," declared William Sharp, "is one
of Mr. Hardy's most noteworthy creations." In 1887 a new one-volume
edition, in red cloth, was issued by Sampson Low, Marston, Searle &
Rivington; and uniform with it were reissues of six of the earlier
novels. *A Pair of Blue Eyes* had already reached a third edition, and
The Trumpet-Major shortly did also. Prosperous winds were beginning
to blow in the direction of Max Gate.

With them came a chill blast from across the Atlantic Ocean. Late
in October of 1886 reports of an article in the New York *World*
reached London and led to Edmund Gosse's writing a letter on
November 19 to William Dean Howells, in which he said:

Thomas Hardy, our greatest novelist over here, as I think, was very much
wounded by what Lowell was reported to have said about him. There are
circumstances in the case which make the sneer at Hardy's personal appearance singularly cruel. I cannot myself believe that Lowell said all that.

Hardy, who has always been a great supporter and admirer of Lowell, is wretched at this supposed snub.

The "sneer" and the "snub" to which Gosse referred are found in a report by Julian Hawthorne, Nathaniel's son, of a conversation he had with James Russell Lowell. According to Hawthorne, Lowell had remarked: "I had been told that Mr. Thomas Hardy was very good, and I took up one of his books—*Two on a Tower*—but I did not get on with it. Afterwards I met him; he is small and unassuming in appearance—does not look like the genius of tradition."

These words, to twentieth-century eyes, are nothing to feel "very much wounded" or "wretched" over, and hardly justify the alarm expressed by Gosse's letter. They will, however, serve to remind the reader that skins were thinner and sensibilities more accessible in Victorian days. Hardy never learned to close his ears to criticism. One of his earliest letters to Macmillan reveals his extreme sensitiveness to adverse remarks, and to the end of his long career this same painful characteristic remained with him. Lowell obviously intended no snub and promptly repudiated Hawthorne's report of their conversation.[3] But wounded vanity does not easily heal, and the Victorians were being constantly hurt. Because he had not been invited to Queen Victoria's Jubilee at Westminster Abbey on June 21, 1887, Robert Browning hurried off to Oxford rather than remain in London. Just because at the Savile there were a number of men who wrote for the *Saturday Review*, which had the day before published a bitter attack on *Tess of the D'Urbervilles*, Hardy wrote on January 17, 1892, to his novelist friend Besant to ask: "Would you resign membership in the Savile Club, if you were in my place?"

Lowell should, of course, have tried *The Mayor of Casterbridge* instead of *Two on a Tower*. The magnificently truthful picture of English life there recorded would have appealed to his England-loving heart. To read *The Mayor of Casterbridge* carefully is as good as— nay, better than—a prolonged visit to Dorchester. Into the rich pages of this novel Hardy had distilled all that his thirty-five-year knowledge of Dorchester had taught him.

[3] See Appendix 7, p. 261.

Those who have been told that there is no humor in this novel should turn to the scene in which Mr. Grower, Constable Blowbody, and Stubberd attempt to find the men who were responsible for the "skimmington" ride. "What can we two poor lammigers do against such a multitude!" exclaim these Dorset successors to Dogberry and Verges. And readers who have been taught to expect nothing but gloom in a Hardy novel, who have been told that though he saw life steadily he did not see it whole, ought to notice that Elizabeth-Jane's adult life was one of "unbroken tranquillity," that she classed herself "among the fortunate," and that her path was "irradiated by rich daybeams" of such continuous "calm weather" that there would have been no novel to write about her. Troubled though he was by human suffering, Hardy was fully awake to the fact that life contains other things besides misfortune and pain.

Among the delighted readers of *The Mayor of Casterbridge* was a Miss Rebekah Owen, of New York City. She and her sister Catharine went to Dorchester in 1892 and became acquainted with Hardy and his wife. The Owen sisters began to read Hardy in New York and continued a systematic study of the Wessex novels after becoming residents of Dorchester.[4] Upon purchasing there a copy of *The Mayor of Casterbridge* Rebekah Owen was surprised to discover that the English version supplied a different ending from that with which she had become familiar in America. When she asked Hardy why he had made the change, he replied that in revising the serial version of the novel for its appearance in book form he had thought that it weakened the story to have Henchard go away twice. Hardy therefore omitted "nearly a chapter" dealing with Henchard's return to Elizabeth-Jane's wedding, his purchase of the caged goldfinch, and the slow starvation of the poor bird after his embittered departure from Casterbridge. Miss Owen maintained that Hardy was wrong in thinking these events weakened the story. She finally convinced him, and he promised her that in a new edition of the novel he would restore the goldfinch, the return to the wedding, and the second departure. He carried out his

---

[4] See Appendix 7, p. 262.

promise in 1895, when *The Mayor of Casterbridge* appeared with a preface in which Hardy called attention to the restoration and stated that it "was made at the instance of some good judges across the Atlantic, who strongly represented that the home edition suffered from the omission."

XI

IN THE LAND OF APPLE TREES

THE FIRST NOVEL which Hardy wrote at Max Gate was *The Woodlanders*. The writing room on the second floor of the new house was the scene of diligent application almost from the moment he moved in. But again he took his time and refused to be rushed. He had a special reason for wishing this next novel to be as good as he could make it. His name was to appear in *Macmillan's Magazine*. It must have been with a good deal of satisfaction that he had received, two years or so before, in London, a request for a novel from the publishing house which had rejected his first two offerings. Macmillan and his editor, John Morley, were now as glad to have the novelist's promise of a manuscript as Hardy would at that earlier date have been pleased to have the publisher's acceptance of one.

Hardy worked hard in planning the new story, some days spending more than twelve hours at his desk. Not content with the fresh ground broken in *The Mayor of Casterbridge*, he planned further original work in *The Woodlanders*. In both setting and time this novel was to be different from all his previous work. For the scene of the story he chose a neighborhood into which he had never ventured before—the wooded region a dozen or fifteen miles northwest of Dorchester; a country which lay, as he afterward specified, "in the hamlets of Hermitage, Middlemarsh, Lyons-Gate, Revels Inn, Holnest, Melbury Bubb, etc.,—all lying more or less under the eminence called High Stoy, just beyond Minterne and Dogbury Gate, where the country descends into the Vale of Blackmore." Minterne Parva and Minterne Magna suggested the names "Little Hintock" and "Great Hintock"; but Hardy made no further attempt to be geographically specific. Years later he confessed: "I myself do not know where 'Little Hintock' is!"

Just as the country of *The Woodlanders* was a new addition to the geography of the Wessex Novels, so the time chosen for the action was a period never before used by Hardy. He had formed the habit of distributing his time charts methodically over the nineteenth century, just as he plotted his settings carefully on the map. Hardy later pointed out that the geographical atmosphere of each of his major novels is distinct and that the settings do not overlap. In the same way the calendars for the various novels are kept separate.[1] *The Mayor of Casterbridge* had dealt with the period 1827-1849. In this novel the quiet mention of Boldwood as a young farmer reminds the reader that *The Mayor of Casterbridge,* though written later than *Far from the Madding Crowd,* deals with an earlier period. Boldwood serves as a link between the two stories. He is twenty years older in *Far from the Madding Crowd,* the action of which begins in 1869 and ends in 1873. The last date Hardy decided to follow up in *The Woodlanders.* He planned the action to cover the two and a half years from Christmas, 1876, to March, 1879.

Hardy also attempted a third innovation in *The Woodlanders.* His earlier novels had expressed with ever-increasing frankness his revolt against the fundamental conditions of existence in a badly constituted world. From his youthful shaking of his fist at his Creator he had progressed in *The Mayor of Casterbridge* to a consideration of the close relationship between defects, not in nature, but in human nature, and man's unhappiness on earth. And now in *The Woodlanders* he turned for the first time to question seriously how far the organization of society itself is responsible for man's unhappiness. When Grace Melbury's marriage proves a failure, Hardy makes her wonder "whether God did really join them together." What man alone had joined, man could put asunder. Hardy's increasingly bitter quarrel with society for its attitude toward sex relationships here makes its first appearance, and for the next twenty-five years the subject is never long absent from his writings, whether prose or verse. *The Woodlanders*

---

[1] See p. 182 and Appendix 7, pp. 259, 263-64.

sounds the initial challenge, and its characters are the first of Hardy's creations to blame neither God nor themselves but human conventions.

At least one writer on Hardy[2] has suggested that this change is closely related to events in Hardy's own life, not only to unhappiness in his own marriage (about which more will be said in a later chapter) but also to unhappiness in "a marriage other than his own . . . Circumstances of this other marriage became known to him after his move to Dorchester" and "one of the partners in it came to have an affection for him." Unfortunately external evidence is almost entirely lacking, and it is extremely dangerous to infer bitter experiences for Hardy from conjectured echoes in *The Woodlanders*.

The hamlet of Melbury Bubb supplied a name for one of the characters; and the numerous Winterbornes in the neighborhood of Max Gate—Winterborne Abbas, Winterborne Came, Winterborne Monkton, and others—supplied the name of a second character. The old formula of "concatenated affections" was again used. Marty loves Giles; Giles loves Grace; Grace loves Fitzpiers; Fitzpiers loves Mrs. Charmond. Three women and two men, set in "one of those sequestered spots outside the gates of the world," are all that Hardy required for presenting a drama "of a grandeur and unity truly Sophoclean, by virtue of the concentrated passions and closely-knit interdependence of the lives therein."

The theme of the story is one that Hardy had already used—the clash between rustic simplicity and urban veneer, between self-sacrificing loyalty and dissatisfied selfishness. George Melbury is eager to make a "good match" for his daughter, and to satisfy him she turns her back on her steadfast rural admirer, Giles Winterborne, and accepts the attentions of the flashy Dr. Fitzpiers. The doctor is a piece of human flotsam who is as unreconciled to the placid life of the woodlanders as Eustacia was, in *The Return of the Native*, to life on Egdon Heath. He marries Grace, but with tragic results. Giles's happiness founders in the shoals of Melbury's blind social ambition, and the representatives of a sophisticated urban society (Dr. Fitzpiers and Mrs. Charmond) come to the woodlands only to bring bitterness and

<hr/>

2 William R. Rutland, *Thomas Hardy*, London, Blackie & Son, 1938, pp. 86-87.

death in their train. The tragedy is relieved by glowing accounts of the humble activities of the woodlanders. The cider making, in which Hardy's father was an expert, is described with an affection and a vividness which leave no doubt as to the group with which Hardy himself sympathized.

Hardy spent fifteen months in writing *The Woodlanders*—from November, 1885, to February 4, 1887. Once the planning was finished, he settled down to more leisurely writing. According to his own declaration he worked at his manuscript once a week—on Fridays. It is indicative of Hardy's mastery that a novel like *The Woodlanders* could be written in this occasional fashion. The story appeared in *Macmillan's Magazine* from May, 1886, to April, 1887; and on March 15, 1887, it was published by Macmillan & Co., in three volumes, bound, appropriately for such a title, in green cloth. Hardy sent Swinburne a copy, which is now in the Harvard University library. Before the end of 1887 the three-volume edition was exhausted, and Macmillan reissued the story in one volume at about the time that a second edition of *The Mayor of Casterbridge* was being published by Sampson Low & Co.[3]

The Woodlanders belongs in the list of Hardy's greatest novels, but of that list it is the one least frequently read. This judgment on the part of the public Hardy thought a mistake. He considered *The Woodlanders* in some respects his best novel. There were other people who agreed with him. One of them, Robert Louis Stevenson, was about to leave England on August 22, 1887. In the excitement of getting ready for the voyage he was chiefly concerned because of his lack of *The Woodlanders*. The afternoon of Sunday the twenty-first was made memorable for Edmund Gosse, for he had to scour London to find copies of the three green volumes. Eventually he found them, "borrowed or stolen somewhere," and Stevenson then felt equipped for the voyage. John A. Steuart declared: "Such a book as *The Woodlanders* is enough to make one feel proud of one's generation." The only reason that will satisfactorily account for the comparative neglect of this novel by modern readers is that there are five other Wessex Novels which

---

[3] See Appendix 7, pp. 261-62.

are provided with more powerfully drawn characters or more strikingly dramatic incidents.

In spite of this admission *The Woodlanders* remains one of Hardy's great works. It is certainly one of the sweetest and tenderest; "his loveliest," Sir Arthur Quiller-Couch called it. Marty South is one of the reasons for the charm of this book. Its opening scene discloses her, and the last scene is wholly hers. She is the real heroine of the novel, not Grace Melbury. Her humble occupation, her quiet contentedness with little, her self-sacrifice and meekness, all make it easy for the reader to overlook her, exactly as Giles Winterborne did. Marty's loyalty and constancy prove that not all Hardy heroines are fickle, vain, irresponsible creatures, and the perfume of her warmhearted character joins with the odor of Winterborne's cider to give this story a fragrance and a quality found nowhere else in the Wessex series. This quality is of course of a more delicate sort. There are no strenuous events like Henchard's fight with Farfrae, Wildeve's drowning, or Boldwood's shooting of Troy. There are no gripping scenes like those between Clym and Eustacia; the domestic life of Grace and Fitzpiers is shown perhaps too little. The man-trap does not prove fatal, as the closed door in *The Return of the Native* and the skimmington ride in *The Mayor of Casterbridge* had done. And although Giles dies (he is, in fact, the only one in all the Wessex Novels to give his life for love), his dying is not the death of a Sydney Carton or of the youth in Browning's poem "In a Gondola," but the quiet death of a rural Socrates.

Much of the charm of *The Woodlanders* comes from the descriptions of Wessex customs, as in the scene in which the Hintock maids go into the woods on Midsummer Eve "to attempt some spell or enchantment which would afford them a glimpse of their future partners for life." And even in scenes of greater dramatic significance—such as that in which Fitzpiers goes riding off to visit Mrs. Charmond, while Grace watches him until horse and rider become a mere speck—even in such scenes, there is quiet picturesqueness. Nothing is more perfectly done than the blending of setting and character, of description and drama; and nowhere are there finer examples of the simple dignity of Hardy's style. Those Fridays of writing at Max Gate were golden days. The picture of Fitzpiers on the sleek mare, set off in distinct relief against the deep violet of the evening sky, is a striking one, but it is not merely a picture.

So the infatuated surgeon went along through the gorgeous autumn landscape of White-Hart Vale, surrounded by orchards lustrous with the reds of apple-crops, berries, and foliage, the whole intensified by the gilding of the declining sun. The earth this year had been prodigally bountiful, and now was the supreme moment of her bounty. In the poorest spots the hedges were bowed with haws and blackberries; acorns cracked underfoot, and the burst husks of chestnuts lay exposing their auburn contents as if arranged by anxious sellers in a fruit-market. In all this proud show some kernels were unsound as her own situation, and she wondered if there were one world in the universe where the fruit had no worm, and marriage no sorrow.

In Grace Melbury's thought nature and man are associated as equally subject to the imperfections of the universe. Nature is not the malign cause of human troubles; there is no talk here, as there had been in *Far from the Madding Crowd*, of "Heaven's persistent irony." The view expressed in *The Woodlanders* is that nature suffers with and like man. That this thought is also Thomas Hardy's is made clear by a passage in which the author speaks. He was writing of the forest:

Here, as everywhere, the Unfulfilled Intention, which makes life what it is, was as obvious as it could be among the depraved crowds of a city slum. The leaf was deformed, the curve was crippled, the taper was interrupted; the lichen ate the vigor of the stalk, and the ivy slowly strangled to death the promising sapling.

Nearly twenty years before, while writing his first novel, Hardy had taken his own rejected poems and broken them down into prose for use in his fiction. Now the reverse order seems to have occurred to him, and he wrote a delightful poem on the lesson to be learned by comparing the forest with the city. He called the poem "In a Wood," and put it aside in the Max Gate study. He also wrote during this same period "The Pine Planters" (or "Marty South's Reverie"). These were not the only instances of Hardy's continued interest in poetry. His friend Edmund Gosse had just published a book of verse (*Liber Cordis*), now little known, in which Hardy noted one poem called

"Two Points of View." He liked the lines, and by omitting the first two stanzas and changing one word in the next-to-the-last line, he found it possible to incorporate the poem into the text of *The Wood-landers*. His mention of "a contemporary poet" in this connection pleased Gosse, but it has often proved puzzling to modern readers. The influence of Keats has sometimes been felt in the description of Giles Winterborne:

He looked and smelt like Autumn's very brother, his face being sunburnt to wheat-color, his eyes blue as corn-flowers, his sleeves and leggings dyed with fruit-stains, his hands clammy with the sweet juice of apples, his hat sprinkled with pips, and everywhere about him that atmosphere of cider which at its first return each session has such an indescribable fascination for those who have been born and bred among the orchards.

The return not of autumn alone, but of each season, has a fascination for Hardy, and no Wessex Novel is richer than *The Woodlanders* in seasonal descriptions.

Giles Winterborne, like Gabriel Oak, is one of Hardy's long-suffering sons of the soil. He is a milder man than Oak, less ambitious, less confident, less forceful. But he has Oak's sterling character. He is loyal to the core and faithful in that loyalty unto death. Set beside him, Fitzpiers is a shallow creature. Although credited with some intellectual capacity, he makes as little use of it as Wildeve in *The Return of the Native* made of his money. Grace Melbury, representing the native woodlander, and Mrs. Charmond, the sophisticated city product, present the same contrast as do Giles and Fitzpiers. In the mutual absorption of these four in their own affairs, Marty South is left alone, like Egdon Heath, "slighted and enduring." From her lips comes that magnificently simple final eulogy of Winterborne: "I never can forget 'ee, for you was a good man, and did good things."

XII

STUDY OF A PURE WOMAN

WITH *The Woodlanders* off his mind, Hardy and his wife set out in 1887 for a month's tour of Italy. The literary outcome of this excursion is a series of eight poems, some written (at least partially) on the spot and others composed later.[1] None were published at this time; not one gives any evidence of being inspired. The reader will look in vain for any

> jewel five words long
> That on the stretched forefinger of all Time
> Sparkles forever.

But as "poems of pilgrimage," as Hardy called them, they are mildly attractive and record his own delight in Shelley, Keats, and Napoleon. Apart from these poems Hardy did little writing in 1887 or early in 1888, when he spent May and June in Paris. The success of *The Mayor of Casterbridge* and *The Woodlanders* had made editors more-than-ever eager for contributions from Hardy, and at least three magazines were provided with short pieces of fiction in 1888.[2] Macmillan & Co. had every reason to be satisfied with the success of *The Woodlanders*, and since no new novel was yet available, they were glad to issue the first of Hardy's collections of short stories, *Wessex Tales*. This publication, in two volumes bound in green cloth, contained five stories and appeared in May, 1888. Not satisfied with this mere reprinting, Macmillan asked for a new novel. *Murray's Magazine,* however, had sent an earlier request, and Hardy promised to try to have something ready by the following year. He no longer needed to feel rushed. He

---

[1] For a list of the titles see Appendix 4, p. 239.
[2] See Appendix 8, p. 266.

could now obtain fifty pounds for the magazine publication of one short story—almost twice the amount Tinsley had paid him for the copyright of *Under the Greenwood Tree*. Even the poorer novels were now selling. *Ethelberta* appeared in a new edition in 1888, and in January, 1889, Hardy was writing a preface for a reissue of *Desperate Remedies*.

Notes for the new work began to accumulate—chance thoughts, a phrase heard in a conversation, an idea at a dinner party, an episode for the plot, a family tradition—and these jottings, made between September, 1888, and July, 1889, eventually took form and shape around a plot and a character into which Hardy put more of his heart than he put into anything else that he ever wrote—*Tess of the D'Urbervilles*. In a sense, Hardy had been getting ready all his life for writing the history of the unhappy milkmaid. The novel was the natural and logical outcome of everything that had gone before.

Thomas Hardy's father was the owner of a farm known as Talbothays. It was situated in the dairy country of the Froom Valley and within easy walking distance of Max Gate. Hardy liked to visit this neighborhood and often invited friends or visitors at his house to walk with him. One of these friends, Mr. Charles J. Hankinson, recalls taking such a walk along the Froom and coming to a farm near Moreton, beyond Talbothays, which caught Hardy's eye. The disrepair into which some of the farm buildings had been allowed to fall led him to stop and, while leaning over the rickety gate, to discourse on the hard life of the farm worker. Hardy had written an article back in 1883 on "The Dorsetshire Labourer." He there told about one family which had recently come under his notice: "The father and eldest son were paid eleven shillings a week each, the younger son ten shillings, three nearly grown-up daughters four shillings a week each, and the mother the same when she chose to go out." He remembered a shepherd boy who had actually starved to death, back in the days before Hardy had begun to attend school. Hardy's own economic position at this time was "one that afforded much to be thankful for," as he had said of Elizabeth-Jane, but it did not blind him "to the fact that there were others receiving less who had deserved much more."

THE ABBOT'S STONE COFFIN AT BINDON ABBEY

There were others—even in his own family. On September 30, 1888, he visited Woolcombe, on the opposite side of Dorchester from Talbothays. Here, where the Hardys had formerly owned a good deal of property, there were more rickety gates and dilapidated buildings to remind him of the decline and fall of the Hardys. He recalled having had a distant relative pointed out to him, the father of "an enormous lot of children," who represented what was once the leading branch of the Hardy family. Not only fences and buildings went to pieces, men did too—and women. "So we go down, down, down," he thought, as he returned to Max Gate.

In any Dorset family with "an enormous lot of children" want and sickness were certainties under the conditions which Hardy saw existing all around him. It was no new problem. T. R. Malthus had written about it in 1798 in his *Essay on the Principle of Population*, and a sixth edition of this work had recently emphasized the difficulties attendant upon large families. Poverty was painful enough when there was only a single person like Marty South involved. But suppose that that heroic soul had had to look after not only her sickly father, John South, but a dozen younger sisters and brothers as well. It took no "wisest wizard" to guess at the inevitable deterioration. In *The Woodlanders* Hardy had written of "dangling and etiolated arms of ivy groping in vain for some support, their leaves being dwarfed and sickly for want of sunlight"; and that in this respect they "show them to men akin" he had recorded in his poem "In a Wood." Large families were certain to produce weak bodies, sickly characters, dwarfed personalities. Let some unscrupulous Fitzpiers enter the situation, and one of society's oldest calamities was certain to be reenacted.

As for the Wessex Novels, the whole truth about seduction had not yet been told. Hardy remembered how the *Spectator* had ridiculed him for supposing (in *Desperate Remedies*) that "an unmarried lady owning an estate could have an illegitimate child!" He remembered how (at the very moment that Tolstoy was working with complete freedom upon his great *Anna Karenina*) Leslie Stephen had insisted on Hardy's handling the account of Fanny's seduction in *Far from the Madding Crowd* in a gingerly fashion. Hence the whispered confidences of Liddy and Bathsheba. Perhaps the time had now come when the author need no longer whisper. A number of things had happened since *Far from the Madding Crowd* appeared in 1874. Trollope, for instance, had again brought forward the problem of seduction in his *Autobiography* and from the preface to one of his novels had quoted these words:

I have introduced in the *Vicar of Bullhampton* the character of a girl whom I will call—for want of a truer word that shall not in its truth be offensive— a castaway. I have endeavored to endow her with qualities that may create sympathy. It is not long since that the very existence of such a condition of life as was hers, was supposed to be unknown to our sisters and daughters.

Trollope explained that his novel was written chiefly with the object of exciting not only pity but also sympathy for the unfortunate woman, and then he added: "I could not venture to make this female the heroine of my story."

To have made her a heroine would have been to anticipate *Tess of the D'Urbervilles*. There was another and more powerful reason for thinking the time had come when an author might write more fearlessly on this theme. Through *A Doll's House* (1879) and *Ghosts* (1881) and other plays Ibsen's influence was beginning to be felt on English thought. An article on Ibsen appeared in the *Fortnightly Review* in 1890, in which he was criticized for using the drama for edification. Hardy read the article and disagreed with the point of view expressed. While he believed that Ibsen's edifying was too obvious, he was far from wishing to exclude all didactic aims from the writer's purpose. Only, Hardy believed, the edification of reader or spectator ought to be accomplished in a less obvious way. As one within whose own lifetime that best of all sermons, Dickens's *Christmas Carol*, had been preached, Hardy never made the mistake of Edgar Allan Poe in thinking that art and morals should never join hands. He was therefore quite ready to welcome Trollope's announcement of the theme on which the Victorian world was greatly in need of edification, and Ibsen's example served as a challenge to English authors to speak out. Shaw's *The Quintessence of Ibsenism* appeared in 1891. Two years earlier Hardy himself had written an article on "Candour in English

Fiction" (printed in the *New Review* for January, 1890), in which he lamented "that the great bulk of English fiction of the present day is characterised by its lack of sincerity" and urged the great desirability of permitting novelists to treat frankly "the position of man and woman in nature, and the position of belief in the minds of man and woman—things which everybody is thinking but nobody is saying." Open eyes and a sympathetic heart were all that were needed to settle for Hardy the theme for his next novel. It was to be: the story of a seduced girl making a futile but heroic effort to help her worthless family in a blighted world, where families go down, down, down.

Stories of seduction were no new thing in nineteenth-century England. Trollope's *Vicar of Bullhampton* has already been mentioned. George Eliot's *Adam Bede*, Dickens's *David Copperfield*, and Scott's *Heart of Midlothian* all dealt with the old theme. But in all these stories the unfortunate victim was a weakling and set in contrast with the heroine, who kept the center of the stage. Scott's Effie, Dickens's little Emily, and George Eliot's Hetty are all overshadowed by their stronger sisters. Hardy's originality lies in advancing the victim to the position of heroine. In *The Woodlanders* he had spoken of the Sophoclean drama sometimes to be found even in rural Dorset, and he now proposed to write his *Electra*. In July, 1889, he was reading Sophocles's *Oedipus Tyrannus* and meditating on the essence of tragedy in literary art. Obviously none of the earlier English novels mentioned above could help him in the invention of a tragic plot on the chosen theme; and critics who attempt to trace relationships here are certain to waste their time.

A more rewarding comparison might be made between *Tess of the D'Urbervilles* and Charles Lamb's almost forgotten *Rosamund Gray*. Lamb's hero was "young Allan Clare." Is it mere accident that Hardy's young man bears almost the same name, Angel Clare? Hardy once told Sir Sydney Cockerell that Angel Clare was partly drawn from Charles Moule, the sixth son of the Reverend Henry Moule, Vicar of Fordington. Charles became president of Corpus Christi College, Cambridge. But Hardy's hero Clare is not wholly Moule, for Clare found it impossible to go to Cambridge because his studies had undermined his religious faith. Lamb's statement that the elder Clare had been "at times betrayed into scepticism" parallels words that Hardy, like many another young man in those Darwinian days, might have written of himself. Angel Clare is Allan Clare brought up to date. Allan became a nomad; similarly, Angel sailed off to Brazil. Lamb's story is a slight and undeveloped piece of work, but the many resemblances to *Tess* in incident and characterization are suggestive.

Hardy's Clare might very well have been the author of a letter that Havelock Ellis wrote in 1878: "I had once some idea of entering the Church, but I begin to see now that I must definitely abandon that idea. I find my views irreconcilable with a position in the Church. If I ever did get there, I suppose my place would be among the 'Nothingarians.' My religious views have during the last three years been very unsettled." The more Hardy himself meditated on the views of the Church, the more he was impressed by the fact that ecclesiastical dogma seemed in complete disagreement with the laws of nature which he had been observing for nearly fifty years. He concluded that an act which might be socially a great tragedy could be in nature not at all alarming. From these meditations emerged the plot of *Tess of the D'Urbervilles*. After the heroine's seduction, she would marry a young man whose religious views were unsettled. After he had deserted her she would be forced by poverty and want into the arms of her seducer. If, in a moment of despair—well, what would a betrayed girl do in a moment of despair?

For an answer to this question Hardy did not have to go back to the story of Clytemnestra in the Greek play he had just been reading. A suggestion was available nearer at hand. When as a boy he had daily tramped to school in Dorchester, he had had to pass an inn kept by a man named Brown. Mrs. Brown was a kindly soul who used to give passing schoolboys cakes and apples. One day a former lover appeared and told Brown about his wife's past. In despair Martha Brown killed the man and was hanged in public. Young Tom Hardy was present at the execution, and he never forgot the sight. Sixty years later he referred to it, in one of the few public speeches he ever made, on November 16, 1910, when he was presented the freedom of the Borough of Dorchester. In the tragic end of Martha Brown Hardy found complete assurance as to what his young heroine would do under somewhat similar conditions. The novelist thus found himself face to face with a situation that had never before arisen in writing any of the Wessex Novels. It occurred to him that perhaps it ought not to be allowed to arise here. He thought carefully and long over the concluding events of the story. As if to anticipate the objections of those who were later to accuse him of loading the dice against Tess, he even made a special trip to Winchester and there walked moodily up and down outside the jail, asking himself what other logical conclusion there was for the situation as it had developed in his mind. He saw no way out but one. "It had to be," he said sadly, and in after years he repeated his conviction: "It had to be. There was no other end possible."

With theme and plot settled, Hardy was now ready for his characters. Three of these have already been mentioned. The heroine assumed definite physical shape as Hardy proceeded. According to Arthur Compton-Rickett, Hardy stated that he built Tess up from three different persons. He recalled having seen a girl once, and once only, driving in a cart on the outskirts of Egdon Heath. She was a handsome girl with "large innocent eyes." Years later he described to J. Henry Harper how he had seen this typical country lass, sitting on the tailboard of a lumbering farm cart, swinging her legs. Compton-Rickett recalls a discussion in which the color of Tess's hair was debated. One man thought it was dark. "Of course it was," said Hardy decisively, "dark and very thick." Another girl, remembered from early years, suggested "the stopt-diapason note which her voice acquired when her heart was in her speech, and which will never be forgotten by those who knew her." Still another feature was of more recent origin. On July 23, 1889, Hardy had been entertained at dinner by Edmund Gosse. The lips and teeth of a lady who had talked with him on that occasion reminded him of an old poem:

> when her lovely laughter shows,
> They look like rosebuds filled with snow.

Not being able to recall off-hand the authorship of these lines, he looked up the poem by Thomas Campion and made use of it a few weeks later, when writing that Angel Clare had beheld nothing on the face of the earth to equal Tess's mouth. "He had never before seen a woman's lips and teeth which forced upon his mind with such persistent iteration the old Elizabethan simile of roses filled with snow." Thus there gradually developed in his imagination the picture of the heroine whom he began by calling Sue Woodrow.

Her three dairymaid companions were recalled from his own Sunday-school days. The one he named Marian was especially easy to remember. Hardy, who had been her teacher, never forgot her amazing ability to quote whole chapters of the Bible by heart. Thoughts of "Marian" carried him back to the Stinsford church, where in memory he could still hear the children singing Thomas Bilby's hymn "Joyful." Its words "Here we suffer grief and pain" were obviously suited in sentiment more to the aged than to the young; but almost from the moment when the hymn was first published in the *Infant School Teachers' Assistant*, in 1832, it became very popular with children because of the catchy tune to which it was set, and it had extensive use in Sunday Schools during Hardy's boyhood. It is now Hymn No. 509 in the *Hymnal Companion to the Book of Common Prayer*, still in print in London. The novelist recalled all this when he reached the point at which Tess asked the four little Durbeyfields to sing. Their phlegmatic performance in singing "Joyful" has elicited sarcastic remarks from critics as to Hardy's exaggerated habits of spreading gloom over the world, even over happy childhood. But as usual Hardy knew what he was writing about. Just such touches as this breathe the breath of life into his characters.

"Sue Woodrow" did not long continue to be known by that name. Hardy had already begun to write her story and had filled many pages of manuscript when an incident occurred which provided a father and a name for those singing children. One day, while Hardy was standing at a street corner in Dorchester, a tipsy man staggered past, saying, "I've a great family vault over at Bere Regis." Hardy's curiosity was aroused. Bere Regis is not far from Dorchester, and upon investigation Hardy discovered that the drunkard's statement was correct. Not only were many of the old Turberville family buried at Bere Regis, but there is a fine Turberville window of stained glass in the church there. Hardy also made the interesting discovery that, although the name "Turberville" had died out, there were still a number of very humble families living in Dorset who were descended from the ancient Turbervilles, and who unwittingly hid their honorable surname under various corruptions. One of the commonest of these was Troublefield. Hardy accordingly decided that he would represent his heroine as belonging to this degenerated Turberville family, and he thereupon crossed out the name "Sue Woodrow" in his manuscript and wrote "Rose Mary Troublefield." Her father was the aged tippler with "a bias in his gait."

Further investigation of the actual Turberville family brought about additional changes in the growing story. Hardy had begun by calling his seducer plain "Smith." In tracing the various ramifications of the Turberville name the novelist came upon a Henry John Turberville who had died as recently as 1875. This man turned out, however, to be no genuine Turberville at all, but the brother of Blackmore, the author of *Lorna Doone*. Born in 1822, Henry John Blackmore had changed his name to Turberville. The information was suggestive. The villain Smith thus became "Smith-Turberville"; and readers of the novel will recall the explanation that his father, having made a fortune as a merchant in the north of England wished to settle afterward in the south as a gentleman of leisure, and that upon discovering that the Turberville family was practically extinct he simply annexed that name to his own in order not to be too readily identified with his commercial past.

Blackmore the novelist, however, was still alive; and Hardy had no desire to suggest, even indirectly, that he had Henry John Turberville in mind. He therefore again changed Alec's name, this time to "Higgs-D'Urberville," and eventually to "Stoke-D'Urberville."[3] Similarly "Troublefield" shifted into "Durbeyfield." Hardy was still dissatisfied with Miss Durbeyfield's first name. Rose Mary was given up. Cissie or "Cis" was tried and discarded. The author's cousin Teresa eventually loaned her name, and the milkmaid became "Tess" at last. Mrs. Hardy

[3] See Appendix 7, p. 264.

once told Rebekah Owen that Tess was called "Rose Mary" so long that it was difficult to think of her as "Tess."

Hardy began by entitling her story "A Daughter of the D'Urbervilles." Once having decided to make John Durbeyfield a forgotten scion of the ancient "D'Urbervilles," the author's memory of that Hardy who had once been pointed out to him as the father of an enormous lot of children came back to him. Thus "Sir John's" wife Joan, and Modesty, Hope, Abraham, and 'Liza-Lu came into being. All that remained was to provide Angel Clare with a family—father, mother, two brothers—and the list of characters, except for such minor figures as might suggest themselves as he went on, was complete.

The family of many children settled another thing too—namely, the locale of the story. The novelist had thought of these Hardy relatives while visiting the country northeast of Dorchester. He had never used the Vale of Blackmoor in any previous novel, although he had known and even written about "this fertile and sheltered tract of country in which the fields are never brown and the springs never dry." Ten years ago he had written those words in an unsigned review of William Barnes's *Poems of Rural Life* (published in the *New Quarterly Magazine* for October, 1879). After Barnes's death he had repeated the same description in an obituary notice he had been asked to write for the *Athenaeum* (printed on October 16, 1886). He now prepared to use his word picture for a third time. Another thought occurred to him. Blackmoor, where he planned to have the Durbeyfields live, was a valley of little dairies. Talbothays, where Hardy's father's farm was situated, was a valley of great dairies. This contrast in the two places suggested contrasting experiences in the projected life of his heroine. Hardy was quick to appreciate the possibility of identifying human experience with geographical setting. Tess's unspoiled childhood is assigned to the unsophisticated village of Marnhull; her betrayal by Alec follows a visit to the "decayed market-town of Chaseborough"; her romantic summer under the eyes of Angel Clare is spent in the lush valley of the Froom where the air is fragrant with the scent of many flowers; at the ancient Wool manor house her own past catches up with her, and in the sterile fields of Flintcomb-Ash she spends her months as a deserted wife. When despair overtakes her and she saves her wretched family by selling herself, Clare finds her in that place of "fashionable promenades," Bournemouth. And finally Stonehenge is chosen for that most beautiful and pathetic of all the scenes Hardy ever invented—that of Tess falling asleep on one of the ancient Druid stones in that place of ancient sacrifice. This artistic harmonizing of man and nature runs through many of the novels, but never more poetically than here.

Having decided upon the place, Hardy like Trollope erected his own buildings, in imagination, thereon. The dilapidated farm near Moreton supplied the dairy where Tess and Clare were to meet, and Talbothays was a good name to assign to the place. He located this dairy house within an hour's walk of Stinsford church. "Two or three miles distant," he wrote at first. After actually walking over the route he crossed out "two or" in his manuscript, leaving the mileage a definite "three." Later, when he thought that readers might demand identification of the precise spot, he added "or four" to the original "three." His decision to use the ancient family of the Turbervilles made possible two more obvious locations for the theater of the novel: the Bere Regis church, where the Turbervilles were buried, and an old residence at Wool, where a former manor house of the family was now serving as an ordinary farmhouse.

For the scene in which Tess discovers the wounded birds and puts them out of their misery, Hardy had only to draw on his acquaintance with the owners of neighboring "pheasant plantations." After the publication of the novel the indignation of these landowners testified to the skill with which Hardy drew his picture of "strangely accoutred" men pointing their guns with "a bloodthirsty light in their eyes." For a long time thereafter these neighbors, so Hardy told H. W. Nevinson, refused to call on him.

Before the actual writing could begin, the customary time chart must be worked out with the customary exactness. The habits of the architect of old thus permit the reconstruction of the work sheet which guided the novelist's labors in the fall of 1889.[4]

---

[4] See Appendix 7, p. 263.

His plans having been carefully and thoroughly made, Hardy wrote freely and rapidly. He was on familiar ground, and the words came easily. His heart came with them. After three months of diligent composition he had enough of the story written to be ready to send it to the editor of *Murray's*. To his amazement the manuscript was returned. He then submitted it to *Macmillan's Magazine*, and on November 25, 1889, it was again returned to him. The double rejection carried his thoughts back twenty years to the time when the same treatment had been accorded *The Poor Man and the Lady*. Then his work had been turned down because, as he had been told, it was too outspoken. Now he was told the same thing over again. A story like *Tess* was simply not wanted in magazines like *Murray's* or *Macmillan's*. "The low growls of British prudery," as Meredith once called them, were still audible enough to make editors timid; and rather than make further efforts to find a magazine that perhaps did not exist, Hardy fell back upon the plan he had followed in disposing of *The Poor Man and the Lady*. During the year 1890 he methodically dismembered his manuscript. One chapter went to the *Fortnightly Review* (which had in March, 1891, printed his short story "For Conscience' Sake"). This chapter appeared in the review in May, 1891, under the heading "The Midnight Baptism: a Study in Christianity." Another chapter excerpted from the manuscript was sent to the *National Observer*, which on February 7, 1891, had printed an article on Hardy. This magazine issued a special literary supplement on November 14, 1891, and there printed, under the heading "Saturday Night in Arcady," the chapter describing the dance at Chaseborough, that "decayed market-town two or three miles distant" from Alec's home. In the process of selecting from this chapter paragraphs that could stand alone, Hardy mislaid three or four pages, which were not printed until as recently as 1912.

After these extractions had been made, he set about covering up the scars by writing new passages. These are more remarkable for their clever surmounting of the difficulties in the road to serial publication than for their harmonizing with the characters as Hardy had conceived them. In order to eliminate the seduction, Hardy substituted mock marriage. This is the story which Tess was made to tell her mother upon her return home:

He made love to me, as you said he would do; and he asked me to marry him, also just as you declared he would. I never have liked him; but at last I agreed, knowing you'd be angry, if I didn't. He said it must be private, even from you, on account of his mother; and by special license; and foolish I agreed to that likewise, to get rid of his pestering. I drove with him to Melchester, and there in a private room I went through the form of marriage with him as before a registrar. A few weeks after, I found out that it was not the registrar's house we had gone to, as I had supposed, but the house of a friend of his, who had played the part of the registrar. I then came away from Trantridge instantly, though he wished me to stay; and here I am.

Since this concession to Mrs. Grundy required corresponding changes in the story which Tess told after her marriage to Angel Clare, that passage too had to be rewritten. Hardy crammed the revised confession into a single sentence: "She entered on her story of the visit with D'Urberville to the supposed Registrar's, her abiding sense of the moral validity of the contract, and her wicked flying in the face of that conviction by wedding again." The psychological ridiculousness of this spurious story was not lost upon Hardy. The situation at Bournemouth, where Clare found Tess living under the same roof with Alec, obviously called for similar emasculation. Instead of the Mr. and Mrs. D'Urberville who took rooms at The Herons, Mrs. Brooks was allowed only one tenant, Miss D'Urberville. Hardy explained that "part of the first floor had been taken for her by a cousin who sometimes occupied another apartment." Living alone, Miss D'Urberville sometimes was made to soliloquize about her cousin, whom she was shortly called upon to murder. Only his sense of humor could have kept Hardy's thought from being equally murderous, as he went about writing such worthless passages. When the botched-up job of revision had been finally completed, the morally "safe" manuscript was offered to The Graphic and accepted—not, however, without some further cause for sardonic amusement. In August, 1891, Arthur Locker, editor of The Graphic, wrote to object to the scene in which Clare carries the dairymaids across the flooded lane. Since The Graphic was intended for family reading, Mr. Locker thought it would be better if the girls were transported in a wheel-barrow. Hardy kept his feelings to himself and obligingly rewrote Angel Clare's offer, as follows:

"I'll wheel you through the pool—all of you—with pleasure, if you'll wait till I get a barrow . . . There's a barrow in that shed yonder." In a minute or two he had fetched the wheel-barrow and rolled it till it stood beneath them. "Now, Marian, attend," he continued, "and sit upon the top, and put your arms round my shoulders, so: or you'll fall off. Now! Hold on. That's well done." Marian had lowered herself upon the back part of the conveyance as directed, and Angel pushed her along.

The Graphic, pleased enough with the mutilated novel, had twenty-five excellent illustrations made for it by Professor Hubert Herkomer, of the Royal Academy, and three of his pupils, Messrs. Wehrschmidt, Johnson, and Sydall. Some of the pictures were dramatic full-page drawings. The novel appeared in *The Graphic* from July 4 to December 26, 1891, and therefore Tess's tragic end ironically greeted the readers of the magazine on the day after Christmas. In the last installment Hardy added a few words as an afterthought. In the manuscript he had written: " 'Justice' was done. The two speechless gazers bent themselves down to the earth." Between those two sentences he now inserted the words: "and Time, the Arch-satirist, had had his joke out with Tess."

Once the story had been published serially, Hardy began to reassemble his dismembered manuscript. The chapters published in the *Fortnightly* and in the *National Observer* were reinserted. The ridiculous substitute readings printed in the *Graphic* were cut out. This labor gave the author a chance to revise his text. Words were changed here and there, and it was improved in phraseology, in sequence of events, and in dialogue. He also decided to discard his afterthought about "Time the Arch-satirist." That sounded too much as if he were blaming the universe for maliciously causing Tess's downfall—as if he believed the Power behind the universe were an imbecile jester. Since he held no such belief, he wished to substitute a poetic statement that would make his idea clearer. He found a way out of his difficulty by attributing the property of a thinking and feeling Being to what he regarded as inanimate, neither good nor bad, neither benign nor malicious. He

HUBERT HERKOMER'S DRAWING OF THE SLEEP-WALKING SCENE IN *TESS*

recalled a phrase in Theodore A. Buckley's 1849 translation of *Prometheus Bound*—the book he had bought with his prize for archi- tectural design. Buckley's words would serve nicely, and so, after "'Justice' was done," Hardy wrote: "and the President of the Im- mortals, in Aeschylean phrase, had ended his sport with Tess." That ought to make it clear. Aeschylus would have explained Tess's fate as due to the "President's" inhuman zest for cruel sport. British law would explain it as due to long-established ideas of "justice." Hardy expected the reader to understand, by his quotation marks around "jus- tice" and his allusion to Aeschylus, that his, Hardy's, own explanation was neither of these. His was an indictment of an intolerant society that could condemn a woman of Tess's integrity and courage and humility. With these last-minute changes, then, the much-battered novel was ready in November, 1891, for the publisher. The firm was the new one to which Hardy had turned earlier in the same year. James R. Osgood, McIlvaine & Co., of 45 Albemarle Street, London, had issued his second collection of short stories, *A Group of Noble Dames*. This house now prepared to publish *Tess* in three volumes. At the very last minute, after reading the final proofs, Hardy had another afterthought. His original title, "A Daughter of the D'Urber- villes," had given way to the more familiar phrasing. He now added the words: "A Pure Woman, Faithfully Presented by Thomas Hardy." That was, he afterward explained, "the estimate left in a candid mind of the heroine's character—an estimate that nobody would be likely to dispute."

To his later amazement it was disputed more than anything else in the book. Those who did not quarrel over his use of the word "pure" selected the other afterthought about "the President of the Immortals" for ridicule and denunciation. It was the result of a disordered liver, readers were told. Its mood was petulant and dogmatic. What would civilization end in, an angry critic asked, if we all came to believe in Hardy's Aeschylean phrase? From the heat generated by discussions of "a pure woman" on the title page and the anger and abuse aroused by the Aeschylean phrase in the final paragraph, the conclusion might have been drawn that Hardy had written only two lines. The 820-odd pages that lay between the two were hardly referred to.

When Osgood McIlvaine issued the three volumes, bound in light tan cloth, neither publisher nor author guessed what was about to happen, for those three volumes sold more rapidly than any novel Hardy ever wrote. A second edition (or printing, as we would now call it) was promptly made and sold; a third and then a fourth were all sold out before six months had gone by. Everyone was talking about *Tess of the D'Urbervilles*. Everyone wanted to read it. Hardy was lifted at once from lukewarm distinction as an English novelist to a position of world fame. He had become one of England's significant authors and would never again be able to get far from the crowd of those who read him or from the crowd of critics whose attacks might have driven any author mad. The *Quarterly Review* announced: "Mr. Hardy has told an extremely disagreeable story in an extremely disagreeable manner." Henry James wrote that Tess was vile, and there were many who insisted that her author must be like her. Even those who had no quarrel with the morality of the novel were inclined to condemn its artistry. George Meredith thought it was "marred by the sudden hurry to round the story; and Tess, out of the arms of Alec into those of the lily-necked Clare is a smudge in vapor." Andrew Lang, unable to express all his displeasure in one attack, condemned the novel a second time in a notorious article which was afterward reprinted. In it *Tess* was denounced "for its forbidding conception, for its apparent un-reality, for its defects of style, so provokingly superfluous."

Edmund Gosse was one of the few who had a consoling word to say. On the first day of 1892 he wrote to Hardy:

In *Tess of the D'Urbervilles* you have achieved the biggest success you have made since *The Return of the Native*. Your book is simply magnificent, and wherever I go I hear its praises. If you could have listened to the things that I have heard said about it, by Walter Besant, by Mrs. Humphrey Ward, by Henry James, by I know not whom else, you would not,—you could not care what the *Saturday's* ape-leading and shrivelled spinster said or thought. Your success has been phenomenal. I have not heard a book so earnestly and honestly praised by word of mouth (and that is the praise that tells) for years. You have strengthened your position tremendously, among your own confrères and the serious male public. Let them rave!

While Hardy was pained and shocked at the violence of the attacks and declared that if this sort of thing went on, "no more novel-writing for me," all this publicity resulted in a great boost in sales. In July, 1892, Osgood McIlvaine prepared to issue a fifth edition in one volume. In this book appeared the first portrait of Hardy published in England. Four years earlier Harpers, in New York, had printed a bearded portrait in *Wessex Tales*, 1888. During the notoriety of *Tess*, Hardy shaved off his beard; and in the fifth edition of the novel the frontispiece portrait presented an author whose unbearded appearance was as strange to his wife as to his readers. For this edition Hardy revised the text again. In addition to minor improvements in phrasing, he made one striking addition to the physical setting. In the *Graphic* for October 17, 1891, there had been a full-page illustration of the sleep-walking scene. The picture, drawn by Hubert Herkomer, showed Clare depositing Tess on the top of a flat gravestone. The accompanying text read: "They reached the cloister-garth, where were the graves of the monks. Upon one of these graves he carefully laid her down." A recent visit to Bindon Abbey suggested to Hardy the use of "the empty stone coffin of an abbot, in which every tourist with a turn for grim humor was accustomed to stretch himself." The stone coffin accordingly replaced the gravestone.

Nearly fifty years have passed since those excited days, and it is now possible to look upon *Tess of the D'Urbervilles* with clearer eyes. Few readers will be disposed to quarrel with the judgment that it is the greatest of his novels. Not the most perfect work of art; that distinction belongs to *The Return of the Native*. Not the most powerful piece of portraiture; that is found in *The Mayor of Casterbridge*. But just as most critics agree that *King Lear* is Shakespeare's greatest work without being his best play, so *Tess of the D'Urbervilles* is Hardy's greatest, without being his most artistic or most nearly perfect novel. Of course there are flaws in *Tess*. The Alec who "twirled a gay walking-cane," who "clenched his lips" and exclaimed "you artful hussy!" is too obviously related to the villain of melodrama. The carpet that "reached close to the sill" and so inopportunely concealed the letter that Tess had slipped under Clare's door discloses the author too openly in the act of setting the stage. Brazil, to which Clare suddenly exiled himself and from which he conveniently returned when the plot needed him, is presented with a disregard for the facts that is equaled only by Dickens's pictures of America in the pages of *Martin Chuzzlewit*. Let all this be freely granted. There still remains in *Tess* an abundance of Hardy at his best. Every aspect of his art and thought is here represented. Wessex superstitions and peasant folklore, delicate descriptions of nature and magnificent accounts of the passage of the seasons, humor and pathos, irony and tragedy, all are here found between the covers of one book. And here there is one thing not found in any of Hardy's previous novels: moral indignation at social injustice. With FitzGerald he had expressed regret over the sorriness of this scheme of things, but not regret such as Wordsworth felt for what man has made of man. Hardy's humanity was never so movingly expressed as in *Tess*. It has become a critical commonplace to maintain that his obvious sympathy for his heroine is an artistic flaw; that he is too openly trying to "edify." But if the free expression of sympathy for those who suffer from human injustice is to be denied an author, how many plays of Shakespeare will have to be condemned! Hardy's open admiration for Tess is one of his noblest acts. In the face of the danger of almost universal condemnation, he exclaims with Shakespeare:

> Poor wounded name! My bosom as a bed
> Shall lodge thee.

Tess is an inspiring figure. Steadfast, loyal, self-effacing, brave, like Marty South, with none of the vanity or deceitfulness so often found in Hardy's heroines, with an emotional fire that would have melted any man's heart except Angel Clare's, with a fortitude in the face of adversity and a self-sacrificing devotion to others that make her the finest woman in all the Wessex Novels, Tess is a figure of tragic strength. In her love for Clare, Hardy truly declares, "there was hardly a touch of earth." She is beaten and crushed at last, but not until she has to choose between her own seemingly worthless body and the life of her mother and her destitute brothers and sisters. Her desperation at Bere Regis, when reduced "to almost her last shilling," sounds in her tragic cry at the entrance to the tombs of the D'Urbervilles: "Why am I on the wrong side of this door?"

Her story is a plea for charity, for a larger tolerance, for a repudiation of social hypocrisy. Its intense moving power led William Sharp to declare that no man or woman could read *Tess of the D'Urbervilles* sympathetically and not thereafter be of broader mind and more charitable spirit. From this point of view it is to be regarded not merely as Hardy's greatest novel, but as one of the great works in English literature.[5] It is an Anglo-Saxon social landmark. "Anyhow," said Hardy, "I have put in it the best of me."

---

[5] See Appendix 7, pp. 264-65.

XIII

AN INTERLUDE

I N THE *Collected Verse* of Rudyard Kipling there is a poem entitled
"The Rhyme of the Three Captains." It is dated 1890, and according to an explanatory note prefixed to the poem it "appears to refer
to one of the exploits of the notorious Paul Jones, an American pirate.
It is founded on fact." Kipling's statement is literally true. The "fact,"
however, was not in the life of the notorious Paul Jones, but in the
literary career of Thomas Hardy. Readers of Kipling have often been
puzzled by "The Three Captains," and Hardy never made any
reference to the poem or to the incident that led up to it. But both
writers are now dead, and the simple facts may be briefly stated.

It should be remembered that when Kipling's poem was written,
in 1890, there was in America no copyright protection for foreign
authors residing outside the United States. Dickens had complained
about the situation, and Hardy certainly had abundant reason for
complaint. It is likely that he was never aware of the extent to which
his novels were printed in unauthorized American editions. By the
end of the century it was possible to buy in America all Hardy's fiction published before 1891 without buying one authorized volume for
which the author received any pay. The last three Wessex Novels—
Tess of the D'Urbervilles, Jude the Obscure, and *The Well-Beloved—*
all came after the enactment of the international copyright law of
1891, and Hardy was thus protected in his rights in these three instances. But with regard to the works that preceded *Tess* it was another story. American publishers laid piratical hands on every one
of them. Hardy was introduced in America by Henry Holt's publication of *Under the Greenwood Tree* in 1873. Following that, Holt

issued in his "Leisure Hour Series" all ten of the Wessex novels, up to and including *The Mayor of Casterbridge* in 1886. But by that time Hardy had become a free hunting ground, in which at least fifteen American firms foraged early and late without authority. As early as 1877 pirated Hardy items began to appear from the press of a publisher who frankly advertised "A $1.50 book for ten cents." In 1887 Holt withdrew from the contest by turning over his Hardy rights to the Harper brothers. In addition to the authorized publications by Henry Holt and by Harper & Brothers, eleven firms in New York and four in Chicago turned out Wessex fiction for ten, twenty, or twenty-five cents.[1]

The shorter stories were subjected to the same sort of perfectly legal but unethical publication. In 1883 Harpers purchased what Hardy called "a short hastily-written novel" entitled *The Romantic Adventures of a Milkmaid*. This story eventually appeared in at least ten different American forms.[2] The total lack of legal protection thus frequently created difficulties for authorized publishers; for, after paying for the right to print an English work, they sometimes found themselves forestalled by a speedier publisher or undersold by one less scrupulous. The appearance of *The Return of the Native*, for instance, in *Harper's Magazine* did not prevent the issue of that novel in book form by at least three other American publishers. Under these conditions American firms sometimes found it impossible to delay action in order to consult foreign authors. During the summer of 1890, while Hardy was at work upon the dismemberment of *Tess of the D'Urbervilles*, Harper & Brothers issued Kipling's *The Courting of Dinah Shadd and Other Stories* as No. 680 in their "Franklin Square Library." This book, made up largely of stories already issued and paid for by Harpers, was put on the market without Kipling's knowledge. When the news reached him in the form of a check from the publishers, he was furious. He blew off steam by sending an angry statement to the London *Athenaeum* for October 4, denouncing the

[1] See Appendix 7, p. 262.
[2] See Appendix 7, p. 261.

American firm and saying: "When an author is unknown to fame, they, it would seem, content themselves with insulting him; when he is celebrated, they insult and rob him."

Within ten days Kipling's blast arrived in New York, and on the fourteenth Harper & Brothers mailed "A Reply" to the *Athenaeum*, which was duly printed in the issue for November 1. They defended their action, explaining the situation that confronted the American publisher of an English author. But Kipling was not to be appeased. He thought that Harpers were incorrect in their statements, and "A Counter Reply" from him appeared in the *Athenaeum* for November 8. There the matter might have ended, but Hardy was not one to remain silent when injustice had been done. He was as ready to speak out in behalf of a foreign publisher as of a Dorsetshire milkmaid. Ever since that meeting in the Green Park, when he had been uncertain what to call *The Return of the Native*, Hardy had been on friendly terms with Henry Harper, and their business relations had always been smooth. Two other English authors, Walter Besant and William Black, men with whom Hardy often dined at the Savile Club, had also had satisfactory business experience with Harper & Brothers. Hardy and Besant had also entrusted their business to the same literary agent, A. P. Watt. When, therefore, the charge of unethical conduct by the Harpers was repeated with all the force of Kipling's invective, the three authors united in sending to the *Athenaeum* a letter of remonstrance, dated November 17, 1890. It was printed in the issue for the twenty-second and read as follows:

It seems a clear duty to us, who have experienced honorable treatment from this firm, to enter a protest against the sweeping condemnation passed upon them. We wish to record the fact that in the course of many years' friendly business relations with Messrs. Harper and Brothers we have always found them as just and liberal in their dealings as any English house.

The letter made Kipling more furious than ever. Hot words boiled from his pen, and before they had cooled off "The Rhyme of the Three Captains" had been sent to the *Athenaeum*, where it appeared on December 6. The poem was an angry allegory, beginning:

>At the close of a winter day,
>Their anchors down, by London town, the Three Great Captains lay;
>And one was Admiral of the North from Solway Firth to Skye,
>And one was Lord of the Wessex coast and all the lands thereby,
>And one was Master of the Thames from Limehouse to Blackwall,
>And he was Chaplain of the Fleet—the stoutest of them all.

After telling in vigorous verse the story of the "lime-washed Yankee brig" that had stolen his own wares, he reported what he had done to "this Yank Yahoo":

>I hulled him once for a clumsy crimp and twice because he lied.

And then the infuriating interference of his three fellow authors came in for attention:

>And the Captains Three called courteously from deck to scuttle-butt:—
>"Good Sir, we ha' dealt with that merchantman or ever your teeth were cut. . . .
>We have sold our spars to the merchantman—we know that his price is fair."

So Kipling wished to wash his hands of such friends. He called to his "crew":

>We'll out to the seas again—
>Then fore-sheet home as she lifts to the foam—we stand on the outward tack.
>We are paid in the coin of the white man's trade—the bezant is hard, ay, and black.
>The frigate-bird shall carry my word . . .
>How a man may be robbed in Christian port while Three Great Captains there
>Shall dip their flag to a pirate's rag—to show that his trade is fair!

"The bezant is hard, ay, and black!" Besant, Hardy, and Black made no further response. On December 13, 1890, the *Athenaeum* printed, under the heading "Copyright and Copywrong," another letter from Harper & Brothers, dated November 2, in final explanation and defense of their position.

In the intervals of dismembering the manuscript of *Tess*, Hardy found time, as the year 1890 wore on, to compose four poems:

1. "Thoughts of Phena," suggested by the death of a cousin
2. "In a Ewe-leaze near Weatherbury," a poem which shows definite improvement in metrical fluency
3. "Lines Spoken by Miss Ada Rehan," an epilogue written by request
4. "Tess's Lament," a poem expressing Tess's feelings at Flintcomb-Ash, and indicating Hardy's interest in stanzaic experimentation, without, however, the attainment of the power possessed by Tess's letters in prose

None of these poems were published at this time.

Once the tedious labor of reassembling the manuscript of *Tess* had been accomplished, Hardy found time to complete the writing of one of his best short stories, "On the Western Circuit," already noticed. One of the results of the bitter and abusive attacks made upon him after the publication of *Tess of the D'Urbervilles* was his determination that his next appearance in print should not offend anyone. He recalled a tale he had sketched more than twenty years before, when he was "virtually a young man, and interested in the Platonic Idea." It now occurred to him that he might dig up this early sketch, modify and develop it; and "bygone, wildly romantic fancy" though it was, he thought it might "please Mrs. Grundy and her Young Person, and her respected husband, by its absolutely 'harmless' quality." This explanation was made to Hardy's friend Gosse to account for the immense contrast between this Platonic story and the novels which preceded and followed it—*Tess* on one side and *Jude the Obscure* on the other. For *The Pursuit of the Well-Beloved* is like neither.

The origin of this story in Hardy's mind goes back to his early days of reading Shelley in London. He had then carried around in his pockets two dumpy volumes of Shelley's Poems, now a prized part of a private New York collection. In them he recorded his feelings and thoughts as he read. Years later, when Sir James Barrie saw these books, he remarked: "There are a hundred, a thousand, pencil marks on those two volumes that look now like love messages from the young poet of one age to the young poet of a past age." After his visit to Italy, during which he visited Shelley's grave, Hardy wrote a poem, "At the Pyramid of Cestius," in which his love for Shelley is recorded. Many years later, when he found himself in Oxford, his hosts expected a man of eighty-three to have little energy for sight-seeing; but Hardy insisted on being shown the Shelley Memorial in University College. Although Shelley never acquired the influential position of Shakespeare in Hardy's thoughts, he was never forgotten. At least six of the Wessex Novels contain quotations from Shelley. Of the poems which Hardy thus remembered, none was more frequently in his consciousness than "Epipsychidion." He quoted it in "An Indiscretion in the Life of an Heiress," its presence there suggesting that it had originally appeared in *The Poor Man and the Lady*. He quoted it again in *The Mayor of Casterbridge*, in *The Woodlanders*, and in *Jude the Obscure*. Two lines from this same poem suggest the "romantic fancy" which Hardy now decided to develop:

> In many mortal forms I rashly sought
> The shadow of that idol of my thought.

Fitzpiers' words, in *The Woodlanders*, show that the theme had recurred to Hardy's mind before 1892. The woodland doctor defines love as a subjective thing—"joy accompanied by an idea which we project against any suitable object." In *The Pursuit of the Well-Beloved* Jocelyn Pierston is the one who feels the joy accompanied by an idea. He was a sculptor. "The study of beauty was his only joy for years." In that pursuit he was not at all unlike Shelley, and it would not have been out of character if he had exclaimed in some Wessex Hymn to Intellectual Beauty ——

> While yet a boy thy shadow fell on me;
> I vowed that I would dedicate my powers
> To thee and thine—have I not kept the vow?
>   O awful LOVELINESS!

Hardy's sculptor, however, made no vow, and there is no awful Loveliness in his fantastic career. Instead, Pierston first pursues his Platonic Ideal in the form of Avice Caro. He is then a young man of twenty, and there is nothing surprising in the pursuit. But later, as a young man of forty, he pursues the Ideal in the form of Avice's daughter; and lastly, as a young man of sixty, in the form of her granddaughter. For nearly a century readers of *Henry Esmond* have had a hard time accepting Esmond's transfer to his affections from daughter to mother, and in Hardy's novel, where the direction of transfer is reversed, the reader's suspension of disbelief is much less willing. And when to mother and daughter, grand-daughter is added, the situation tends to become farcical. The author meant it to be fanciful, but his habits of composition interfered. True, he did dispense with the customary time chart; but graphic allusions to London, Bayswater, and Pennsylvania Castle do not help to lift the narrative into the region of fantasy. Nor is the play of imagination encouraged by explaining that Pierston's nature is due to his being a native of Portland—"a spot apt to generate a type of personage like the character imperfectly sketched in these pages."

When "The Pursuit of the Well-Beloved" was finished, Hardy sent it to the *Illustrated London News*, which had taken two of his stories in the past. Walter Paget, who had illustrated "On the Western Circuit," was asked to make two drawings for each of the twelve weeks during which the novel was to appear. It ran in the *News* from October 1 to December 17, 1892. That Hardy himself was not overconcerned with the fate of this development from the Platonic conception of his youth is indicated by his delay in putting it out in book form. Five years elapsed, and not until several of the chapters had been rewritten did Osgood, McIlvaine & Co. issue the story in book form. The title was then shortened to *The Well-Beloved*. With a quotation from Shelley on the title page, it was published in 1897 in one volume, bound in blue-green cloth. Even with its rewritten chapters it remains an impossible story. Impossible, not only in the sense that the incidents are incredible: there is a monotony and an inventive sterility about the events amazingly in contrast with Hardy's work elsewhere; but impossible also in the sense that the characters are stone cold. Pierston might be given a place among the statues of a museum, and there is more vitality in one day of Tess's life than in all the lives of the three Avices rolled together. *The Well-Beloved* is not the same sort of failure that *Ethelberta* and *A Laodicean* are, but failure it is, nonetheless. It has never been reprinted except as a part of Hardy's *Collected Works*.

XIV

SAD MUSIC OF HUMANITY

URING THE FALLOW MONTHS between the Italian journey of 1887 and the commencement of *Tess of the D'Urbervilles* in 1889, Hardy from time to time jotted down notes and memoranda for various novels, stories, and poems. Among these notes was one suggested by a death that occurred in 1887. He thought of telling the story of a young man who could not go to Oxford, who after heroic struggles and ultimate failure committed suicide. Hardy felt that in this theme "there is something the world ought to be shown, and I am the one to show it to them." The idea recurred to him while at work on the manuscript of *Tess*. It has already been mentioned that the milkmaid's physical appearance was suggested by the memory of a girl riding in a cart on the outskirts of Egdon Heath. Hardy's thoughts also went back to another and similar picture—a baker's cart driven by a Dorchester boy who worked for a widow baker. Hardy remembered him because the boy had one day stopped Hardy and asked whether he might borrow Hardy's Latin grammar. The youngster's studious habits sometimes interfered with his driving the baker's cart, and the conflict between his occupation and his ambition for a university education impressed the future novelist. In 1890 Hardy jotted down a scheme of events illustrating such a conflict. The story of the girl who rode in a milk cart could be rewritten, he thought, transferred to the other sex, in order to present the sad fate of the boy who rode in a baker's cart. In place of the two men, Alec and Clare, supply two women, Arabella and Sue, presenting the same sort of contrast between selfish sensuality and fastidious aloofness. For *Jude the Obscure* is *Tess of the D'Urbervilles* turned round about.

Corresponding to the death of the horse at the beginning of Tess, the killing of the pig serves to set events in motion. Jude's failure to mention to Sue his marriage to Arabella corresponds to Tess's similar failure to speak of her past to Angel Clare. Just as the scene of former property holdings of the Hardys suggested an environment in which to place the shiftless Durbeyfields, so past history in his own family again provided him with a suitable spot to which to transfer the ambitious but impecunious boy. This past history may be briefly summarized.

Hardy's father died in 1892. It was the first time death had visited the novelist's immediate family since he was a boy. His grandmother Hardy had died when he was seventeen. She is the "One We Knew" in the poem of that title (1907). He recalled her stories of the first thirteen years of her life, when as a little girl named Mary Head she had endured such hardships at Great Fawley, in Berkshire, that she had never been willing to go back to that spot after she had once left it. As the possibilities of the new story grew upon him, Hardy went (in October, 1892) to visit Great Fawley and acquaint himself with the country of his grandmother's melancholy memories. Then he began to write an outline of the Story of an Ambitious Boy. He decided to call the lad Fawley; the place of Mary Head's girlhood he renamed "Marygreen."

Jude Fawley's desire to borrow a Latin grammar obviously suggested thoughts of Oxford or Cambridge. Oxford was not far away from Great Fawley. When Hardy had been a young assistant architect in London, his sister Mary had visited Oxford several times. He remembered writing her: "Oxford must be a jolly place. I shall try to get down there some time or other." Apparently the desire to visit Oxford had never been satisfied,[1] but Hardy easily recalled the intellectual ferment of those days. The British Association for the Advancement of Science met at Oxford in 1860, when Bishop Wilberforce and Huxley had their famous meeting. In 1863 Benjamin Jowett

---

[1] Clive Holland suggests (in *Thomas Hardy, O.M.*, London, Herbert Jenkins, 1933, p. 54) that Hardy had been at Oxford in 1864, but the evidence is slight and unconvincing.

was prosecuted for heresy in the Vice-Chancellor's Court, and a year later there was a debate in the Oxford "Congregation," in which Jowett was charged "with holding and affirming doctrines subversive of the Church's faith." It is more than possible that Hardy, in London, knew that Professor Maurice had been expelled for heresy from King's College, London, ten years before the Jowett affair.

But if the university were to figure in the new story, knowledge of its streets and colleges was imperative. "I always go to a place first before attempting to describe it," Hardy once declared. Hence, to Oxford he went in June, 1893—almost thirty years to a day before he returned to that "city of light" as an honorary fellow of Queen's College. He stayed in Oxford through the "Commemoration" period, passing unnoticed in the crowds assembled there for the festivities. He watched the boat races, strolled about the quadrangles, and stocked his memory with knowledge of the main thoroughfares—the High, "the Corn," and Broad Street. When he left Oxford he was ready to give Jude Fawley a vivid Oxonian setting.

A quarter of a century earlier Hardy had written to Cambridge to find out what steps were necessary for matriculation. Although his own failure to go to the university was due neither to rebuff by Cambridge nor to opposition by his father, the memory of those blighted early leanings toward a formal university education was still clear. An echo of his own decision has already been heard in Angel Clare's words: "I will do without Cambridge." Hardy had made the same renunciation, and it marked a milestone in his life. There is a milestone, too, in *Jude the Obscure.*

Jude drew near it. He remembered that once on his way home he had proudly cut an inscription on the back of that milestone, embodying his aspirations. By the light of a match he could still discern what he had cut so enthusiastically so long ago:

THITHER

J. F.

The sight of it, unimpaired, lit in his soul a spark of the old fire.

Likewise the old fire of twenty-five years before was not forgotten by Thomas Hardy. Reminiscently he now wrote in his new novel: " 'It is a city of light,' he said to himself. He was silent a long while, till he added: 'It would just suit me.' "

Without making the mistake of thinking that Jude and Thomas Hardy are to be identified as one and the same person, readers naturally feel justified in surmising that in some of Jude's longing for Oxford may be found traces of Hardy's own inner life. In the biographical volumes by his second wife readers are told that in *Jude the Obscure* there is not a scrap of personal history. But Jude, who is described as "earnestly reading from his Griesbach's text," certainly recalls Hardy's purchase about 1859 of Griesbach's Greek Testament. Jude reads in the *Iliad* the same passages as those that Hardy marked as his favorites in the Clarke edition of 1818, which he bought while studying architecture under Hicks. And in Jude's frustrated ambition may be found echoes of Hardy's disappointment at having been, like Jude, "diverted from his purposes."

These thoughts of Oxford and Cambridge brought back to him memories, too, of another place. His sisters, Mary and Katherine, had gone to a Teachers' Training School at Salisbury, where he had once visited them in the eighteen-sixties. He never forgot that visit, nor the painful restrictions to which he found his sisters subjected. He was reminded of their plight by a visit in 1891 to the Training College for Schoolmistresses at Whitelands, where the young women inspired in him "not reverence but protective tenderness. Their belief in the rightness of things which you know to be wrong makes the heart ache." It was with this same aching heart that he came to describe in *Jude the Obscure* that "species of nunnery known as the Training School at Melchester" (Salisbury) which Sue Bridehead enters. It was "a pretty, suggestive, pathetic sight."

With theme and characters, plot and settings thus fixed in his mind, Hardy returned from Oxford to Max Gate and set about the business of writing the novel. As he warmed to the task, his heart ached even more than it had over the similarly unjust way in which the world had treated Tess. Here was another character of genuine nobility—obscure and weak, it is true, but of high ideals, true humility, steadfast courage, and affectionate loyalty. As Tess had been betrayed by Alec and then deserted in her moment of need by Clare, so Jude was to be trapped by Arabella and deserted in his moment of need by Sue. But there is one important distinction between the two treatments of the same theme. In the end Tess had been crushed into a shell of her real self, so that Clare had hardly recognized her when he found her at Bournemouth. But nothing can stamp out the manhood in Jude's character. Scourged, disgraced, starved, deserted, ridiculed, tricked, despised, even when he has been plied by Arabella with "plenty of good liquor," he refused to bow his head. "Don't say anything against my honor!" cried Jude hotly, standing up, when he had hardly strength enough in his legs to stand with. "Listen to me, Arabella. You think you are the stronger; and so you are, in a physical sense, now. You could push me over like a ninepin. But I am not so weak in another way as you think. I made up my mind . . ."

And Hardy had made up his mind. He was going to write his *King Lear*. There would be no room now for amusing rustics; no idyllic descriptions of apple orchards; no dallying with sensational feats of sword play, sleepwalking, or conjuring; no sorting out of ill-mated couples at the end; no soothing sop of faith in a life hereafter in which the wrongs of this world would be righted; no pretense that the worthy receive any other reward than that which Cordelia shared with Goneril and Regan—death. And if some reader of his novel should, like Kent, ask: "Is this the promised end?" he would find his answer in the book: "Somebody might have come along that way who would have asked him his trouble, and might have cheered him. But nobody did come, because nobody does."

As Hardy went on with this tragic theme, he began to realize that as a novel it was not going to prove satisfactory to any magazine editor. His recent experience with *Tess* and the contemporary growls about the "Ibscene" drama were enough to show how far English readers still were from being willing to take what he had to give. The editor of *Harper's Magazine*, in offering to accept a new novel by Hardy, explained that his was a family periodical and that he could not publish a serial along the lines of *Tess*. Hardy had assured him that the novel he had in mind "would not bring a blush to a school-girl's cheek" (the phrase is J. Henry Harper's); but after the story got under way, Hardy found that "the characters had taken things into their own hands," and the result was not what he had expected. In April, 1894, he therefore asked *Harper's* to release him from his agreement to supply that magazine with a serial. Harper was not eager to lose the chance of having so famous an author appear in the pages of his magazine, and he therefore advised delay. If Hardy would go on with the story, they might talk it over again when the manuscript was completed. In October, 1894, the two men met in London, with the result which Hardy had foreseen. His story was much too strong for the magazine. Readers would think that Hardy was taking Tennyson's sarcastic advice quite literally:

Authors—essayist, atheist, novelist, realist, rhymster, play your part,
Paint the mortal shame of nature with the living hues of art!
Rip your brothers' vices open, strip your own foul passions bare;
Down with Reticence, down with Reverence—forward—naked—let them
    stare!
Feed the budding rose of boyhood with the drainage of your sewer;
Send the drain into the fountain, lest the stream should issue pure!

The outcome was that Hardy agreed to mutilate his novel, as he had mutilated *Tess*, by rewriting certain passages at which magazine readers might take offense, deleting others, and patching up the scars. Back to Max Gate he went, and spent another month at the distasteful task.

To understand this willingness to yield to the dictation of editors one must remember Hardy's oft-repeated statement that he never really wanted to write novels anyway. He wanted to write poetry, but he could not support himself by it. He turned to fiction as some people turn to teaching or to clerking in a bank or to writing advertising copy. It was a way of making a living. He took that way seriously enough to work hard at it, but never with any stubborn insistence upon having his own way. This acquiescent attitude enabled him to meet editorial demands with a grim humor. Hardy was as much amused by London editors as by Dorset rustics. John Durbeyfield walking with a bias in his gait was no funnier than Editor Locker prodded and goaded by his board of directors on the road of propriety. If in the course of yielding to Mrs. Grundy a magazine portrait degenerated into a gargoyle, the grotesque transformation amused the author, although the necessity for it annoyed him. Everyone who knew Hardy testified to his ever-ready sense of humor. Distasteful though he found the labor of adding the blue-ink revisions, easily distinguished to this day in his manuscript, the distortions of plot and of character were, according to Mrs. Hardy, as amusing to him as they are to us. When, therefore, the editor asked him to revise *Jude the Obscure* so as to make it acceptable for publication in *Harper's*, Hardy set about doing what the editor wished. By the end of 1894 the manuscript was all in the hands of the publisher.

The first installment appeared in December. The title given the novel, "The Simpletons," aroused immediate comment because of its resemblance to Charles Reade's "A Simpleton." When the second installment appeared in January, 1895, the name had been changed to "Hearts Insurgent," a style of title which Kipling was to use two years later in *Captains Courageous*. W. Hatherell was employed to make twelve illustrations for the novel. On November 10, 1895, Hardy wrote to Hatherell: "Allow me to express my sincere admiration for the illustration of 'Jude at the Milestone.' The picture is a tragedy in itself, and I do not remember ever before having an artist who grasped a situation so thoroughly." As the magazine proceeded with the publication of the tragic tale to its conclusion in the November number, Hardy busied himself with restoring the manuscript to its original state. He found this labor particularly onerous, because the year 1895 had been already crowded full of proofreading and manuscript correction caused by the plan of Osgood, McIlvaine & Co. to issue a uniform Collected Edition of all his works. In August, 1895, he prepared a preface for the book edition of the novel, in which he tried to disarm criticism by reminding readers that the story was "addressed by a man to men and women of full age." Osgood, McIlvaine & Co. printed the novel in one volume, and bound it in blue-green cloth. The title of the reassembled work was changed to *Jude the*

Obscure. Interest in the story had already been so aroused by its serialization that the volume was published in November, 1895, in spite of the "1896" on the back of the title page. In New York, Harpers issued the novel at the end of 1895; in place of the etching by Macbeth-Raeburn which appeared in the London edition, they copied the twelve illustrations by W. Hatherell from the magazine.

Immediately bedlam broke loose. Reviewers and critics were violent in their denunciations. The clergy and the genteel world tore their passions to tatters. The noise of alarm arose, too, in America. In the New York *World* for December 8, 1895, Jeannette L. Gilder hysterically announced:

Thomas Hardy has scandalized the critics and shocked his friends. What has gone wrong with the hand that wrote *Far from the Madding Crowd?* I am shocked, appalled by this story. *Jude the Obscure* . . . is almost the worst book I have ever read . . . No wonder that Harper's Magazine could not print it all. The only wonder is that it could print any of it . . . I do not believe that there is a newspaper in England or America that would print this story . . . as it stands in the book. Aside from its immorality, there is its coarseness which is beyond belief . . . Mr. Hardy's mind seems to be grovelling all through this story. He goes out of his way to write of nastiness . . . When I finished the story I opened the window and let in the fresh air.

In the January, 1896, *Blackwood's* Mrs. M. O. W. Oliphant "screamed" (the word is Hardy's own) her charge that the novelist was trying to establish a wicked "anti-marriage league." *The Bookman* called it "a novel of lubricity," and *The Critic* announced that Professor Harry Thurston Peck "brands it as one of the most objectionable books he has ever read."

Hardy lived in constant perturbation. He scarcely liked going to the Athenaeum. He told William Rothenstein that one day, while he was sitting there quietly reading, he was suddenly aware of the menacing figure of a bishop who was striding toward him. Now he was in for it, he thought! Happily the bishop passed him by, but the fear of being assailed was always with him. Some readers became abusive, and anonymous letters began to appear in the Max Gate mailbox. Hardy was pictured as a very fat man in pumps aimlessly trampling a rose in the mud and spattering his shoes and socks in the process. His characters were similarly vilified. One reader exclaimed: "If these men and women and their companions are to be taken as true to modern life, we may as well accept a cage full of monkeys as a microcosm of humanity." The Rev. W. W. How, Bishop of Wakefield, threw Hardy's book into the fire—at least he publicly announced having so done—and sent a scandalized remonstrance to London with the result that *Jude the Obscure* was withdrawn from Smith's Circulating Library. A lecturer at Liverpool, discussing Hardy at some length, told his audience that "this author has a curious mania for exploiting sewers; filth and defilement he faces with the calm, unshrinking countenance of a Local Board laborer."

In the uproar two or three quieter and saner voices could hardly be heard. Swinburne wrote to Hardy to say: "The tragedy is equally beautiful and terrible in its pathos." In a new magazine called *Cosmopolis*, Hardy's friend Gosse wrote: "*Jude the Obscure* is an irresistable book," but he explained, somewhat apologetically, that in it Hardy had "aimed higher than he ever aimed before, and it is not to be maintained that he has been equally successful in every part of his design." Havelock Ellis defended the novel in an article in *The Savoy* in October, 1896, but at this time his name was a doubtful support for Hardy.

After a while the novelist came to see that not all his readers agreed with the noisy reviewers, but it took him some little time to regain his composure. At a luncheon in London he found himself seated beside Edith Wharton. She asked Hardy whether it was really true that the editor of *Harper's* had insisted on his transforming the illegitimate children of Jude and Sue into adopted orphans. With a sardonic smile Hardy answered yes, it was a fact; but he added that he ought not to have been surprised, because the editor of a Scottish magazine which had published one of his short stories had objected to his making his hero and heroine go for a walk on a Sunday, and obliged him to transfer the stroll to a weekday.

Other critics and reviewers evidently found it impossible to appraise the book disinterestedly. For either they were shocked into in-

sensibility by Phillotson's proposal to set his wife free, allowing her
to rush, if she wished, into the arms of her lover, or their critical eyes
were so fixed on the piece of pig's flesh and their critical ears so deaf-
ened by the Nicene Creed recited in the tavern to the lady nicknamed
Bower o' Bliss, that they were unable to notice that, weak though
he was, Jude maintained to the end an idealistic vision of the possibilities of human life. That vision had beckoned him, just as the gleam-
ing city of light had called to him in his youth. It was a vision of a
society in which law and conventions would more nearly coincide
with individual needs. "Is there anything better on earth than that
we should love one another?" At least one of Hardy's critics has had
the insight and the courage to declare: "The love of Jude and Sue,
with all its error and its agony, most nearly approaches the ideal love,
and this is the one love that we are allowed to see persisting into
years of married life." But most critics have been blind to this fact.
The persistence with which Hardy stuck to the marriage theme convinced early readers that there was malicious intent in his writing.
There had been talk of the "untenable redemptive theolatry" of the
Church in *Tess of the D'Urbervilles*, but there was so much else in
that novel that even prejudiced readers could find much to admire.
But in *Jude the Obscure* Hardy refused to be diverted. Again and
again the subject comes up. Sue is made to "feel more than ever
how hopelessly vulgar an institution legal marriage is." Jude declares, "Wifedom has not yet squashed up and digested you in its
vast maw as an atom which has no further individuality."

In art there is nothing more difficult than to breathe life into an
ethical theory. That is what Hardy was attempting to do in *Jude*.
Over and over again Sue is made to argue about the desirability of
a different attitude toward marriage; but until her viewpoint shall
have become commonly accepted, readers will continue to accuse
Hardy of special pleading. That is the price he has to pay for attempting like Clym to adopt an ethical code ahead of his fellows. In vain
readers will be reminded that the arguments are Sue's or Jude's,
not Hardy's. They appreciate the fact that Shakespeare is not proved
to have believed that life is a tale told by an idiot, full of sound

and fury, signifying nothing, just because Macbeth said so. Shakespeare, however, wrote within the bounds of ethical comprehension of his time. Hardy was daring enough to stride out beyond them, and he suffered from the abuse that is always heaped upon the intellectual pioneer. He wrote in a compassionate spirit and was accused of immorality. With sympathy and loving kindness for all men into whose souls the iron of thwarted ambitions and defeated aspirations has entered, he tried to point the way to a happier society, and in return was charged with enjoying filth and defilement.

Under the impact of misfortune Sue failed to develop the fortitude which her obscure cousin maintained to the end. In the rigid economy of the novel Jude is denied the dramatic dignity of a dying speech. But if it had been allowed him, he might, like de Neuvillette in *Cyrano de Bergerac,* have recited another man's words. Cyrano's dying speech would express Jude perfectly: "Spite of your worst, something will still be left me when I go hence. Despite of all, I carry forth unblemished my own integrity!"

Sue's words give Hardy's own judgment of Jude's simple and direct character. "You are Joseph the dreamer of dreams, dear Jude. And sometimes you are St. Stephen, who, while they were stoning him, could see Heaven opened." Sue, on the other hand, is far from simple. "So sensitive that the very wind seemed to blow on her with a touch of difference," she is the most complex woman Hardy ever drew. He afterward explained that Sue was a type of woman which had always had an attraction for him. Sometimes she reminds one of Eustacia, as when she says:

I feel that I shouldn't have been provided with attractiveness unless it were meant to be exercised. Some women's love of being loved is insatiable; and so, often, is their love of loving; and in the last case they may find that they can't give it continuously to the chamber-officer appointed by the bishop's license to receive it.

At other times there seems to be none of Eustacia in her; as when Jude tells her: "You, Sue, are such a phantasmal, bodiless creature, one who has so little animal passion in you!" People had told her she was cold-natured, sexless. She herself talks about her "fanciful fastidiousness." Phillotson recognized in her love for Jude "an extraordinary affinity, or sympathy, which somehow took away all flavor of grossness. Their supreme desire is to be together—to share each other's emotions, and fancies, and dreams."

This novel, more than any other of the Wessex series, is full of "fancies and dreams." There is more talk and less incident. The one startling event of the story, the slaying of the children, stands out with all the greater power to shock. With the violence of an earthquake, *Jude the Obscure* upset the normal reactions and conventional codes of the Victorian world. This was partly Hardy's intention, but he had no idea how impossible most of his countrymen would find it to read his book with the equanimity necessary for sane appraisal.

Naturally Hardy was disappointed. Many years later he remarked that it had always been his misfortune to presuppose a too-intelligent reading public.

In my own eyes [he wrote] the sad feature of the attack [on *Jude*] was that the greater part of the story—that which presented the shattered ideals of the two chief characters, and had been more especially, and indeed almost exclusively, the part of interest to myself—was practically ignored by the adverse press of two countries; the while that some twenty or thirty pages of sorry detail deemed necessary to complete the narrative, and show the antitheses in Jude's life, were almost the sole portions read and regarded.

In presenting the shattered ideals of his characters Hardy had hoped to be able to influence the world's way of thinking and doing. In this he failed. "The only effect of it on human conduct that I could discover," he grimly remarked years later, was "its effect on myself—the experience completely curing me of further interest in novel-writing." He never wrote another. Ten years later, in a copy of *Jude* which afterward found its way into the library of Jerome Kern, the New York song writer, Hardy inscribed:

The criticisms which this story received in England and America were a monumental illustration of the crass Philistinism of the two countries, and were limited to about twenty pages out of more than 500. It was left to the French and Germans to discover the author's meaning, through the medium of indifferent translations.

The "crass Philistinism" he never forgot; for he had found it not only in readers who were strangers to him but also in friends and others who knew him well. In one of the poems published three years after *Jude,* Hardy expressed the wish that his heart had shrunk like his skin, so that he might not suffer so much from observing "hearts grown cold to me."

The book can now be read with a quieter pulse, even though the critics still disagree. H. C. Duffin calls *Jude* "the greatest of Hardy's novels." He finds in it "a vastness, an inexhaustibility, that . . . carry us out into the illimitable spaces of thought. . . . I cannot see how *Jude the Obscure* should ever die for any man or any age."[2] W. R. Rutland, on the other hand, sees in *Jude* "Hardy's deliberate determination to create a nasty taste." He finds the description of the pig-sticking "physically sickening," and thinks that Hardy "deliberately did all he could to horrify and outrage his readers."[3] In the long run Swinburne's judgment is likely to prove the best. *Jude* is a great tragedy, "beautiful and terrible in its pathos." It is Hardy's most sustained effort, his bitterest piece of fiction, the one in which he was most seriously in earnest. In it he tried, as he declared in 1895, "to deal unaffectedly with the fret and fever, derision and disaster, that may press in the wake of the strongest passion known to humanity; to tell, without a mincing of words, a deadly war waged between flesh and spirit; and to point the tragedy of unfulfilled aims." It is an unpleasant and at times a painful work; so is *King Lear.* But any reader of mature mind may take it up with the assurance "that certain cathartic, Aristotelian qualities may be found therein." This was Hardy's hope in writing the novel.

[2] H. C. Duffin, *Thomas Hardy,* University of Manchester Press, 1st ed., 1916, p. 203; 2d ed., 1921, p. 188.

[3] W. R. Rutland, *Thomas Hardy,* Oxford, Blackwell, 1938, p. 249.

XV

THE FIRST MRS. HARDY

IT WAS INEVITABLE that *Jude the Obscure*, with its frequent bitter attacks on marriage, should result in many a silent guess or whispered surmise about Hardy's own marriage. The world has always tried to read backward from work to author in this fashion. Shakespeare once wrote:

> Let still the woman take
> An elder than herself; so wears she to him,
> So sways she level in her husband's heart.

With the knowledge that Anne Hathaway was eight years older than Shakespeare, readers of *Twelfth Night* have insisted on seeing in the lines above evidence of the playwright's marital unhappiness. Similarly Hardy's novels, particulary *Jude*, have been cited as evidence of lack of domestic harmony. Readers have felt that there must be some explanation of the fact that the decay of love is a favorite theme in the Wessex series. Hardy could point out to a friend in private that the only remarks in *Jude* which can be said to bear on the general marriage question occur in dialogue and comprise no more than half a dozen pages in a book of five hundred. But he made no explanations for the enlightenment of the general reader. The public ought to have remembered that the subject of marriage and divorce had been on everyone's lips only a few years before, when the Parnell Case (in 1890) filled the newspapers. Hardy saw no need to tell his readers that the subject had been again called to his attention as a theme for a novel by a conversation in July, 1893, when Lady Londonderry, the Duchess of Manchester, and Lady Jeune discussed in his hearing the problems presented by the British laws. They

had brought up the difficulties of separation, the problems involved
when there are children, and the rigidity of the legal principles involved. This conversation was continued at the home of Lady Jeune,
when one of those present was the Duchess of Abercorn, to whom
Hardy afterward sent a copy of *Jude,* knowing that she would "understand and sympathize with the shadowy personages it concerns." But
the general public saw only the shadows cast by the hypothetical unhappiness at Max Gate. Henry Van Dyke merely put into plain
words what many a reader thought, when he remarked:

Some say that the sombre tone of Hardy's books is a reflection of a certain
unhappiness in his life. His first marriage, I have heard, was not altogether
a congenial one. It cast a shadow of discontent upon his mind. I do not pro-
fess to know whether this explanation is true or not.

Hardy's own silence at this time of bitter attacks upon him is evidence enough of his feeling that his private life was his own and that
he shared Robert Browning's dislike of public intrusion into his own
domestic affairs.

> Sonnet-sing you about myself?
> Do I live in a house you would like to see? . . .
> Unlock my heart with a sonnet key?
>
> No: thanking the public, I must decline.
> A peep through my window, if folk prefer;
> But, please you, no foot over threshold of mine!

So long as Hardy or his wife remained alive, they were entitled to all
the privacy that Browning demanded in "House." But not only are the
builder of Max Gate and his wife now both dead, but there are two
additional reasons for no longer hesitating to set foot over threshold of
his. In the first place, Hardy deliberately decided to take the world
into his confidence after Mrs. Hardy's death, and no one who has read
the "Poems of 1912-13" will feel that their author was asking the
reader to remain content with a mere peep through the windows of
Max Gate. In November of 1913 Hardy told A. C. Benson at Cambridge that he had written some poems about his wife, but didn't
know whether he ought to publish them or not. They were "very
intimate, of course—but the verses came; it was quite natural; one

looked back through the years and saw some pictures; a loss like
that makes one's old brain vocal!" Hardy finally decided to give them
to the world. When a poet invites his reader in to listen to hearth-side
reminiscence and anecdotal reverie, it is no discourtesy to accept the
invitation.

In the second place, to preserve silence on the subject of Hardy's
private life, in the face of the whispers, even the slanders, that have
been printed about him, is to do him no service. One of the most
frequently repeated questions asked by curious readers has been: How
much truth is there in Somerset Maugham's *Cakes and Ale*? In this
novel, published two years after Hardy's death, Herbert Driffield was
obviously patterned after Thomas Hardy, but no attempt was made to
indicate where fact ended and fiction began. In a reprint of the novel
in 1934 Mr. Maugham denied that Driffield was any more a portrait
of Hardy than of Meredith or of Anatole France. That statement still
left readers free to guess and invited false and uncharitable inferences.
Hardy was no stranger to this sort of mischievous fiction and left
no room for doubt as to what he thought of it. About twenty years
before Maugham's book had appeared Hardy wrote:

What should certainly be protested against is the mixing of fact and fiction
in unknown proportions. Infinite mischief would lie in that. If any statements in the dress of fiction are covertly hinted to be fact, all must be fact,
and nothing else but fact, for obvious reasons. The power of getting lies
believed about people through that channel after they are dead, by stirring
in a few truths, is a horror to contemplate.

If readers listen respectfully and sympathetically to the novelist's
words, they will immediately learn that Hardy's attitude toward marriage has been absurdly exaggerated and misrepresented. "My opinion
was what it is now," he declared in 1912, "that a marriage should be
dissolvable as soon as it becomes a cruelty to either of the parties."
Hardy's marriage sometimes caused him pain, but it never became
continuous cruelty to him, and there is no ground for supposing that
he wished it dissolved. Readers who are looking for some Shelleyan
or Byronic scandal will have to go elsewhere. This does not mean,
however, that Thomas Hardy and Emma Lavinia Gifford were an-

other Browning and Elizabeth Barrett. The psychological and temperamental congeniality of the famous Wimpole Street couple was not reproduced at Max Gate. But the Dorset union was solidly founded; it lasted. Browning maintained his idolatry for fifteen years, but Hardy's life with Emma Gifford continued for thirty-eight. Although he never remarked as did Tennyson, "The peace of God came into my life when I married her," he was a much more considerate husband than was the poet laureate. No manuscript of a Wessex Novel is known to exist prefaced with the sort of dedication that was written on the manuscript by the author of *Adam Bede*: "To my dear husband I give the MS. of a work which would never have been written but for the happiness which his love has conferred on my life." But that celebrated "happiness" was all the more prized by George Eliot because of the social ostracism that partly accounts for it—an isolation to which the Hardys were never subjected. In short, Thomas Hardy and his wife were neither cruelly mismated nor ecstatically enraptured with each other as life partners.

Emma Gifford became Mrs. Thomas Hardy on September 17, 1874. She was then 33; Hardy was 34. There was a difference of only six months in their ages. Ignorance of this fact has permitted guesses that Hardy's inferred unhappiness with his wife was due to a disparity in their ages—guesses which, in the absence of definite knowledge about Mrs. Hardy's age, were partly based on *A Pair of Blue Eyes*. In that novel Elfride was drawn, in appearance and in some of her habits and activities, after Emma Gifford. Elfride is described as being nineteen, or "sweet-and-twenty," when the young architect in the novel arrived. Emma was actually ten years older. When Hardy put in his first appearance at St. Juliot, neither he nor Miss Gifford had quite reached the age of thirty. They had more than parity of age to bring them together. Between the date of that first meeting and their marriage four and a half years later Miss Gifford supplied the would-be author with enthusiastic encouragement. It was a period when he described himself as feeling his way to a method in novel writing. She gave practical assistance as well, in making fair copies from sheets of revised manuscript, in discussing themes and plots, and in lending a sympathetic ear. After her marriage she continued these professional services, and loyally put up with that aspect of an author's life that is most likely to strain human relations to the breaking point—the long hours of solitude, hours of what a selfish woman would call indifference or neglect. There was, therefore, no disparity in age or lack of sympathetic interest in a literary career to interfere with the happiness of the Hardys.

In one respect, however, the two were different. His lowly origin on the edge of Egdon Heath, the thatched house which he did not like to hear called a cottage, in which his humble parents continued to reside for many years after his marriage, his lack of a university degree, all served as reminders of the difference in social station of which he was as conscious as she was. In *The Poor Man and the Lady*, written before meeting Miss Gifford, he had already shown sensitiveness to social levels, and after the romantic meeting in Cornwall the conversation quoted on pages 5-6 shows that Miss Gifford's social background had removed none of his self-conscious touchiness on the subject of his own class. She did not forget that her father was a solicitor, that her uncle was a canon of Worcester Cathedral and Archdeacon of London, that her brother-in-law was a rector. When Hamlin Garland visited Hardy's birthplace, the owner repeated to him the local belief that Mrs. Hardy had taken more pride in being the niece of an archdeacon than in being the wife of Thomas Hardy. Her father had taught her to ride, but when Hardy made his first appearance at St. Juliot, she discovered that he did not even know how to help her to mount. While she rode her mare, he walked. Little points, dropped in conversation, frequently reminded him of the difference in their backgrounds. An echo of this discovery is found in the conversation between Egbert and Geraldine in "An Indiscretion in the Life of an Heiress":

"How long does it take to go to Westcombe?"
"About two hours."
"Two hours—so long as that? How far is it away?"
"Eight miles."
"Two hours to drive eight miles—who ever heard of such a thing!"

"I thought you meant walking."

"Ah, yes; but one hardly means walking without expressly stating it."

"Well, it seems just the other way to me—that walking is meant unless you say driving."

And the reader is told that they both were then conscious of the same thought. "It was that horrid thought of their differing habits and of those contrasting positions which could not be reconciled. Indeed, this perception of their disparity weighed more and more heavily upon him as the days went on." These words, which Hardy published in 1878, after four years of married life, led to the remark in the same story: "Thus they mutually oppressed each other, even while they loved." Fifty years later he was still sensitive on the subject of "those contrasting positions." In his poem "A Question of Marriage" a proposal receives this answer:

"Come, Dear, and be queen of my studio."

"We dine our artists; but marry them—no!"

One of the results of Mrs. Hardy's social origin was a very normal and very feminine delight in polite society. She liked to meet people, especially those whose names were well known. She liked to entertain and to be entertained. While her husband was a struggling young novelist there was not enough money to indulge these social proclivities very far; but once he had become a famous author and money came more easily, the social engagements multiplied. Hardy himself got very little out of them. It has already been mentioned that conversations in two London drawing-rooms supplied *Jude the Obscure* with its much-talked-of theme. But usually Hardy found the talk of the genteel world so much idle chatter, from which he was glad to slip away as soon as possible. The dozens on dozens of socially prominent but otherwise unimportant names upon their calling lists indicate not only the patience with which Hardy yielded to this demand for society on the part of his wife, but also her persistent effort to change her "poor man" into a "gentleman," as London understood the term.

A second difference between Hardy and his wife soon made itself apparent to him. He learned that the spontaneity with which Dorsetshire natives expressed their feelings was not paralleled in high society. Instead there was suppression or concealment. Wordsworth had made the same observation when comparing the natives of rural Westmorland with the dwellers in towns and cities. Hardy had been "taken" with the young lady in brown almost from the instant of first seeing her. He made no attempt to hide his interest, and four days later

> crimson one cheek of hers burned
> When we came in together.

But he soon learned that a woman's conduct could be more circumspect, if not frigid. He failed to find the same physical warmth in response to his own spontaneous overflow of feeling. Where he looked for Juno (or Lucina, about whom he wrote in *Far from the Madding Crowd*) he found Diana. He learned that the cold moon goddess still had human devotees. Some of this discovery escaped into his description of Bathsheba:—

Although she scarcely knew the divinity's name, Diana was the goddess whom Bathsheba instinctively adored. That she had never, by look, word, or sign, encouraged a man to approach her—that she had felt herself sufficient to herself, and had in the independence of her girlish heart fancied there was a certain degradation in renouncing the simplicity of a maiden existence to become the humbler half of an indifferent matrimonial whole—were facts now bitterly remembered.

Written in 1874, the word "bitterly" belongs of course exclusively to the story of Bathsheba's alliance with Troy. The instinctive adoration of Diana, however, may be given broader application; for Mrs. Emma Hardy, like Bathsheba, "felt herself sufficient to herself." Like Grace Melbury in *The Woodlanders* she was "a woman who had more of Artemis than of Aphrodite in her constitution." Like Sue, who "drew back stringently" when Jude "could not help putting out his arm towards her waist," she allowed desire to play only a secondary part in her attachment. Two years after their marriage the Hardys settled at Sturminster Newton and for the first time had a house to themselves. On August 13, 1877, Hardy recorded in his notebook: "We hear that Jane, our late servant, is soon to have a baby. Yet never a sign of one is there for us." Hardy wanted children. His early sketch on "How I Built Myself a House" contained provision for a nursery. The absence of children to bless his marriage is to be taken into account not only in connection with this disappointment of his hopes but also in explaining the absence of convincingly drawn children in the Wessex Novels and the presence of the startling figure of Father Time, that allegorical symbol of a child, in *Jude the Obscure*. Nowhere does Hardy show any recognition of the charm and happy innocence of childhood; rarely does he portray the sanctity and tender self-abnegation of motherhood. Before he was fifty Hardy jotted down in his notebook: "I discovered several years ago that I was living in a world where nothing bears out in practice what it promises incipiently." Marriage had not borne out in practice what he thought it had promised him.

In addition to his disappointment in having no children and the chagrin of having to face recurring reminders of his own social "inferiority" (Rebecca West once reported that Mrs. Hardy had said: "Try to remember, Thomas Hardy, that you married a lady!"), there was a third source of friction between the two occupants of Max Gate. One of the results of Mrs. Hardy's assisting her husband in revising and in copying his manuscripts was the development of her belief that she too could write. Hardy modestly welcomed her criticism of his work. Like Hawthorne and Mark Twain, he was quite sincerely ready to listen to whatever comments his wife had to offer; but his very humility gave her an exaggerated idea of her own powers. As time went on and Hardy felt less and less in need of critical help, Mrs. Hardy turned to original composition of her own. She wrote poems on her pet cats—she had very beautiful ones which she liked to show to visitors; and some of these verses she sent to the local newspaper. One visitor at Max Gate recalls Hardy's reference to these poetic efforts of his wife, and the "rather wry smile" with which he alluded to them. Ford Madox Ford called one day at Max Gate, but found Hardy out. Therefore, instead of talking with the novelist, he listened to Mrs. Hardy, "in her Junonian blondeness," read her own "innocuous poems." Mrs. Hardy told one friend of the family that she had also written novels, or at least stories of considerable length. She explained on another occasion that these stories were in a box some-where at the top of the house, because her husband would not let her publish them. The impression she gave was that the world had been thus deprived of works that were just as good as any in the Wessex series. Sometimes she left no doubt about her view of relative values. Desmond MacCarthy, for instance, remembered her saying to him sharply at tea: "If you listen to what I am saying, you will find it as well worth hearing as Mr. Hardy's remarks." She also gave many visitors the impression that she not only copied but also helped to write her husband's books. T. P. O'Connor heard her declare: "I say to his mother, 'Mother, you wrote Thomas's books.' 'No, Emma,' Mother says, 'it was you wrote Thomas's books.'" And then, so O'Connor said, she added, "I have it all here," pointing to her ample bosom, "but I have not the power of expressing it." She told Dr. Fred B. Fisher (the Hardys' physician) that her husband always submitted his novels to her. "She gave me the impression she revised them pretty freely." A French visitor was given the same impression. M. Henri D. Davray noted her willingness to have it believed that it was her hand that put the finishing touches to her husband's rough drafts. Hardy maintained an attitude of simple dignity at such times, and his French caller thought him timid and resigned to a situation he could not improve. When Mrs. Hardy spoke of collaborating with her husband, he remained silent.

The reader will be able to estimate the critical acumen of Mrs. Emma Hardy by recalling that when Sir George Douglas referred to *The Trumpet-Major* as his favorite Wessex Novel (*Tess* and *Jude* had not yet appeared), Mrs. Hardy replied, "Ah, yes! that's one of the pretty ones." The hopeless inadequacy of the adjective may justify the suggestion that some of the "pretty" passages in those Wessex Novels which the world has called failures may be those in which the author yielded to his wife's judgment with respect to the pro-prieties. Douglas reported that Hardy invariably referred to his wife's criticism with a deference which it did not deserve, whereas she showed no corresponding deference to him. She held strong opinions and expressed them vigorously. When some bull-fights were held at

Boulogne-sur-Mer on September 3, 1899, a steamer carried many English excursionists across the Channel to see the gory sight. Mrs. Hardy exploded to the *Daily Chronicle* in London as follows:

Many Englishwomen must have felt a painful shock on learning that a thousand English men and women could so far forget their English birth and breeding as to go to the disgusting spectacle at Boulogne. Can it be found out who were the English men and women who have thus trailed our national reputation in the dirt, that decent people may keep clear of them?

There was still another ground of disagreement. As the niece of an archdeacon and the sister-in-law of a rector, Mrs. Hardy had every reason to be strictly orthodox and conventional in her religious views. Her husband's knowledge of the Bible, his interest in church music, and his experience as a Sunday-school teacher and as a church architect served for a while to disguise for her his complete rejection of the doctrine and dogma of the Established Church. Successive novels wore the disguise increasingly thin; and by the time that she had become acquainted with the basic ideas of his mind, it was obvious that intellectual sympathy between them was impossible. He was familiar with Darwin and Huxley, with Mill and Spencer, with Kant and Schopenhauer, with Comte and Frederick Harrison. Mrs. Hardy was interested in none of these. She was not a thinker. Her expressed belief in an "Unseen Power of great benevolence" made it hard for her not to feel irritation at her husband's repeated references to that power as "a counterfeit of straw," and worship of Him as only empty "mockery." To Hardy's trenchant theological arguments her reply was, "I have some philosophy and mysticism."[1] He believed that death ends all; she preserved a devout confidence in a life beyond this present one. She would have been perfectly suited to be the wife, instead of the sister-in-law, of the Rector of St. Juliot's. Her kind and charitable acts, her gracious manner, had endeared her to many people in the Cornish parish. Unfortunately she found at the head of her Dorsetshire dinner table a man who refused to conceal his doubts, who seemed to her to take a perverse delight in exposing his apostasy.

[1] See Appendix 9, pp. 268-69.

Visitors at Max Gate recall numerous occasions when Mrs. Hardy endeavored to tone down her husband's frank and outspoken language. When she failed in accomplishing this, she sometimes had recourse to another device. Mr. Charles J. Hankinson recalls taking Madame Sarah Grand, author of *The Heavenly Twins* (1893), to call on Hardy at Max Gate. Mrs. Hardy expressed warm approval of this book, while Hardy looked on with a sardonic smile. At the lunch table the conversation drifted on to general philosophical views of life. Hardy stated his abhorrence of pious pretensions which have no counterpart in conduct. Mrs. Hardy was shocked; Madame Grand was amused. The next morning Hankinson received a note from Mrs. Hardy, saying that she hoped he would not take any of Mr. Hardy's remarks seriously; that he really didn't mean them; that he was a very religious man who read his Greek Testament regularly; and that his religious beliefs were in reality quite orthodox. Mr. Hankinson records having received similar notes from Max Gate "on several other occasions."

This religious incompatibility made it increasingly impossible for Hardy to defer to his wife's judgment in his later literary work. His views seemed quite pagan, and his growing popularity seemed to her only to make him more stubborn and opinionated. T. P. O'Connor recalled that, after entertaining the Hardys at dinner, Mrs. Hardy returned the following day to talk about her husband. "She was full-blown, with an ample figure, a large rubicund face, and a defiantly jolly expression." O'Connor reports her words: "You know, he's very vain and very selfish. And these women that he meets in London society only increase these things. They are the poison; I am the antidote." To T. P. O'Connor her whole bitter purpose seemed to be to belittle, irritate, and discourage her husband. No wonder Hardy's face was ribbed with wrinkles of thought and sadness.

Gertrude Atherton also remembers Mrs. Hardy in those days when she thought the London ladies were spoiling her husband by their flattery. At an afternoon reception given for her by William Sharp and his wife, Mrs. Atherton met Hardy and noted his "almost excessive refinement of feature and air of gentle detachment." Later, at the home of the Duchess of Sutherland, she again saw him. "In his wake was an excessively plain, dowdy, high-stomached woman with her hair drawn back in a tight little knot." It was Mrs. Hardy. At first Mrs. Atherton thought that "no doubt Hardy went out so constantly to be rid of her." Obviously this guess was wrong, for everyone who knew Hardy was familiar with his constant desire to "take her along," not only in making calls, in paying visits, in sight-seeing and traveling, but even in his thinking and writing, where he was certain to meet with rebuff. Yet "an excessively plain, dowdy woman" might become tired of the observations her husband made after these social gatherings. When he looked at his wife, he saw

an ageing shape
Where beauty used to be;
That her fond phantom lingers there
Is only known to me.[2]

But it was a different story when he looked upon the society belles who rained invitations upon him. He attended their luncheons, dinners, and garden parties, but rarely did he get any food for thought from them. The people he met were just like so many portraits in an art gallery—to be observed and studied and then set down in his notebook, exactly as he had studied Rembrandt and Rubens and Romney years before. The Duchess of Manchester was a "laughing-eyed woman." Lady Cynthia Graham was "something like my idea of Tess." Lady de Grey was "handsome, tall, glance-giving, arch, friendly." Lady Grove was beautiful. Lady Portsmouth's black brocaded silk gown fitted her well. Lady Yarborough was "very rich and very pretty." Lady Stracey "looked remarkably well." Lady P— was "the most beautiful woman there." Miss — was a "handsome girl" with a "cruel small mouth." Mrs. Jeune "looked handsome." Mrs. T— "and her great eyes" was "the most beautiful woman present." Mrs. Thorny-croft's mouth recalled an Elizabethan poem. Mrs. R. C. and Mrs. A. G. were "a pair of beauties"; the latter "with her violet eyes was the more seductive." Even the most generous-minded wife might sour under the endless succession of implied comparisons between her faded self and

[2] "Memory and I."

the ladies whose portraits her husband was studying. Mrs. Hardy found
it increasingly difficult to respond sympathetically and affectionately
to her husband—increasingly easy to reply sharply or not to speak at
all. A visitor recalls how she presided at the Max Gate tea table without once entering into the conversation.

When, therefore, Hardy began writing *Jude the Obscure*, with its
outspoken "vulgarities," its description of Arabella as "a complete
and substantial female animal," and its bitter attacks on marriage,
and when he passed the pages of his manuscript over to his wife to
read, it was too much. The breaking-point had been reached. In disgust she threw the pages away from her, so she told Dr. Fisher, and
said "she'd never have anything more to do with any book he
wrote." It was unfortunate that she did not read on. Toward the
end she would have come to sentences that might have sounded to
her as if they were Hardy's own words addressed to her:

My own too suffering dear!—there's no evil woman in you. Your natural
instincts are perfectly healthy; not quite so impassioned, perhaps, as I could
wish; but good, and dear, and pure. And as I have often said, you are absolutely the most ethereal, least sensual woman I ever knew to exist without
inhuman sexlessness. Why do you talk in such a changed way? I have not
been selfish, except when no one could profit by my being otherwise. You
used to say that my nature was noble and long-suffering, not vile and corrupt. Now you seem to take such a much lower view!

Brief though her examination of *Jude* may have been, Mrs. Hardy
had read enough to convince her that it was vile and corrupt. If her
husband had sunk to this low plane, something ought to be done
to stop him. She had always been a prompt, resourceful woman.
Elfride's energetic rescue of Knight, when he had slipped over the
cliff in *A Pair of Blue Eyes,* is Hardy's testimony to this quality as
he had noted it in Miss Gifford. During their two-year residence at
Sturminster Newton, when their servant Jane was once discovered
after midnight in the act of admitting a man to the house, while
Hardy had stood perplexed, Mrs. Hardy was downstairs taking command of the situation. The door was locked and the maid ordered back
to her bed, before the novelist had thought what to do. When they

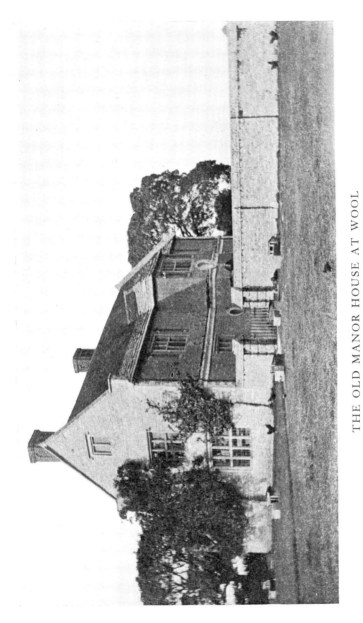

THE OLD MANOR HOUSE AT WOOL

had gone to Wool to inspect the old manor house where Hardy planned to have Tess and Angel Clare spend their honeymoon, he was unsuccessful in obtaining entrance to see the two "horrid life-size portraits" that figure in the novel. He was turning submissively away when Mrs. Hardy pretended to faint. Nothing served to revive her until she had been carried into the house. During her slow recovery the novelist found time to inspect the two paintings.

In the crisis presented by *Jude the Obscure* similar energy and promptness seemed called for. Finding her husband obdurate, Mrs. Hardy made a special trip to London and applied to Dr. Richard Garnett at the British Museum for aid in inducing her husband to burn his vicious manuscript. She had already written to no avail; now she implored Dr. Garnett; she wept. The young Garnetts, on hearing the story, were appalled or amused, depending upon their own individual leanings. But between gasps and snickers the news got around in the British Museum that Dr. Garnett had been appealed to, as Dean of Letters, for aid in suppressing this horrid book. In the end Mrs. Hardy returned, defeated, to Max Gate.

The Hardys continued to live together; they bicycled and toured the continent; they entertained and were entertained. But there was an unseen wall between them. For Hardy, as for Browning's Andrea del Sarto, a common grayness silvered everything when he noticed that his wife was no longer

> at the point of your first pride in me;
> That's gone, you know.

In the poem "The Division" Hardy records his feeling that, though living under the same roof,

> —I am here, and you are there,
> And a hundred miles between!

> O were it but the weather, Dear,
> O were it but the miles
> That summed up all our severance,
> There might be room for smiles.

> But that thwart thing betwixt us twain,
> Which nothing cleaves or clears,
> Is more than distance, Dear, or rain,
> And longer than the years!

Under the surge of his own pent-up feelings his verse acquired a spontaneity and power that it had often lacked.

Years later Edmund Gosse wrote Hardy to ask a question about Helen Paterson. She had illustrated *Far from the Madding Crowd* in 1874 and had married William Allingham about the time of Hardy's marriage to Miss Gifford. Hardy's reply was: "Your inquiry makes me feel 'quite romantical' about her (as they say here). You might hunt her up. If you do, please give her my kind regards, but you must not add that those two almost simultaneous weddings would have been one but for a stupid blunder of God Almighty."

With Hardy's cessation from novel writing the situation at Max Gate was somewhat eased. Later poems were to recall his own anguish of soul, but at least there would be no more novels to cause domestic discord. He preferred to think of his wife

> not as you were
> When you had changed from the one who was all to me,
> But as at first, when our day was fair.[3]

Looking back on these bitter experiences, he later wrote:

> What have you now found to say of our past—
> Summer gave us sweets, but autumn wrought division?
> Things were not lastly as firstly well
> With us twain, you tell?[4]

And that there had been blindness and misunderstanding on both sides is indicated by his words in another autobiographical poem:[5]

> Some heart-bane moved our souls to sever
> And misconceits raised horrid shows,
> And agonies came thereof.

Hardy was not one to insist on his own rights. Twenty-five years

[3] "The Voice."
[4] "After a Journey."
[5] "The Spell of the Rose."

of yielding to timid magazine editors and conventionally minded publishers had created no desire in him to "make a scene." True, *Jude* was published; but once in print, Hardy was ready to forget it. "No more novel-writing for me!" The extent to which his own mildness was appreciated may be judged by recalling his visit in 1907 to Windsor Castle. Earlier in that year Mrs. Hardy had gone up to London, to march in the suffragist parade on February 9. On such occasions she would hurry off from Max Gate without bothering to say good-bye.

> When you'd a mind to career
> Off anywhere—say to town—
> You were all on a sudden gone
> Before I had thought thereon,
> Or noticed your trunks were down.[6]

On this occasion, however, there was need for more careful preparation. For Mr. and Mrs. Thomas Hardy had been invited to the Royal Garden Party at Windsor Castle on June 22, 1907; and they had, in turn, invited the French portrait painter, Jacques-Emile Blanche, and his wife to go with them. M. Blanche had already (in 1906) made a sketch of Hardy, and was at this time engaged upon a second, more carefully studied portrait. The two couples entrained at Paddington station and shortly arrived at Windsor. Blanche had heard from others that in Mrs. Hardy's youth there had been a blithe, rosy freshness about her which he now failed to see. She was thin and shrunken, and forced a stereotyped smile on the face which Mrs. Atherton had observed to have a severe cast. She urged M. Blanche to proceed with the portrait of her husband, "but," she added, "don't make him look miserable!" Blanche noticed Hardy's white hands, with fingers a little swollen and weak; his bald head and wrinkled skin; his face so deeply lined that it looked like the back of a leaf; his eyes deep set, his cheeks thin. He was pale and seemed tired and gloomy. On their arrival at Windsor they discovered that they were only a very small part of the large number of people arriving for the Court festivity. The crowd was so great that there were not enough conveyances

6 "Without Ceremony."

to carry them all from the station up the steep hill to the Castle. However, Mrs. Hardy, wearing a long green veil, took a place in one of the royal carriages and invited Madame Blanche to come with her. The latter declined, urging Hardy to take the seat and spare himself in the July-like heat. The author had just passed his sixty-seventh birthday and looked even older. Rheumatism had so lamed his back that on a previous occasion he had found it impossible to walk downstairs. He was obviously frail. Other guests headed for Windsor Castle followed Madame Blanche's example in urging Hardy to ride. But Mrs. Hardy settled the matter. "Mr. Hardy ride? That walk up the hill in the sun will do him a lot of good." So up the stony hill Thomas Hardy and his portrait-painter trudged on foot, following the open carriage with its driver in King Edward's scarlet livery and its lady in a green veil, seated under a bright silk umbrella.

Two years later Hardy published his poem, "The End of the Episode." There his advice to himself is:

> Ache deep; but make no moans:
> Smile out; but stilly suffer:
> The paths of love are rougher
> Than thoroughfares of stones.

Even though he was determined to make no moan, none of his intimate friends long remained unaware of the profound melancholy that weighed down his spirits. Even his own writing had no power to lift the depression. He once told T. P. O'Connor that he did not care if every book he had ever written were burned and never seen or heard of again. That remark may well be the most tragically sad one ever made in the history of English literature. He later wrote of

> —that wound of mine
> Of which none knew,
> For I'd given no sign
> That it pierced me through.[7]

In his poem "Had you wept" he spoke of "deep division" and "dark undying pain." The pain he might be able to keep to himself, but the division was harder to conceal from the eyes of others.

[7] "The Wound."

In his lines on "A Poet" Hardy later declared that he did not care for loud acclaim, that he did not need attentive eyes,

> Nor urgent writs to sup or dine,
> Nor pledges in the rosy wine.

But urgent writs he received and was urged into accepting. A visitor to the Hardy home remembers the little gray man, hawk-nosed, keen-eyed, gentle-mannered, with a kindly smile at times lighting up his furrowed face as they talked about his books and the characters in them; and he also remembers how Mrs. Hardy broke off her husband's conversation with the visitor, to remind him that he had a garden-party engagement some miles away. "Do you know what marriage is?" Edward FitzGerald asked, shortly after his own wedding. "I'll tell you. It's standing at your desk, all ready for your work, with your brain clear, and then seeing the door open and a great big bonnet asking you to go for a walk with it." On the other hand, when Mrs. Hardy was laid up in September, 1897, as the result of a bicycle accident, Hardy wrote that it had "thrown our household machinery out of gear for a time." In March, 1908, he wrote to a friend: "Emma has been in bed with bronchitis nearly a week, and the house is rather disorganized." Without her there to run things, Hardy surrendered to confusion.

Four years after the royal garden party the *Fortnightly Review* for April, 1911, printed twelve short poems entitled "Satires of Circumstance."[8] These are the most mordant and cynical comments Hardy ever made on marriage, mismating, and death. True, none of these poems refer to his own life or experience, and we need not make the mistake of those "geese [Hardy's description of them] who devoutly believe that everything written in the first person has been done personally." But the spirit in which these poems are written is bitter and hard. Three years later they were collected in a volume entitled *Satires of Circumstance, Lyrics, and Reveries*, about which Hardy's friend Gosse remarked: "The wells of human hope have been poisoned for him by some condition of which we know nothing." Attempts have

[8] See Appendix 4, pp. 239-40.

been made to pass these *Satires* off as humorous productions which
Hardy had issued with a light heart; but the true state of his heart
is revealed in a letter. To his friend Gosse he wrote: "The little
group of satires cost me much sadness in having to reprint them in
the volume. The scales had not fallen from my eyes when I wrote
them, and when I reprinted them they had." That is to say, between
April, 1911, and October, 1914, "the scales fell from his eyes." Mrs.
Hardy had died of heart failure on November 27, 1912, three days
after her seventy-second birthday.

Immediately the atmosphere was cleared. For as soon as the irrita-
tions and disappointments of the present were removed, Hardy's
memory eagerly fell back upon the past "when our day was fair."
He forgot the physical coldness, the social snobbery, the literary jealousy,
the intellectual narrowness, the religious conventionalism. He thought
only of what Emma had meant to him, back in those days when she
was a high-spirited girl "with bright hair flapping free." Once again
she became "The woman whom I loved so, and who loyally loved
me."[9] Those words were truthfully written. There had been loyal
love on both sides, and no account of discord and division should be
allowed to obscure that more important fact. Their affection had been
genuine. Each had been called upon to sacrifice something to the other,
but their attachment was strong enough for each to be resigned to
that sacrifice. Emma's death caused him real sorrow; and in an affectionate nature like Hardy's, sorrow at times assumed some of the
features of remorse. Three weeks after his wife's death he wrote: "In
spite of the differences between us, which it would be affectation to
deny, and certain painful delusions she suffered from at times, my life
is intensely sad to me now without her." He could now recognize that
there had been blindness on both sides.

> I did not know, nor did she infer
> How much there was to read and guess
> By her in me, and to see and crown
> By me in her.

[9] "Beeny Cliff."

Wasted were two souls in their prime
And great was the waste, that July time.[10]

Poem after poem poured from his heart in the months immediately
following her death—poems that are as distinctively individual as any
series of love lyrics in the language. It is entirely possible that these
"Poems of 1912-13" will outlive anything else that Hardy has done,
with the exception of three or four of his best nature poems. The
title "Poems of 1912-13" is convenient but colorless. They ought to be
known by their secondary and more moving title: "Veteris Vestigia
Flammae." The poet's bereavement is here recorded with a beauty,
a tenderness, and a wistful restraint that attain an effect unique in
English literature. No lover of poetry can read these verses without
feeling tempted to regard the discord at Max Gate as well worth while.
With Amiens in *As You Like It* one might say:

> Happy is your Grace
> That can translate the stubbornness of fortune
> Into so quiet and so sweet a style.

And happy was Hardy, all the rest of his life, in living over again
the events of his Cornish romance. As Sir Arthur Quiller-Couch has
observed, all who knew Hardy in his later years were reverently
aware that he had constructed a pure fairytale of that youthful time,
bathed in romantic color: and that it took only a word from a friend
or a sight of a familiar scene to set him off retracing, reclothing, re-
living the happy events of his dream.

The quintessence of those wistful memories was distilled off into
the "Veteris Vestigia Flammae," published in *Satires, Lyrics, and
Reveries* in 1914. In addition to these twenty-one poems there are
nineteen which should be read in this connection.[11] Five appeared in
1917 in *Moments of Vision*; eight appeared in *Late Lyrics*, in 1922;
and six were published in *Human Shows*, in 1925. There are, then,

[10] "We sat at the window."
[11] The list of these nineteen is given in Appendix 4, p. 240.

forty autobiographical poems in which Hardy's Cornish romance is tenderly enshrined.

In the St. Juliot church in Cornwall, in which Emma Gifford had once played the organ, there now hangs a memorial tablet erected by her husband. It reads:

> TO THE DEAR MEMORY OF EMMA LAVINIA HARDY, BORN GIFFORD, THE WIFE OF THOMAS HARDY, AUTHOR, AND SISTER-IN-LAW OF THE REV. C. HOLDER, FORMERLY INCUMBENT OF THIS PARISH: BEFORE HER MARRIAGE SHE LIVED AT THE RECTORY 1868–1873, CONDUCTED THE CHURCH MUSIC, AND LAID THE FIRST STONE OF THE RE-BUILT AISLE AND TOWER: SHE DIED AT DORCHESTER 1912, AND IS BURIED AT STINSFORD, DORSET. ERECTED BY HER HUSBAND 1913.

The poem "The Marble Tablet" refers to this "cold white" record of bygone days. No marble, however, can recapture her "Voice like the purl of a brook," and Hardy never forgot the day when he first heard that voice. On March 7, 1924, he made this entry in his notebook: "E. first met 54 years ago." In "Looking at a Picture on an Anniversary" he recalled that on

> —this day of the year
> (What rainbow-rays embow it!)
> We met, strangers confessed,
> But parted—blest.

On her gravestone in the Stinsford churchyard he placed these words: THIS FOR REMEMBRANCE. To the end of his days, "calm of mind, all passion spent," he remembered what "E" had done for him:

> She opened the door of Romance to me,
> The door from a cell
> I had known too well,
> Too long, till then, and was fain to flee.

MRS. EMMA LAVINIA GIFFORD HARDY

She opened the door of a Love to me,
  That passed the wry
  World-welters by
As far as the arching blue the lea.

She opens the door of the Past to me
  Its magic lights,
  Its heavenly heights,
When forward little is to see!

XVI

THE END OF PROSE

IN THE CHAPTER devoted to *Tess of the D'Urbervilles* it was stated that in 1891 Hardy transferred his business to the publishing house of Osgood, McIlvaine & Co. After the unprecedented and unforeseen commercial success attained by the publication of *Tess*, Osgood and McIlvaine were more than ready to carry out a suggestion that had once been made to Hardy by George Murray Smith, of the firm of Smith, Elder & Co., to issue a collected edition of his works in uniform bindings. The project was accepted by the publishers, and as soon as *Jude the Obscure* was off his hands Hardy began to prepare copy. The plan called for more than merely reprinting the novels. A map of Wessex was to be prepared, an etching for each of the volumes was to be made by H Macbeth-Raeburn, and Hardy, in addition to revising his texts, was to write a preface for each of the seventeen volumes. The number seventeen was obtained by adding three books of collected short stories to the fourteen full-length novels. In connection with the preparation of the map of Wessex, Hardy amended the texts of all the earlier novels, harmonizing the place names so that when a spot appears in more than one story it may always be known by the same name.

This editorial labor was spread over twenty-five months, from January, 1895, to January, 1897. The year 1895 was especially busy. In addition to helping Macbeth-Raeburn find the places he was to draw for the etchings, Hardy had an immense amount of proofreading to do at the very time when he was restoring the mutilated manuscript of *Jude the Obscure*. At this time, too, he was attempting to dramatize *Tess*.[1] In January he wrote a new preface to *Tess*, in February to *The Mayor of Casterbridge*, in March to *A Pair of Blue Eyes*, and in April to *Far from the Madding Crowd*. After a May season in London he went on with the work. A preface was written in June for *The Return of the Native*, in July for *Two on a Tower*, in August for *Jude*, in September for *The Woodlanders*, in October for *The Trumpet-Major*, and in December for *The Hand of Ethelberta*. His task was not merely a matter of a preface a month; the entire text of each novel was carefully combed, and in some cases hardly a page in the book escaped revision. Syntax was strengthened, metaphors added, dialect revised, awkwardness removed, and various infelicities deleted. Miss Rebekah Owen had won her point with regard to *The Mayor of Casterbridge*, and the caged goldfinch reappeared in that novel. The year 1895 might have taxed the strength and endurance of even a stronger man than Hardy, but until the job was finished there could be no let-up. The same exhausting pace was kept up in 1896. In January there was a preface to *A Laodicean*, in February to *Desperate Remedies*, in April to *Wessex Tales*, in June to *A Group of Noble Dames* and *Life's Little Ironies*, and in August to *Under the Greenwood Tree*. He spent a welcome vacation in Belgium in the fall of 1896, and the last of the prefaces was written—for *The Well-Beloved*—in January, 1897.

An eighteenth volume was added in the year 1913, when in *A Changed Man and Other Tales* Hardy collected a dozen short stories which had been scattered over a period of twenty years or more. The publication of this volume was a part of Hardy's final tidying up of all his prose. The enterprise of Osgood, McIlvaine & Co., begun in 1895, had not lasted very long. After their publication of *The Well-Beloved*, in 1897, the business of this firm was passed over to Harper & Brothers, who continued in London as the sole authorized publishers of the Wessex Novels until 1902. Then all Hardy's publishing

[1] See pp. 222-224 and Appendix 12, p. 277.

in England was at last permanently lodged with the firm which had rejected his very first manuscript—Macmillan & Co. They issued the second collected edition in 1902-3; and, after *The Dynasts* had appeared they proposed to Hardy a definitive edition of his works. In October, 1911, he accordingly wrote a General Preface, and in the following year he prepared new or revised prefaces for those novels that seemed to need them. In March he added a new prefatory note to *Tess*, explaining the addition of a few pages to the novel at this time—the three or four pages described heretofore as having been lost in the process of dismembering that novel. In April he wrote new prefaces for *Jude* and for *The Return of the Native*; in May for *The Mayor of Casterbridge* and for *Wessex Tales*. In August a new prefatory note for *Desperate Remedies* completed Hardy's labor in the field of prose fiction, with the exception of a very short note added in June, 1919, to the preface of *Wessex Tales*.

It should not be assumed that in all this later handling of the novels Hardy's work was confined to proofreading and preface writing. Comparison of the text of the definitive edition of the novels with earlier versions shows that Hardy put a vast amount of thought and care into his revisions. His deprecatory remarks about his own novels, especially those uttered in moments of extreme depression of spirits, cannot conceal the patience with which he toiled through the novels line by line. He was tireless in the attempt not only to correct punctuation and grammar (Lionel Johnson once sadly observed that Hardy, like Miss Burney, was "an inveterate patron of the split infinitive"), but also to strengthen diction, beautify rhythm, clarify thought, and enrich the suggestive power of his lines. Learned allusions were added, quotations were identified, geography was made more specific and accurate, and the handling of dialect was greatly improved. In the revision of all the novels Hardy gave increasing care to the speech of the Dorset natives, and among his many historical services this deserves more attention than it has received. Some of the novels (*A Pair of Blue Eyes*, for instance) emerged from the grooming with a text not wholly unlike that which appeared in the first serialization of the story. In other cases the revision has been extensive. Of the 508 pages in the modern Harper edition of *Tess*, only 160 carry no trace of revision.

This late polishing of Hardy's style accounts for some of the differences between recent praise of his prose and the sneers of some of his critics sixty years ago. Hardy's style was self-taught, and, as J. H. Fowler observes, it "betrays the lack of that academic training which perhaps produces its greatest triumph in the finished art of Thackeray." The burrs and brambles, the rank weeds and the thistles in Hardy's prose garden are obvious enough; some of them are still there, in spite of all his cultivating. But his self-taught style also has great merits, and among the thistles there are many luscious fruits and fragrant blossoms. In company with Bunyan and Defoe, Hardy uses words that are often as simple and as unexciting as the Egdon landscape; but in the white heat of his emotion they are sometimes fired until they glow, in the great passages, with unexpected brilliance. Hardy's style, without the clever turns, the nimble tricks, the bright epigrams of other artists in words, is equal to the working-day-world demands of his stories.

In the general preface of 1911 Hardy selected one topic as worthy of special mention. "The geographical limits of the stage here trodden were not," he declared, "forced upon the writer by circumstances; he forced them upon himself from judgment. I considered that there was quite enough human nature in Wessex for one man's literary purpose." This concentration upon Dorset and the neighboring counties was wise in more than one sense. Whenever Hardy let his imagination range far abroad, he allowed errors and incongruities to creep into his stories. Yet such ranging is found in almost all his novels. In *A Pair of Blue Eyes* Stephen Smith goes off to Bombay. In *Far from the Madding Crowd* Troy works his passage to the United States, where he makes "a precarious living in various towns as Professor of Gymnastics." In *The Return of the Native* Wildeve announces that he has "kindred in Wisconsin." In *Two on a Tower* the young astronomer "landed at Boston," but taking no interest in cities he "went immediately on to Cambridge"—just across the Charles River. Years later, when Hamlin Garland mentioned Harvard to the Wessex author, the

American writer was astounded to have Hardy hesitatingly inquire: "Is that a girls' school?" In *The Mayor of Casterbridge* Newson went to Canada, where he was conveniently washed overboard, but he "got ashore at Newfoundland." Most incongruous of all is "that South Carolina gentleman of very passionate nature" who appears in the moonlit pages of *The Woodlanders*, only to shoot Mrs. Charmond at a moment convenient to the plot. The most grotesque distortion of foreign lands in all the Wessex Novels is that found in the five chapters of *Tess* in which Brazil figures. During the three years immediately preceding the publication of *Tess*, hundreds of thousands of agricultural laborers had emigrated from Europe to Brazil. In August, 1890, as Hardy and his brother were setting out from Southampton to cross the English Channel on their way to Paris, they passed a huge Brazilian ship. The little channel steamer (so Hardy thought) was "almost overwhelmed by the enormous bulk" of the South American vessel. He thought too of the notices published in *The Times* throughout the preceding year, warning emigrants about the epidemics, fevers, fraudulent agents, heat, rain, and other hardships to be encountered in Brazil. Hardy also recalled, from his early days in London, previous emigration to that empire. In 1868-69 there had been a large exodus of Algerian French to a spot near Curitiba, and about 1880 two thousand Russians from the Volga settled in the neighborhood of Curitiba. Both these colonizing attempts resulted in failure. The outcome of all these recollections, mixing vaguely in Hardy's memory, was the fantastic land to which Angel Clare emigrates. Hardy never bothered to learn that Curitiba, delightfully situated on a high and healthful plateau, is two thousand miles south of the rainy clay lands of the Amazonian plain. To represent Clare, on mule back near Curitiba, as riding on Amazonian clay and under Amazonian heat and rain is as curious a mixture of climates as it would be to describe Mayor Henchard, staggering down a Dorchester street under the heat and over the sands of the Sahara. Whenever Hardy forsakes his own native region, the result is unconvincing.

On the other hand Hardy was no Egdon recluse, ignorant of the outside world because he never came into contact with it. He spent a month or two in London every year for nearly a third of a century, and he visited Ireland once, Scotland on several occasions and the Continent at least six times. He went to Rouen and to Paris in 1874; in 1876 he toured the Rhine regions; and in 1880 he visited Normandy. He went to Italy in the spring of 1887, and a year later and again in 1890 he was in Paris. It was not lack of opportunity for observation that accounts for the ineffective presentation of people and places outside Wessex; it was lack of sympathy. At home he studied the Dorset native with his heart as well as with his head. Abroad he observed the world through critical if not satirical spectacles. Just as Dickens looked upon the poor and unfortunate mortals of London with a sympathetic eye, but saw only what was offensive and repulsive in their brothers and sisters in New York, Baltimore, and Ohio, so Hardy, like Clym Yeobright, left his heart behind when he went traveling.

In Wessex, however, Hardy is supreme. There his knowledge is not only extensive, it is intimate and accurate in detail and amazingly varied. There could be no more skillful artistry than Hardy has shown in dealing with the geographical variety in the small compass of Dorset. When Donald Maxwell was engaged in making his "artist's anthology of the landscape of the Wessex novels" (published in *The Landscape of Thomas Hardy*, 1928), Hardy advised the artist to concentrate his attention on ten of the novels. He explained the omission of four of his fourteen full-length novels by stating that in these four he had not had "much chance of getting a complete atmosphere for each"—*Desperate Remedies, The Hand of Ethelberta, A Laodicean,* and *A Pair of Blue Eyes.* Maxwell discovered that the settings for the ten recommended by Hardy differ essentially, the two most nearly alike being *Under the Greenwood Tree* and *The Woodlanders.* Each has a different geographical atmosphere—a different literary climate, as it were. The maps of "Wessex," as published with the novels for the past fifty years, have been so crowded with names (there are, for example, forty-eight place names in *Tess* alone) that this atmospheric aspect of Hardy's work has been obscured. The distinctive nature of the settings of the ten novels, those in which Hardy felt that he had been able to carry out his purpose, may be better represented by a simplified map such as is here given.

The same ten novels show that Hardy was equally alert to the possibilities of historical atmosphere. The periods of time are kept just as distinct as are the geographical regions. In one of the earliest magazine articles on Hardy, Barrie called him the "historian of Wessex." That Hardy covered almost the entire nineteenth century is made clear by examining a list of the ten novels in the order of the historical decades to which they refer. The action of the stories is dated as follows:

The Trumpet-Major	1800-1808
Under the Greenwood Tree	1835-1836
The Return of the Native	1842-1843
The Mayor of Casterbridge	1846-1849
The Well-Beloved	1852-1892
Jude the Obscure	1855-1874
Two on a Tower	1858-1863
Far from the Madding Crowd	1869-1873
The Woodlanders	1876-1879
Tess of the D'Urbervilles	1884-1889

By common consent Hardy's readers have reduced his list of ten by dropping into the second rank four of the titles: *The Well-Beloved, Two on a Tower, The Trumpet-Major,* and (regretfully) *Under the Greenwood Tree.* Many who share Tinsley's feeling that the last-mentioned story is "the best little prose idyll ever" will still agree that its slightness must prevent its being classed among the greatest novels. The remaining six titles are those on which Hardy's fame must depend. Critics have disagreed and doubtless will continue to disagree about the order in which the great half dozen are to be ranked. *The Woodlanders,* for instance, the novel least frequently referred to and, of the six, least widely known, is by some regarded as the best. We have Hardy's own word for it that "as a story" he liked it best of all. One hundred years from now, when the world is celebrating the second centenary of Hardy's birth, these are the six which are most certain to be remembered:

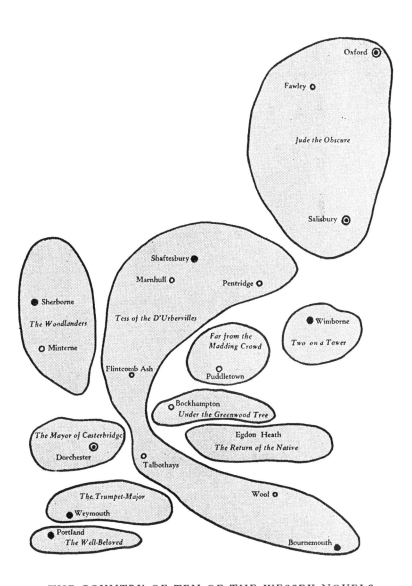

THE COUNTRY OF TEN OF THE WESSEX NOVELS

1. *Tess of the D'Urbervilles*   4. *Far from the Madding Crowd*
2. *The Return of the Native*   5. *Jude the Obscure*
3. *The Mayor of Casterbridge*   6. *The Woodlanders*

That is a list on which any novelist might be willing to risk his chance of survival. It is a list which tells why Hardy has been called the Shakespeare of the English novel.

His elevation to that rank is the more easily understood when it is noticed that five of the six books are tragedies. Hardy himself indicated that it is important to call them tragic rather than pessimistic. In the General Preface of 1911 he wrote his answer to all who had condemned his books as "pessimistic." "Differing natures," he pointed out, "find their tongue in the presence of differing spectacles. Some natures become vocal at tragedy, some are made vocal by comedy, and it seems to me that to whichever of these aspects of life a writer's instinct for expression the more readily responds, to that he should allow it to respond." Hardy made of the English novel—as no other English novelist has done—a completely satisfactory medium for high tragedy.

XVII

THE FIRST BOOKS OF POEMS

VARIOUS MOTIVES and forces combined to make Hardy turn his back upon the business of novel writing to which he had devoted a quarter of a century of successful labor. The agonized outcries of readers of the later novels, combined with his wife's disgust over *Jude*, made the thought of writing more fiction distasteful to him. "A man must be a fool to deliberately stand up to be shot at." Nor does a man approaching sixty have the zest for battle that a young man might feel. Economic pressure was likewise lightened by the immense boost which notoriety gave to the sale of all his books. If he had been a man of indolent habits, he could easily have withdrawn for the rest of his life to the seclusion of Max Gate and never have written another word.

Had he been asked why he chose a more energetic course, he might well have used Hamlet's words in reply:

> Sir, in my heart there was a kind of fighting
> That would not let me sleep.

Pent up within him there was still something crying for expression, something that none of the fourteen novels had satisfied. Poetry had been his chief literary interest before he wrote a word of fiction, and throughout the thirty years since his student days in London, he had never wholly given up the practice of writing verse. The poems composed in London, the lines written after the pilgrimage to Italy, and by-products of the novels, such as the delightful poem "In a Wood," have been mentioned. In 1890 he had written "In a Ewe-leaze near Weatherbury" and other poems; in 1893, "He Wonders about Himself," "The Young Glass-stainer," "Rake-hell Muses," and "A Thunderstorm in Town"; in 1894, "The Slow Nature"; in 1895, that significant poem "In Tenebris," to which he added a supplement in the following year. In 1896 he wrote "Wessex Heights," and in 1897, "The Dead Quire" and "In Gibbon's Old Garden." By the time the seventeen volumes of his collected works were in print, Hardy thus had in his hands a considerable number of poems in manuscript, and the consequent revival of his early desire to publish his verses was natural. He still held ideas which he knew ran counter to the inert crystallized opinion of the public; but that opinion, he thought, might be less offended by poetry than by prose fiction. On October 17, 1896, he recorded his guess that to cry out in a passionate poem that the Supreme Mover must be either limited in power, or unknowing, or cruel, would cause merely a shake of the head; whereas he knew from his own experience that to put the same idea into argumentative prose would make his foes sneer or foam at the mouth and would set them all "jumping upon me, a harmless agnostic." By February 4, 1897, his plans for a book of poems had progressed beyond the mere collecting of his manuscripts. He had decided on a title for the volume, "Wessex Poems," and he planned to make sketches of the scenes of the poems himself.

The project developed. When Harper & Brothers took over in 1897 the business of Osgood, McIlvaine & Co., Hardy brought forward his book of poems and offered to assume the financial risk of the publication. Harpers, however, were ready to trust the commercial value of Hardy's name, even in a new field, and accepted full responsibility. *Wessex Poems* appeared in 1898 with thirty-one illustrations drawn by the poet. The book, bound in blue-green cloth (some copies were bound in white buckram and had gilt edges), contained fifty-one titles. Thus, at the age of fifty-eight Thomas Hardy embarked upon a second career —one which was to end only with his death thirty years later.

The appearance of *Wessex Poems* was greeted by exclamations of surprise. No one except Hardy and his wife knew of his thirty-year devotion to versification. To the public it looked as if an old man were trying to learn the rules of an art in which success has ever depended upon practice in early life. To ears accustomed to Tennysonian sweetness Hardy's vocabulary seemed particularly unpoetic. It is true that the novels had already supplied evidence of Hardy's occasional verbal awkwardness. In *Tess* there are, for instance, horrible Latinizations like "dolorifuge," "heliolatries," "arborescence," and "noctambulist." Angel Clare talks to Tess about a "grotesque prestidigitation"; and words like "photosphere," "concatenation," and "ecstasise" have little propriety in the Valley of the Great Dairies. But in the novels such words are lost sight of in the sweep of the narrative; in the poems they are like sand in honey. Not only can they not be missed, but they may make the reader grit his teeth and conclude too promptly that Hardy was no poet. Nouns like "fantocine," "fulth," "swage," and "wanzing"; adjectives like "baldachined" and "chasmal"; verbs like "to bygo," "to inbe," "to lection," are accompanied by a whole series of unfamiliar negatives, the meaning of which is often obscure: "unbloom," "unheed," "unhope," "unknow," "unreason," "unsight," "untouch," and "unvision." Even when the meanings are clear, some words seem harsh and inappropriate: "cresive," "fulgid," "checkless griff," and "afterhaps."

Some of Hardy's poetic vocabulary is easily explained. His lifelong study of Shakespeare gave him words like "bias," "cess," "cicatrize," "eyne," "fetch" (noun), "forethink," "mow" (deride), "phantastry," and "softling"; and Hardy's practice of the Shakespearean sonnet is far from being the only other mark of Shakespeare's influence upon the Wessex poems. There was, however, another influence at work. Hardy's reputation as a pessimist has obscured his indebtedness to the great optimist Robert Browning. The unlikeness of the two men in disposition and spirit—the aggressive faith of the one as opposed to the resigned agnosticism of the other—has concealed their true relation.

As a young man of twenty-one Hardy went to London just when Robert Browning was returning to his native city after the death of his wife in Florence. A new collected edition of his poems, issued in 1863, brought him to Hardy's attention. Hardy liked to recall that in 1865 he and Browning lived almost within a stone's throw of each other. In the poem "Hap," written the following year, he showed that he had already adopted the hard consonantal cacophony of

Browning's verse. In "John Jones," Swinburne's amusing and all too inaccessible parody of Browning, a single sentence serves to indicate what Swinburne thought a characteristic feature of Browning's verse:

> Ah, how can fear sit
> And hear as love hears it
> Grief's heart's cracked grate's screech?

Browning's typical line,

> Irks care the crop-full bird? frets doubt the man-crammed beast?

had appeared in his 1864 volume, *Dramatis Personae*. That Hardy as well as Swinburne caught its tones is shown in "Hap":

> Know . . .
> That thy love's loss is my hate's profiting.
> Crass Casualty obstructs the sun.

Years later Hardy confessed to Gosse that he had felt that the jeweled line in poetry was effeminate and that he wished to avoid it. Before he had gone far, however, in following Browning's example of indifference to smooth and pleasant-sounding verse, Hardy was lured aside into writing prose.

In *The Poor Man and the Lady*, of 1868, or at least in the remnant of that novel published ten years later, he quoted Browning twice: once from "Instans Tyrannus" and once from "The Statue and the Bust." This last-named poem supplied two additional quotations for *Desperate Remedies*, and that it was one of Hardy's favorite poems became clear when in *Far from the Madding Crowd* it appeared for the fourth time, in a reference to "the mouldering gentlefolk of the poet's story."

In the eighteen-eighties Hardy met Browning at the home of Mrs. Anne Procter (wife of "Barry Cornwall," the poet) in London. In the following year Browning's lines

> There shall never be one lost good! What was, shall live as before;
> What was good shall be good, with, for evil, so much good more,

reappeared in Hardy's notebook as: "Conserve the existing good, supplant the existing bad by good"; and in the pages of *Two on a Tower* he paraphrased lines from "Rabbi Ben Ezra." Browning and Hardy were both guests at a luncheon given by Lord Houghton in June, 1883, and the two poets again talked with each other a few days later at Mrs. Procter's. In 1885 and 1886 they frequently met at that same hospitable home. While writing *The Woodlanders* Hardy once more quoted his old favorite, "The Statue and the Bust"; and in April, 1887, when he and Mrs. Hardy went to Italy, one of the first things he did in Florence was to hunt up the scene of the events in that poem. He also visited San Lorenzo in the same city and was afterward vexed at not recalling until too late its connection with other poems by Browning. Back in London, he again met Browning three or four times at Mrs. Procter's and shared with him their common interest in Shelley. In writing "The Waiting Supper" that fall, he quoted "The Statue and the Bust" for the sixth time. The frequent reappearance of this poem in Hardy's prose does not mean that the novelist was using over and over again a single phrase or thought, as he used Shakespeare's oft-repeated apothegm, "All's well that ends well." Browning's poem supplied a variety of phrases, lines 51-53, 138, 160-62, 214-18, 222-23, and 246, all having been quoted.

In May, 1888, Hardy's *Wessex Tales* were published in two volumes. Hardy set aside a copy of each, and in Volume I he inscribed: "To Robert Browning, Esq., D.C.L., from Thomas Hardy, May, 1888." On Browning's seventy-sixth birthday he sent the collection of short stories with the following letter:

Savile Club,
107, Piccadilly, W.
May 7, 1888

Dear Mr Browning,

May I ask you to do me the honour of accepting a copy of my "Wessex Tales"—sent under another cover to-day? I send this little collection in preference to a regulation novel, in the hope that the varied character of the stories may enable you to find one among them to your liking, if you should have time to look into the volume.

Believe me,

Yours very faithfully
THOMAS HARDY.

Hardy was forty-nine when in the following year he read in the newspapers that Browning had died in Venice. In his notebook he recorded Browning's words: "Incidents in the development of a soul: little else is worth study!" Hardy was at this time at work upon *Tess of the D'Urbervilles*. In it he quoted Browning's "By the Fireside" and "Pippa Passes" and paraphrased a passage in "Rabbi Ben Ezra"— a poem which stood second only to "The Statue and the Bust" in his affections. In writing *Jude the Obscure* Hardy quoted Browning at least four times—lines from "By the Fireside," "Too Late" (twice), and "The Statue and the Bust" (which had been quoted six times in other works). Following the publication of *Jude* Hardy received many an unwelcome letter, among the number being one from an American reviewer who had written a violent and abusive attack in the New York *World*. In replying to her request for an interview, Hardy quoted Browning's "The Worst of It":

> I, never the worse for a touch or two
> On my speckled hide.

As the lines clearly seem to be quoted from memory, this letter illustrates the familiarity of the novelist with even the less-well-known poems of Browning.

Much as Hardy admired the author of "Rabbi Ben Ezra," he could not reconcile Browning's oft-expressed views with scientific truth as Hardy himself had learned to see it. He could not avoid the suspicion that Browning had been insincere. On March 6, 1899, Hardy wrote Gosse the following letter:[1]

The longer I live the more does Browning's character seem *the* literary puzzle of the nineteenth century. How could smug Christian optimism worthy of a dissenting grocer find a place inside a man who was so vast a seer and feeler when on neutral ground? You, from your intimacy with Browning, could probably answer all that, if any living man can; and don't think me officious if I say that you ought to give an explanation to the world. One day I had a theory which you will call horrible—that perceiving he would obtain in a stupid nation no hearing as a poet if he gave himself in his entirety, he professed a certain mass of commonplace opinion as a bait to get the rest of him taken. Well, "the Riddle of Browning" is what I want to read from your pen.

[1] See Appendix 10, p. 269.

Two years later, in a conversation with William Archer, Hardy's thoughts were still centered on Browning. Archer reports him as saying:

I believe that a good deal of the robustious, swaggering optimism of recent literature is at bottom cowardly and insincere. My pessimism, if pessimism it be, does not involve the assumption that the world is going to the dogs. On the contrary, my practical philosophy is distinctly meliorist. Whatever may be the inherent good or evil of life, it is certain that men make it much worse than it need be. When we have got rid of a thousand remediable ills, it will be time enough to determine whether the ill that is irremediable outweighs the good.

In 1904 Hardy referred in private correspondence to Browning's "Childe Roland to the Dark Tower Came," and in the General Preface to his works he quoted "The Last Ride Together." Even in his own notebook he continued this habit of quoting Browning: fifty-five years after first becoming acquainted with the puzzling optimist, he copied a line from the "Epilogue" to *Asolando*: "Never dreamed though right were worsted wrong would triumph." In the painful uncertainty and depression of the World War period, Hardy added, on January 16, 1918: "Well, that was a lucky dreamlessness for Browning."

After the war was over Hardy somewhat recovered from the gloom into which it had plunged him. On May 14, 1920, he visited Exeter Cathedral and enjoyed listening to a beautiful anthem. He recorded his feeling at that time that he would prefer to be a cathedral organist rather than anything else in the world, just to be able like Browning's Abt Vogler to sit,

> Bidding my organ obey, calling its keys to their work,
> Claiming each slave of the sound.

After quoting these words he wrote his poem "The Chapel-Organist," in which he imitated the anapestic meter of "Abt Vogler." The record of numerous similar echoes and imitations does not make for fluent reading, but those who are interested in further details of Hardy's tribute to Robert Browning will find them given in an appendix.

On the night before he died Hardy asked to have "Rabbi Ben Ezra" read aloud to him. He wanted none of the thirty-two stanzas skipped. Riddle though he was, Browning had fascinated Hardy's mind for sixty-five years; and now upon his deathbed the novelist poet wanted to hear again the words of that enspiriting poem after which so much of his own work, in thought, in phrase, and in meter, had been patterned. He might well have used Browning's own words, to say:

> Yes, I have loved you so, followed you, honored you,
>   Lived in your mild and magnificent eye,
> Learned your great language, caught your clear accents,
>   Made you my pattern to live and to die.

Curiously enough, none of this was known to those who read *Wessex Poems* in 1898. All that was evident then was the great contrast between Browning's zest for life and Hardy's lack of it. Browning's cheerfulness was an enigma to many people; it had puzzled the sage of Chelsea just as much as it did Hardy. Carlyle had written: "There's a great contrast between him and me. He seems very content with life, and takes much satisfaction in the world. It is a very strange and curious spectacle to behold a man in these days so confidently cheerful." With Browning all things worked together to justify faith, hope, and love; Thomas Hardy saw no assurance whatever that wrong will be righted. This striking contrast, however, between Hardy's quiet waiting and Browning's enthusiastic, almost defiant certitude ought not to be allowed to obscure the close resemblance of the two poets in other respects. Both took the dramatic way of handling a theme. Both were particularly attracted by the little ironies of life, those little

> Things we have passed perhaps a hundred times
> Nor cared to see

until a Browning or a Hardy came along to call our attention to them. Thus not only in the matter of harsh diction, rough rhythm, and twisted syntax is Hardy to be recognized as a true follower of Robert Browning, but likewise in these more important matters of literary form and human material. Both men liked to write about people—not about mankind in the mass, as did Wordsworth and Shelley, but about individual personalities. Hardy's "crusted characters" and Browning's *Men and Women* are more closely related than their outside clothing might seem to indicate.

In spite of the lack of enthusiasm shown by those who read *Wessex Poems*, Hardy persevered in his efforts, and after four years he had a second volume, one of ninety-nine poems, ready to print. Harper & Brothers again served as publishers. *Poems of the Past and the Present* appeared in 1902, bound in blue-green cloth. Detailed consideration of these verses will be postponed to a later chapter, in which Hardy's entire poetic output may be more conveniently examined. The publication of 1902, however, served notice on the critics that there was no longer any possibility of refusing to recognize Hardy as a genuine poet. Although a Shakespearean vocabulary and a Browning-like harshness were by no means absent, *Poems of the Past and Present* showed undeniable poetic growth. "God-Forgotten," whatever readers might think of its thought, was phrased with the vividness and directness of one of Browning's dramatic episodes. "The Lost Pyx" showed that, in spite of having some difficulties with the anapests, Hardy could use internal rhyme freely without destroying the animation of his narrative.

There is no reason for debating which is the best poem in the book, for "The Darkling Thrush" is one of the best that Hardy ever wrote. Even his most dubious readers were ready to call it perfect. It was possibly suggested by W. H. Hudson's *Nature in Downland* (1900), in which a thrush "in rough or gloomy weather . . . singing his best" brought to Hudson's mind the thought that "such sounds" indicated a "contentment and bliss" beyond our own. The idea expressed in Hardy's poem is the same as Hudson's, but the music is the poet's own. Hardy repeated the wistful tenderness of its tone in other poems, but never did he excel the perfect fusion of subject, mood, and technique here shown. A fellow-poet, Alfred Noyes, declared:

Hardy's poem, "The Darkling Thrush," is a lyric of rugged strength, that peculiar strength which comes from understatement and the sense of something in reserve; a lyric of such pathos and beauty as can be compared with the best that has ever been done in our great lyrical language; and that is to say one of the finest lyrics in the world. From the first line to the restrained and intense rapture of the close, the poem bears upon it the stamp of a truth and sincerity beyond praise.

Hardy was now ready, at the age of sixty-two, for the most ambitious undertaking of his life. He had always preferred the large intention of an unskillful artist to the trivial intention of an accomplished one. He was, as he himself put it, "more interested in the high ideas of a feeble executant than in the high execution of a feeble thinker." Here again he was echoing Browning, who had written:

> That low man seeks a little thing to do,
>   Sees it and does it:
> This high man, with a great thing to pursue,
>   Dies ere he knows it.
> That low man goes on adding one to one,
>   His hundred's soon hit:
> This high man, aiming at a million,
>   Misses an unit.

Thomas Hardy was a "high man." He might miss by a unit; he might die ere he attained his great thing; but he had such a goal to pursue, and in *The Dynasts* he pursued it.

XVIII

THE DYNASTS

NOTHING ILLUSTRATES BETTER than *The Dynasts* the slow incubation of literary projects in Hardy's mind. In a very literal sense he spent sixty years getting ready for this massive effort. As a boy he had listened to his grandmother's accounts of the time of the French Revolution. His father had pointed out traces of the excitement of Napoleonic days still to be seen in Wessex in the shape of bullet-holes, beacon-keepers' huts, and the like. His mother told him of one member of their family who had been a volunteer during the war with Napoleon. Hardy happened to be in London when the Franco-Prussian war broke out in 1870, and in the feverish atmosphere of those war days he paid a visit to the Chelsea Hospital and there enjoyed talking with veterans of the Battle of Waterloo. He meditated, too, on the contrast between war hatreds, as still felt by these old soldiers, and the old, old story of love of man for maid. A visit to Miss Gifford in Cornwall at this time (1870) suggested the theme of a poem, "In Time of 'The Breaking of Nations'"—a poem which (characteristically enough) he carried around in his mind for forty-five years before writing it down on paper. It took the World War to recall to life Hardy's poetic reaction to the Franco-Prussian War. In 1870, however, he was young and shared some of Wordsworth's feeling about an earlier European crisis:

> Bliss was it in that dawn to be alive,
> But to be young was very heaven!

His visit to the Chelsea Hospital proved so enjoyable that on three later occasions he returned. In 1875, 1876, and 1878 he found keen pleasure in listening to the aged soldiers fighting the battle all over again. When, in May, 1876, Hardy visited Belgium, he lingered with particular interest in Brussels. He tried to identify the exact spot of the Duchess of Richmond's ball and explored in detail the battlefield at Waterloo.

All of this preceded the writing of *The Trumpet-Major*, but the publication of that novel in 1880 by no means ended Hardy's interest in the Napoleonic era. Two years later he wrote his short story on "A Tradition of Eighteen Hundred and Four" (published in *Life's Little Ironies* in 1894, but in 1912 transferred to the more appropriate collection, *Wessex Tales*). He not only wrote but read. His purchase of Gifford's *History of the Wars* has already been recorded, but he was not satisfied with an occasional random book. He began systematically to acquire a Napoleonic library, and by the end of his life he owned an extensive collection. Most of it is now preserved in the museum at Dorchester.[1]

In March, 1891, Hardy spent intervals during his work on *Tess of the D'Urbervilles* in meditating an original drama on the time of Napoleon. The magnitude of the stage of such a drama he felt would be in marked contrast with the circumscribed orbit of the Talbothays milkmaids. No sector of Wessex coast would suffice for an epic equal in size to the commanding figure of Napoleon: the entire map of Europe would have to be brought into play. When he finally turned from writing fiction, the Napoleonic struggle again and again left its marks on his verse. Three of the *Wessex Poems* dealt with one aspect or another of those stirring times. "The Alarm," "Leipzig," and "The Peasant's Confession" refer to 1804, 1813, and 1815, respectively. In September, 1896, Hardy was back in Brussels again, attempting to clarify his Napoleonic drama on the spot. "Europe in Throes" he now thought of calling it; and, recognizing the impossibility of holding so momentous a period within the limits of a single play, he thought of writing the drama in three parts, each one to have five acts. The climax of the drama would come in the third part—the Battle of Waterloo. On October 2, 1896, he made another visit to the battlefield

---

[1] For a partial list of titles see Appendix 11, pp. 276-77.

and there walked about alone, identifying the lines of the English and the French forces and fixing in his memory the whole lay-out of the countryside. Even then he was not ready to set to work. For another five years he continued to mull over the subject.

One of the causes of this extended rumination was Hardy's feeling that he did not want to write a mere historical record, no matter how massive its sweep. He wished to work, not as a historian, but as a dramatic poet, as Shakespeare had done in *Henry IV*, and Browning in *Strafford*. And yet neither of these poetic dramas supplies a perfect analogy to what Hardy had in mind, for neither was on the massive scale which the figure of Napoleon required. He was of Homeric stature, and Hardy wished his drama to be of epic grandeur as well as of dramatic vividness and power. The impression of massive significance given by the story of ancient Troy is partly achieved by the concern which the gods and goddesses show over the outcome of the human struggle. Hardy thought of using a similar supernatural framework for his epic drama of human strife, but he found that he was at once faced with further difficulties. The old Greek theology was of course impossible in a modern poem. The Hebrew Lord God of Hosts was equally inapplicable. Hardy's own post-Darwinian views made it impossible for him to think of presenting Napoleon and his foes against a background of orthodox Christian faith. Belief in Crass Casualty obstructed that plan. Hardy eventually decided to try to invent a new supernatural chorus of his own—one which he hoped might represent the best human intelligence and sympathy of his own day in a sort of quintessential form. He realized that this would involve him in inconsistencies, that the thought of his own day might be proved wrong, and that he would probably be condemned for trying to express in poetry a philosophy which had never been expressed in poetry before. "I expect I shall catch it hot and strong!" But this high man, aiming at a million, was not to be deterred by such fears. His private correspondence shows that he had Browning's "Childe Roland" in mind at this time; and like that imperturbable knight, "Dauntless the slug-horn to his lips he set, and blew."

Thus the Phantoms came into existence, through whose eyes the spectacle of Europe in Throes was to be observed. They were to take no part in the action and exercise no control over the events; but all of the vast human tragedy was to be observed from their point of view. "The Spirit of the Years," representing the stoically-minded "enlightened" modern intellect, and the "Spirit of the Pities," representing long-suffering common humanity with its futile sympathies and impotent sense of injustice and wrong, were to be allied with "It"—the modern conception of mechanistic force or urge, which Hardy felt had displaced God in the universe. (Shortly after *The Dynasts* he wrote a poem on "God's Funeral.") He knew that the Prime Cause had never before been called "It" in poetical literature, but he found it hard to use "He" or "She" for that vague purposeless blind thrusting which he found at the center of everything. The nearest he could come to finding a satisfactory word was Schopenhauer's "Will." Hardy was quite ready to agree that "Immanent Will" did not perfectly fit the idea he wished to convey. But Schopenhauer and Hartmann had made the term more widely known than any other, and Hardy himself had no better one to offer as a substitute. He proceeded, therefore, to present the drama of Napoleon's meteoric career as seen through the framework of the Pities, the Years, and "the all-urging Will, raptly magnipotent."

Beginning his action shortly before the date he had reached at the end of *The Trumpet-Major,* Hardy worked away at the story of Austerlitz and Trafalgar throughout 1902 and much of 1903. His original plan had been a gigantic epic drama in fifteen acts; but by September, 1903, when he had finished only six acts, he felt so exhausted by his labors that he began to think he would not carry the undertaking any further. Hardy was no Trollope. Strenuous labor left him physically exhausted and mentally depressed. He wondered whether *The Dynasts* was worth the effort. Before regaining his interest in the huge undertaking which he had mapped out, he impulsively sent his manuscript of the six acts to Macmillan, and publication was immediately arranged for. In December, 1903, Part I of *The Dynasts* came from the press, but the belated discovery of some errors delayed the publication of the book until January, when it was issued with a cancel title page.

From that date Macmillan & Company published all Hardy's new works, both in England and in America, and no further reference to the author's business arrangements is necessary.

After a few months of rest Hardy felt more interested in trying to complete the drama. Its reception by the public could not be called cordial, but in March, 1904, he wrote to his friend Clodd that he was nonetheless inclined to go on with it. In May he was busy reading in the British Museum, and a year later he was energetically at work upon the second part, in which the Battle of Jena and the Peninsula Campaign figure. He used the occasion of a visit to his old critic, George Meredith, to ask whether *The Dynasts* was worth finishing. Meredith's reply is recorded in a letter he wrote on July 2, 1905:

Hardy was here some days back. I am always glad to see him, and have regrets at his going; for the double reason, that I like him, and am afflicted by his twilight view of life. He questioned me as to *The Dynasts*. I spoke (needlessly) in favor of his continuing it, now that it had a commencement. It was useless to say, as I think, that he would have made it more effective in prose, where he is more at home than in verse, though here and there he produces good stuff. Of much of Browning I could say the same.

Meredith, like every other reader who begins *The Dynasts* and is at once sent running to the dictionary, did not have to read beyond the second page before finding cause for annoyance. In the line "You cannot swerve the pulsion of the Byss," the meaning of "byss" may be guessed by the student of Greek as being the opposite of "abyss"; but that is only the beginning of the trouble. "Fugle," "incarn," "walm," and "inkle," are samples of the difficulties presented by the vocabulary of *The Dynasts*. Even words that have a familiar sound are likely to appear with strange new meanings. "Finite" means "final," and "voidless" means "unavoidable." The perplexing use of "un-," already noticed in *Wessex Poems*, again causes the reader to stumble; for Hardy does not mean a negative reversal of an action, as in "tie" and "untie," but the mere absence of such action. He writes, for instance: "His projects they unknow, his grin unsee." What he means is: "They do not know his projects, nor do they see his grin." Readers also found abundant reason for sharing Meredith's feeling that Hardy was not at home in metrical composition. Apart from the idiosyncrasies of diction, his verse read like the product of a conscientious workman rather than like that of an inspired poet. Not only was the blank verse frequently flat and undistinguished, but the passages in which the action by contrast most easily came alive were written in racy, idiomatic Dorset prose. Jems Purchass and John Whiting, the two old men who tend the beacons on Egdon Heath, are as real as Jan Coggan and Henery Fray in the novel; they seem to have come direct from Warren's Malthouse in *Far from the Madding Crowd.*

The master of Max Gate went on with his labors and by October of 1905 had completed Part II. Like Part I it was divided into six acts. It was published early in 1906 (except for half a dozen copies published in America in December, 1905). This volume was more warmly welcomed than its predecessor. The supernatural "phantom intelligences" were no longer startling and disturbing innovations, and there was above all some of the finest sort of realism in this second part. Perhaps the most vivid passage in *The Dynasts* is the episode of the wretched deserters hiding in a cellar near Astorga, on the retreat from Corunna after the battle of 1809. Here again there was vigorous, colloquial prose; and readers who didn't care anything about the pulsations of the unconscious all-urging Will were thrilled by the vitality and humanity of this scene. Hardy felt encouraged to proceed.

He now had the end in sight. In June, 1906, he was again at work in the British Museum, equipping himself with detailed facts about the retreat from Moscow. About the great climax of Part III, however, he was little in need of historical research. The Battle of Waterloo was too vividly present in his imagination for him to feel hampered or uncertain. He approached the crisis of 1815 with the same assurance, based on long and intimate acquaintance, that he felt in dealing with the Dorset natives. All the stories of the Waterloo veterans came back to him from those Chelsea visits in the seventies. His own two trips to the battlefield provided him with the topographical details that he always found necessary. In March, 1907, he was busily at work. He found that six acts were not enough; even seven would be crowded. In the nineteen acts of the complete drama there are 130 scenes. By September his manuscript was completed; and in January, 1908, Part III was published.

It brought about an immediate change in the attitude of the reading public toward *The Dynasts*. The swift and unrelaxing tension of this final part, the animation of all its scenes, and the hopeful note which Hardy sounded at the close—all served to make many a reader suspect that he had been previously blind and deaf to one of the great surprises of modern literature. The vitality of these final scenes, leading up to the resonant climax of Waterloo, now led many to be willing to forget the tedious road of prosaic poetry, and the rocks and stones of freakish vocabulary and jangled syntax, over which they had had to pass to reach the glorious conclusion.

Hardy sent a copy of the book to George Meredith, whose acknowledgment of the gift supplies a brief but sound appraisal of the entire work:

The book was welcome all the more as being a sign that this big work was off your mind. How it may have been received I cannot say, but any book on so large a scale has to suffer the fate of Panorama, and must be visited again and again for a just impression of it to be taken. I saw that somewhere in your neighborhood it was represented in action. That is the way to bring it more rapidly home to the mind. But the speaker of Josephine's last words would have to be a choice one.

Meredith correctly recognized that Hardy's drama is an immense panorama. The human eye cannot in a single glance take in such a work, and a single reading will not serve to indicate the varied riches of *The Dynasts*. Its wealth of historical details alone calls for close inspection, and students of history have frequently testified to Hardy's masterful grasp of fact throughout the momentous decade of 1805-15. More essential, however, is the artistic effect gained by his use of his materials. Some lines of *The Dynasts* are obviously out of place. Here, for example, are four that sound as if they belonged in Gilbert and Sullivan:

> Should the corvette return
>   With the anxious Scotch colonel,
> Escape would be frustrate,
>   Retention eternal!

It is important, therefore, to approach this work with a just critical attitude. One of the earliest commentators on *The Dynasts* was Sir Henry Newbolt. While not blind to its defects, he found much in it to praise, and his words elicited an appreciative reply from Hardy:

You approach the book from the right side, which so few critics have done. Instead of saying to themselves, "Here is a performance hugely defective: is there anything in it notwithstanding the huge defects?" they have mostly contented themselves with picking out bad lines, which any child could do, there being myriads of them, as I knew too well before they said so.

The modern reader may well take his clue from Hardy's own critical dictum regarding *The Dynasts*. Is there anything in it? Most assuredly there is. It succeeds in giving a stirring impression of the Napoleonic wars in their entirety. That alone is a notable achievement. But individual scenes in the drama rise to greater heights—the death of Nelson and the burning of Moscow, the soldiers found frozen by the fireside in Russia, the ball at Brussels, the insane George III receiving the news that he had won a battle, Josephine being told of the intended divorce, Napoleon's interview with the Queen of Prussia, the colloquy between Lord Uxbridge, hit by a cannon ball, and Wellington:

"I have lost my leg, by God!"
"By God, and have you! I felt the wind o' the shot—"

the contemptible Regent's frenzied perplexity as to how to "get over this infernal woman."

Meredith's reference to Josephine's last words indicates his appreciation of the moving scene of her death, and she is merely one of the many characters who are drawn with sympathy and insight. Most of Hardy's characterizing labor was expended upon drawing the contrast between Wellington and Napoleon. Beginning with a conviction that England's part in the Napoleonic struggle had never received adequate treatment in previous literary accounts of the era, Hardy carefully built Wellington up into a commanding dramatic figure, well qualified to stand as the impressive emblem of England's implacable resistance to Napoleon's selfish ambition. Equally skillful is the portrayal of Bonaparte's gradual deterioration, both physical and spiritual.

Hardy's earlier study of the great English epic of the human race had acquainted him with Milton's skillful reduction of Satan from a figure of heroic proportions to the despicable wretch who is eventually hissed by his own followers. Hardy similarly traces Napoleon's slow decline. The emperor looks well at first, but soon we read that he is growing fat. In Spain his unhealthy face is mentioned. In the second part his "stoutening figure" is accompanied by unchivalrous conduct. In Part III his puffed calves and continual cough are merely the physical counterparts of a psychological brutality which shows itself again and again. Hardy's little poem "In a Wood" had concluded with the glowing recognition that among men, now and then, are found "life-loyalties." Napoleon's final spiritual collapse is symbolized by his seeing infidelity in everyone around him, even in those who have served him most faithfully.

The lyrics scattered throughout the poem often contrast strikingly with the woodenness of the blank verse. These lyrics vary from stirring martial rhythms like "Budmouth Dears" and exuberant songs like "My Love's Gone a-Fighting" to dignified choruses of surprising intensity. One of the most characteristic of these lyrics is the Chorus of the Years before Waterloo, in which Hardy recalls an idea from *The Woodlanders.* Using the meter of "The Statue and the Bust," and beginning with the line "The eyelids of eve fall together at last," he associates the swallow and the lark, the snail and the worm, even the butterfly and the "flowers in the bud," with the sickness of the whole earth, of which man's sufferings are only a pathetic part.

As for the philosophy of the drama, inherent in the supernatural framework of the poem, a great deal too much emphasis has been placed upon its alleged pessimism. One critic thought the entire work was written just to enforce the philosophy of Schopenhauer. Another found in it just one line which excused it from the charge of utter pessimism. Hardy's quiet observation in a letter was: "My pages show harmony of view with Darwin, Huxley, Spencer, Comte, Hume, Mill, and others, all of whom I used to read more than Schopenhauer." To one writer who had criticized Hardy for making Pitt give utterance to Schopenhauerian ideas of the Immanent Will, Hardy pointed out that he had used Pitt's actual words, his last public ones, uttered before Schopenhauer was ever heard of. A more serious objection to the philosophical commentaries scattered throughout the play is that they fail to accomplish a complete fusion between the two worlds—the mundane and the supernatural. The view of the Will, working Its listless aim unconsciously, conflicts with the political theory which must be held if the historical aspect of *The Dynasts* is to have any force or significance. England's part in the conflict is no nobler than Napoleon's, if all alike, English and French, "obey resistlessly the purposive, unmotived, dominant Thing." Hardy himself urges the reader not to make too close an inspection of his phantoms. They "are but tentative, and are advanced with little eye to a systematic philosophy."

One thing at least was brought about by the completion of *The Dynasts* in 1908. In spite of some discriminating appreciation of his earlier books of poetry, most readers had been inclined to regard Hardy as a novelist who was trying rather ineffectively to learn to write verse. After all three parts of *The Dynasts* had appeared, Hardy the poet was given general recognition. Many who felt *The Dynasts* to be a failure still regarded it as a truly significant achievement, worth more than some successes. Hardy had himself observed that "the failure may be greater than the success. To have strength to roll a stone weighing a hundredweight to the top of the mount is a success, and to have the strength to roll a stone of ten hundredweight only half-way up that mount is a failure. But the latter is two or three times as strong a deed." *The Dynasts* did not reach the top of the mount, but it was a ten-hundredweight attempt and certainly carried Hardy more than half way up. The world was all the more ready to applaud because the heroic task had been attempted by a man of sixty-eight. The acclaim of the public was appropriately signalized on July 19, 1910, when Hardy was invested by the King with the Order of Merit.

XIX

INDIAN SUMMER

GEORGE MEREDITH, Hardy's early critic, did not live to see him attain the honor of the Order of Merit. Shortly after Meredith's death in 1909 Hardy wrote an eighteen-line poem to commemorate a friendship that had grown from the meeting "forty years back." The poem, containing a characteristically inept adjective "vitiate," was written in the modified *terza rima* of Hardy's favorite "The Statue and the Bust." A few months later it was collected into his third volume of poems (not counting *The Dynasts*). This volume he called *Time's Laughingstocks and Other Verses*. Like its predecessors it contained not only contemporary compositions but also work written as early as 1866. The volume as a whole cannot, therefore, supply a basis for judging Hardy's poetic development unless the dates of individual compositions are carefully studied. One of the most significant personal lyrics is the "country song," with its sober optimism, beginning:

> Let me enjoy the earth no less
> Because the all-enacting might
> That fashioned forth its loveliness
> Had other aims than my delight.

Among Hardy's readers many ears remained deaf to this song in praise of the loveliness of earth. One reviewer announced: "Hardy has turned his back on the sunrise and his songs are all of the night." Two of the poems give tender pictures of the poet's family: "One We Knew," dealing with Hardy's grandmother, and "A Church Romance," in which he recorded how his father and mother met. However, the most distinguished poems in the book are not the lyrics but the narratives.

Three of the titles in *Time's Laughingstocks* belong in the list of Hardy's most successful stories told in verse: "The Curate's Kindness," a typical "little irony"; "A Sunday Morning Tragedy," another *Tess* story reduced to miniature proportions; and "Panthera," a rationalization of the traditional stories told about the birth and death of Jesus. Even though Hardy had banished God from the world of *The Dynasts* and had written a poem about His funeral, he found it very easy to slip back into the comfortable language of tradition. He was quite ready to say with Gamaliel Bradford,

> I sometimes wish that God were back
> In this dark world and wide;
> For though some virtues He might lack,
> He had His pleasant side.

This wistful note of "sometimes wishing" has already been noticed in "The Darkling Thrush," and was to be heard again in other poems. It became one of Hardy's distinguishing poetic characteristics.

His increasing success in metrical composition and the greatly increased cordiality in the public reception of his poems encouraged him not only to continue producing—that he would have done without encouragement, just because he liked to write verses—but to share his work with the public. Five years after *Time's Laughingstocks* he had enough in hand to make a fourth volume of verse. Then came the World War, and after it there were four more volumes. Exclusive of *The Dynasts* and *The Famous Tragedy of the Queen of Cornwall*, both of which are in dramatic form, these eight volumes provide a mass of poetry which makes it quite ridiculous to regard *The Dynasts* as a huge but isolated poetic monolith. It is surrounded by nearly a thousand lesser titles, which if taken individually may often seem to be of negligible importance, but which in a body represent a high achievement. The eight collections are as follows:

Title	Publication Date	Number of Poems
PRE-WAR		
Wessex Poems	1898	51
Poems of the Past and the Present	1902	99
Time's Laughingstocks	1909	94
Satires . . . Lyrics and Reveries	1914	106

POST-WAR

Moments of Vision	1917	160
Late Lyrics and Earlier	1922	151
Human Shows, etc.	1925	152
Winter Words (posthumously published)	1928	105
Total		918

Some account has already been given of the "Satires of Circumstance" and of the "Poems of 1912-13," which by their bitterness (in the case of one group) and their poignancy (in the case of the other) distinguish the *Satires, Lyrics and Reveries* of 1914 from all the other volumes. This same book contained a pleasing metrical tribute to Swinburne, "A Singer Asleep," and an autobiographical statement in which Hardy's words on "A Poet" clearly refer to himself. These lines, written a few months after his second marriage, begin:

> Attentive eyes, fantastic heed,
> Assessing minds, he does not need,
> Nor urgent writs to sup or dine,
> Nor pledges in the rosy wine.

"A Poet" also illustrates Hardy's attention to the technical aspects of poetry. The habits of revision acquired in his days of writing prose stayed with him. In "A Poet" he originally suggested for his own epitaph:

> "Whatever the message his to tell,
> Two thoughtful women loved him well."
> Stand and say that amid the dim:
> It will be praise enough for him.

Dissatisfied with the wording of these couplets he revised them so that they now read:

> "Whatever his message—glad or grim—
> Two bright-souled women clave to him;"
> Stand and say that while day decays;
> It will be word enough of praise.

The same autobiographical note is struck in the succeeding volume, *Moments of Vision*. There, in "For Life I Had Never Cared Greatly,"

Hardy wrote his companion piece to Browning's "Epilogue" to *Asolando*. He reveals that, although at the beginning of life he had not had "much zest for its dance," he, like Browning, was "One who never turned his back but marched breast forward," and that now, at the age of seventy-seven, he had

> no humor for letting
> My pilgrimage fail.

As he thinks of the approaching end of his "pilgrimage," he wonders what people will say of him after he is gone. In "Afterwards" he suggests an epitaph different from that of "A Poet." He now wonders whether, when

> the May month flaps its glad green leaves like wings,
> Delicate-filmed as new-spun silk, will the neighbours say,
> "He was a man who used to notice such things"?

No other book of his verse contains as much evidence as is found in *Moments of Vision* that he "noticed such things." His eye for nature is recorded in "To the Moon," "The Wind Blew Words," "A January Night," "The Wind's Prophecy," "During Wind and Rain," and "The Upper Birch-Leaves." Some of his best nature poems throb with his sympathy for birds. This single volume contains "The Blinded Bird," "The Robin," "The Caged Goldfinch," and "Her Love-Birds." While none of these equals "The Darkling Thrush," "The Oxen" strikes the same note of wistful hope and will rank with "The Darkling Thrush" among the poems that will keep Hardy's name alive. Originally published in the London *Times* on Christmas Eve, 1915, in one of the darkest periods of the World War, its last lines

> I should go with him in the gloom,
> Hoping it might be so,

leave an impression of that perfect fusion of affectionate regard for the past and courageous readiness to face the future which is one of Hardy's finest spiritual attributes. *Moments of Vision* also contains a penetrating poem "To Shakespeare," written for the tercentenary of the poet's death in April, 1916.

To Shakespeare

After Three hundred years.

Bright-baffling
~~Brasznosse~~ Soul, least capturable of themes,
Thou, who display'dst a life of commonplace,
Leaving no intimate word or personal trace
Of high design outside the artistry
Of thy penned dreams
Still shalt remain at heart unread eternally.

Through human orbits thy discourse to-day,
Despite thy formal pilgrimage, throbs on
In harmonies that ~~howl~~ Oblivion,
And, like the wind, with all-uncared effect
Maintain a sway
Not fore-desired, in tracks unchosen & unchecked.

And yet, at thy last breath, with mindless note
The borough clocks ~~in sameness~~ tongued the hour,
The Avon ~~~~ tower,
just as always glasses the
thy age

THE MANUSCRIPT OF HARDY'S POEM
TO SHAKESPEARE

Thy age was published on thy passing-bell
            But in due note
With other dwellers' deaths accorded a like knell.
        _____

    And at the strokes some townsman (met, maybe,
    And thereon queried by some squire's good dame
    Driving in shopward) may have given thy name,
    With, "Yes, a worthy man & well-to-do;
            Though, as for me,
I knew him but by just a neighbour's nod, 'tis true.

    "I' faith, few knew him much here, save by word,
    He having elsewhere led his busier life;
    Though to be sure he left with us his wife."
        —" Ah, one of the tradesmen's sons, I now recall....
            Witty, I've heard....
We did not know him ... Well, good-day. Death comes to all."
        _____

    So. like a strange bright bird we sometimes find
    To mingle with the barn-door brood awhile,
    Then vanish from their homely domicile —
    Into man's poesy, we wot not whence
            Flew thy strange mind.
Lodged there a radiant guest, & sped for ever thence.
February 14. 1916.
        _____

Hardy's interest in poets of the past was again evidenced in 1922 in *Late Lyrics and Earlier*. This time Keats was celebrated. "At a House in Hampstead" and "At Lulworth Cove a Century Back" are not only interesting memorials of 1820 but also good poems in themselves. "The Chapel-Organist" shows that Hardy still retained his story-telling ability, but the most significant part of *Late Lyrics* is the group of reminiscent poems which make up almost a third of the volume. Hardy was now an old man of eighty-two who found pleasure, as he says, in sitting and thinking "of things I have done." His reminiscences found their way into poem after poem, which thus have a biographical interest even when they are not of high poetic quality. Whether the large number (large by comparison with other volumes) of philosophical poems indicates an old man's return to the subject which interested him in his youth or whether these are recovered remnants of earlier poetic activity is not clear. Among the poems written in the nineteen-twenties are the "Epitaph on a Pessimist" and "The Absolute Explains." Hardy was preparing to issue his eighth book of verse when death overtook him. He had written: "So far as I am aware, I happen to be the only English poet who has brought out a new volume of his verse on his . . . birthday." But before his eighty-eighth anniversary his work was over. *Winter Words* appeared in November, 1928, adding nothing new in subject or style, unless both may be found in Hardy's Christmas epigram:

> "Peace upon earth!" was said. We sing it,
> And pay a million priests to bring it.
> After two thousand years of mass
> We've got as far as poison-gas.

The increasing recognition of Hardy as a poet was marked in October, 1916, by the publication of a small volume of *Selected Poems* in Macmillan's Golden Treasury Series. Hardy made the selection of the verses included in this volume, which was reprinted a number of times before his death. In his last year he prepared an abridged edition. By eliminating fifty of the titles in *Selected Poems* and making several substitutions, he prepared in September, 1927, his final selection, which was published in London as *Chosen Poems* in 1929. It represents Hardy's own idea as to which of his poems are most interesting rather than the world's estimate as to which are his best.

The first volume of Hardy's *Collected Poems* was issued in 1919, to which subsequently published verse was added in 1923 and in 1925. In 1930 the posthumous *Winter Words* was also included, and a much-needed index to the 918 titles was added. Ten years have since passed without any marked increase in general knowledge of or interest in Hardy's poetry. Whatever its merit may be, its reputation on this one hundredth anniversary of his birth is assuredly lower than that of his prose. This is partly due to the fact that there are many more novel readers than there are readers of poetry; but novels go out of style much more quickly than do poems. When Hardy's second centenary arrives, some of his poems may stand higher than the novels in general estimation. Time will weed out some of the chaff, and it will then be easier to read—

> Seeing only what is fair,
> Sipping only what is sweet.

A chronological arrangement of Hardy's poems is difficult. In every one of the eight volumes late verse is mixed with early. Sometimes the dates of composition are available, and at other times they can only be inferred from the places named. "Weymouth," subjoined to the poems "Her Father" and "The Contretemps," thus implies composition in 1869-70; and "Pentargan Bay," in 1913. Bath, Exeter, Kingston-Maurward, and Chard supply similar hints. However, even an approximation of a chronological arrangement will make it clear that throughout the sixty-five years during which Hardy wrote verse his viewpoint, his interests, his subject matter, and his methods remained surprisingly unchanged. He improved in technical ability, but the poet of twenty-three was father of the poet of eighty-eight.

The modern *Collected Poems* may therefore be examined with little thought of chronology. There are eight general categories into which Hardy's poems naturally fall. Two of these can be quickly dismissed. Hardy wrote a number of war poems, one series during the Boer

War and another during the World War. As patriotic expressions of
national feeling they are of interest, but as poetry they are quite unimportant. None of them come up to the quality of "Budmouth Dears"
and "My Love's gone a-fighting" in the third part of *The Dynasts*.
Closely allied to these war poems is a group of songs, not more than
5 per cent of Hardy's total output, in which he made an ineffective attempt to write a lyric to rank with Ben Jonson's "Drink to Me Only
with Thine Eyes." The most distinctive group of poems, those that
Hardy alone could have written, those that will never suggest Browning or Swinburne or Shelley or Keats to any reader, may be called
"philosophical," for want of a better designation. Here Hardy is
emotionally intellectual, rather than intellectually emotional. He is thinking and explaining rather than rejoicing or sorrowing. "Hap" is one
of the earliest in this class of poems and "The Absolute Explains" one
of the latest. They were written fifty-six years apart. The persistence
of this type throughout volume after volume has resulted in a mis-
conception as to its importance in the sum total of Hardy's poetic work.
Actually only about 7 per cent are philosophical. "Nature's Questioning," "God's Education," "God-Forgotten," and "By the Earth's
Corpse" are good representatives of this class.

Almost equal in number are the poems which Hardy wrote on special
occasions—on the anniversaries of poets, on the deaths of friends, on the
occasion of visits to historic spots, on crises and catastrophes, such as the
sinking of the "Titanic" in 1912. Many of these memorial poems are
more successful than such "occasional" verse usually is; and the
poems on Shakespeare, Keats, Gibbon, Meredith, and Swinburne deserve to be more widely known than they are.

One of the great surprises of Hardy's poetry is the relatively small
number of lines devoted to nature. Of his 918 poems, less than one hundred remind us that "he was a man who used to notice such things."
The comparatively small number is concealed by the fact that in this
category are found some of Hardy's very best poems. "The Darkling
Thrush," "The Oxen," "In a Wood," "Afterwards," and "The Blinded
Bird" are all of such unquestioned superiority that they lead to the false
inference that much of Hardy's metrical composition was inspired by

nature. But in fact, all five classifications already mentioned (songs, war, philosophy, memorials, and nature) taken together do not account for more than one-third of his poems. Two-thirds of his work falls into three categories: poems of love (or sorrow), personal poems (autobiographical reminiscences and records), and narratives of one kind or another.

Under the heading "Love Poems" must be grouped a wide variety of verses. Many are very far from being new songs on the old theme of "My love's like the red, red rose." Some are tender and sympathetic, but others are plaintive and poignant. Irony and even bitterness are not always absent. There is as much variety in form as in tone. Some are personal lyrics; some, dramatic dialogues; some, monologues in Browning's style; and some might with equal propriety be classed among the narratives. The best of the love poems were inspired by the first Mrs. Hardy. Most of them were written after her death. The most distinguished love poem not intimately connected with his own experience is "A Broken Appointment." Of the personal verses, mention has already been made of "A Poet" and "Afterwards," of "Let Me Enjoy" and "I sometimes think," of "Waiting Both" and "For Life I had never cared greatly." In this same class and of almost equal quality are "I look into my glass" and "The Impercipient," both in the first volume, *Wessex Poems.*

Fully a quarter of all the titles fall into the somewhat heterogeneous class designated as narrative. Some are in dramatic form; some are dialogues; but all tell a story. These narratives offer the widest variety. Some are flippant and frivolous, some are caustic and bitter; in some, plaintive and poignant experiences are recounted; in others, the ironies of life are emphasized. In all, however, there is something striking and unusual. Hardy was not interested in trying to set down drab, flat everyday experience. His own artistic principle he made perfectly clear:

A story must be exceptional enough to justify its telling. We tale-tellers are all Ancient Mariners, and none of us is warranted in stopping Wedding Guests (in other words, the hurrying public) unless he has something more unusual to relate than the ordinary experience of every average man and woman.

In the large list of narrative poems Hardy wrote with this dictum constantly in mind. "The Curate's Kindness" and "Panthera" are two strikingly different representatives of this class.

In all these poems on whatever subject one may expect to come upon words that belong to science or philosophy, to rhetoric or logic. These terms are usually clear enough in meaning, but they do not throb with the life of poetry. Just as in *The Dynasts* one reads that Marshal Ney's ignominious death was "But technically deserved," so in the poems one may come upon a "culminating sight" or may read of something that is "warranted up to date." In one poem day dawns with such a chill "As to render further cheerfulness intolerable now." It ought not, however, to be supposed that Hardy never achieved a lovely line. In landscape painting he could write: "The yachts ride mute at anchor, and the fulling moon is fair." In portrait painting he could sketch a girl

> With cheeks whose airy flush outbid
> Fresh fruit in bloom.

In the poetry of action he could picture "a ghost-girl-rider" who still rides gaily, "Draws rein and sings to the swing of the tide." In a philosophizing mood he could remark that "The vows of man and maid are frail as filmy gossamere."

No English poet ever spent more time than Hardy did in the study of verse forms. His approach to metrics was through music. In a note written in 1909 to a friend Hardy said: "To be honest, I am never tired of music." When he wrote up an account of himself for the 1916 edition of *Who's Who*, he mentioned as his recreations cycling (at the age of 76) and "old church and dance music." Ever since his early joy in going with his father to play at country dances, tunes ran through his head. Rhythms stayed by him, even without words or music. Many of his original stanzaic inventions were first worked out, with an architect's clarity and precision, in skeleton forms showing stressed and unstressed syllables, rhymes and pauses, with no words at all. This sort of devotion to metrical technique strikes some readers as evidence of lack of qualification for writing poetry. Yet for most poets the shape of a poem is not an extraneous attribute but part of the poem itself. The testimony of a poet is available on this point. Edna St. Vincent Millay, whose poetry Hardy admired more than that of any modern American poet, declares:

When the image of the poem rises before the suddenly quieted and intensely agitated person who is to write it, its shadowy bulk is already dimly outlined; it is rhymed or unrhymed; it is trimeter, tetrameter, or pentameter; it is free verse, a sonnet, an epic, an ode, a five-act play. To many poets, the physical character of their poem, its rhythm, its rhyme, its music, the way it looks on the page, is quite as important as the thing they wish to say; to some it is vastly more important.

To Hardy the music was as important as the thought. His final product indicates certain definite rhythmical preferences. He almost never wrote trochaics; and when he did, as in "News for Her Mother," it was with experimental designs.

> One mile more is
> Where your door is . . .
> Old brown gable,
> Granary, stable.

Dactyls are almost equally rare. Among his best known poems, the only one to use this rhythm is "In a Wood," in dactylic dimeter lines. The occasional awkwardness shown in this poem, dating back to 1887, had been entirely overcome by the time he wrote another, "The Voice," where the dactyls are used with consummate appropriateness and skill: "Woman much missed, how you call to me, call to me!" Much more commonly do anapestic rhythms occur. The influence of Browning and Swinburne may be felt here, particularly in the long lines of "Afterwards" and "The Chapel Organist." The use of the anapest in this last-named poem and its appearance in "The Bride-Night Fire," "The Curate's Kindness," and "The Lost Pyx" suggest that Hardy felt this rhythm particularly suited to animated narrative, and the influence of "The Statue and the Bust" seems clear. Most of Hardy's work, however, was done with slow iambics. The poems on Shakespeare, Keats, Gibbon, Swinburne, and Meredith, together with the lines "At the Pyramid of Cestius near the Graves of Shelley and Keats," are all in iambic lines. All the poems recently mentioned as illustrating the philosophical group are in iambic meters. Of the chief nature poems, all except "In a Wood" are in iambics. Of approximately forty poems chosen in the course of this book as representing Hardy's best, thirty-one are in iambic rhythm.

Yet there is no rhythmical monotony about Hardy's lines. Analysis of his stanzaic forms reveals an abundant power of invention. Couplets, triplets, quatrains are all represented. Five-line stanzas, numerous six-line forms, eight-line schemes, Spenserians: he used them all. They do not all appear, however, with equal success. The more obvious the effort for originality, the more likely the poem is to seem a failure. The numerous ineffective rhythmical experiments point to the same conclusion as that indicated by his songs: Hardy was not instinctively lyrical. Like Robert Burns, he did his best singing when he used some one else's metrical form. Hardy's best teacher was the Church. The hymns and Sunday-school songs which he knew so well provided the rhythms for most of his best poems. The old ballad meters of the doxologies—the Long Meter, the Short Meter, and the Common Meter—are those which he handled most skillfully. "A Sunday Morning Tragedy," "A Poet," "Let Me Enjoy" can all be sung to Long Meter refrains. "I look into My Glass" is the familiar Short Meter of "A Charge to Keep I Have." And the Common Meter ballad stanza is found, in its pure state or with slight modifications, in "The Darkling Thrush," "The Oxen," "God's Education," "Epitaph on a Pessimist," "The Impercipient," and many other poems.

When he was a young man Hardy had wished to become a clergyman. But though he did not enter the Church, the Church entered him. Its forms and phrases, its melodies and rhythms, were stamped upon his memory in early life; and throughout his poetic career the echoes resounded clearly. At a time when he had very little money for books or for anything else, Hardy bought a copy of *Psalms and Hymns*, 1858, and in it wrote his name and the date "1860." This book, still extant in a private collection in America, he kept in use for sixty-eight years. Sidney Lanier once wrote that "Music is love in search of a word." For Hardy poetry was often a tune in search of words. His own definition read: "Poetry is emotion put into measure. The emotion must come by nature, but the measure can be acquired by art." When the measure fitted his own mood and the words fitted both mood and measure, great poetry was the result.

XX

"AFTERWARDS"

D URING HARDY'S LONG INDIAN SUMMER he was able to produce four volumes of verse. This achievement after he had reached the age of seventy-five is to be attributed largely to the happiness he found in his second marriage.

Florence Emily Dugdale was one of the five daughters of Edward Dugdale, headmaster of a church school at Enfield, just north of London. Her mother was Emma Taylor. Born on January 12, 1879, Miss Dugdale grew up in an educational atmosphere, but ill health prevented her from following her father's profession. She therefore turned to writing and earned a modest reputation as the author of children's books. Many an English child learned to associate the name of Florence Dugdale with stories such as *Cousin Christine* (in William Collins' Sons & Co.'s "Silver Lion Library"), *In Lucy's Garden* (Oxford University Press), and the *Adventures of Mr. Prickleback* (Oxford University Press). Before her marriage she also published *Old Time Tales, Tim's Sister,* and the illustrated *Book of Baby Birds* and *Book of Baby Beasts.*

One day Miss Dugdale came across *Half Hours with Living Writers.* In this book there was a selection from *A Pair of Blue Eyes*—the sensational chapter in which Knight falls over the cliff and is saved by Elfride. That was Miss Dugdale's introduction to the name Thomas Hardy. She proceeded to read all the Wessex novels, and she was equally delighted with the short stories, of which "On the Western Circuit" was her favorite.

Miss Dugdale was more interested in the Wessex stories than an ordinary reader would be, for she learned from her father that the

Dugdales were an old Dorset family and that they and the Hardys were distantly related. In Hardy's minor story "Alicia's Diary" (1887) he wrote of "old feeble Mr. Dugdale." When Florence Dugdale was in her early twenties, she was introduced to Hardy by their common friend Mrs. Arthur Henniker, who presented her as a distant relative of the novelist. Hardy, however, preferred not to talk about family matters and instead asked her if she had ever read Crabbe. Miss Dugdale soon made the acquaintance of Mrs. Hardy and learned that she, too, was a writer. When the younger woman encouraged Mrs. Hardy to think that it might be possible to publish her work, invitations to Max Gate followed. The difference of thirty-nine years in their ages did not prevent the two women from becoming attached to each other. As the guest of Mrs. Hardy, Miss Dugdale used to visit the novelist's home, sometimes staying for weeks at a time. During such visits she found opportunity to assist her hostess in many ways. She proved helpful to the novelist, too, and when trouble with his eyes made it impossible for him to write letters, she typed them at his dictation. Upon her return from Max Gate to London, Miss Dugdale continued to be helpful by looking up references in the British Museum reading room. Some of the material supplied by her found its way into Part III of *The Dynasts*. After a time Hardy began to refer to Miss Dugdale as his "assistant," and she has often been spoken of as his secretary. Actually she was never a paid employee of Hardy. Her research for *The Dynasts* was entirely voluntary, but her pleasure in helping the author was so real and so unconcealed that she suspected Hardy of sometimes inventing little jobs for her, just to give her happiness.

Miss Dugdale rendered fairly continuous assistance for more than a decade, before Mrs. Hardy died, in November, 1912. Hardy had got into the habit of turning to her for help, and her quiet efficiency encouraged this increasing dependence upon her. At the time of Mrs. Hardy's death Hardy was alone in the house, except for his servants. Never having accustomed himself to the administration of household affairs, he was more than commonly distracted. Not knowing what to do, he telegraphed for Florence Dugdale. She came at once to

Max Gate, quietly made all the arrangements for the funeral, and then slipped quietly away again.

After the funeral Hardy was left alone in Max Gate, with no one to protect him from the ever-increasing crowd of celebrity seekers who forced their way in to his front door. Hardy later told his friend Newman Flower, "There was no end to these people." He recalled that one day, years before, a visiting card was brought in by the servant and that on it he read "Herbert Spencer." " 'Well,' I thought, 'it's odd that he should be in this neighborhood.' But I had him shown into the drawing-room." When Hardy went into the room, he found that the caller was not Herbert Spencer at all. When these strange people failed to obtain a glimpse of the author, they walked about his grounds, they tore branches from his bushes, they even rooted up his flowers and carried them away as souvenirs. His lonely life at Max Gate became a plague to him. Work under such conditions was an impossibility. Once again he turned to Florence Dugdale for help. On Christmas Day she was at Max Gate, writing letters at Hardy's dictation. One letter went to Swinburne's friend, Watts-Dunton, saying that Hardy had had to give up both reading and writing.

He felt that he must get away from the lonely house, and in January, 1913, he fled. On the thirtieth he was at Margate looking out upon the fogs of the North Sea. In March he made a sentimental journey to Cornwall, where he went over all the ground connected with his romance of 1870. He then went into Suffolk for a visit of a week or so with Mrs. Arthur Henniker, with whom he had collaborated in 1896 in writing "The Spectre of the Real" (the only case of his collaboration). At Mrs. Henniker's he was joined by Miss Dugdale. There, under the eyes of his former collaborator and of his "assistant," he recovered some peace of mind and responded to a sympathetic interest in his own literary work—a sympathy which for some years he had not enjoyed in his own home. "The scales fell from his eyes."

Miss Dugdale's happiness in being of service to Hardy, her sincere belief in his genius, and his own unconcealed delight in finding some one who really cared about his work and who had so efficiently demonstrated her ability to put his affairs in order, brought the two closer than ever together. On February 10, 1914, in the presence of his brother Henry and her sister Margaret, they were married at Enfield. She was 35 and he nearly 74, but the common bond of their interest in literature was strong enough to go far in surmounting the barrier of a great disparity in age. In one of his personal poems[1] he recalled that

> one did care,
> And, spiriting into my house, to, fro,
> Like wind on the stair,
> Cares still, heeds all, and will, even though
> I may despair.

"Heeds all" was a correct description. Nothing escaped Mrs. Hardy's solicitous observation, for she had an eye for everything. She noticed Hardy's indifference to food and his not knowing what kind of wine he was drinking. When a friend sent him a case of fine champagne, Mrs. Hardy jestingly asked: "How do you like this brand of cider?" Hardy replied: "It's very nice, but rather drier than we usually have."

None of the great figures of literature ever had a finer and truer helpmate than Hardy enjoyed from 1914 on. His wife gave him that understanding which made of his second marriage a great companionship. She kept the marauders from the front door. "Florence is my chucker-out," Hardy once remarked to St. John Ervine. His home, with its secluded garden, became a place where there were feet

> That were light on the green as a thistledown ball,
> And those mute ministrations to one and to all
> Beyond a man's saying sweet.[2]

In 1917 he inscribed a volume of his verse "To the First of Women, Florence Hardy." The world can thank the second Mrs. Hardy and her tender care of the poet for much that he accomplished in the years following the World War which broke out six months after his marriage.

On a man of Hardy's tender and sensitive spirit the war was certain to inflict more than ordinary pain. His distress was somewhat allevi-

---

[1] "I Sometimes Think."
[2] "After the Visit."

ated by his pleasure in the war-time performances of scenes from *The Dynasts.* A presentation at Dorchester in 1908 has already been mentioned in the letter from Meredith; but a more ambitious setting was given the epic drama in London in November, 1914, and the scenes that deal with the Wessex natives were produced with great effectiveness in Dorchester and in Weymouth in June, 1916. In February, 1920, the Oxford University Dramatic Society produced the play in Oxford. This revival of Hardy's early interest in the drama bore fruit in other ways. For a Christmas performance in 1920 he drew on his memory of the old play which he had used in *The Return of the Native,* the play of "St. George and the Dragon," in which Eustacia Vye played a part disguised as a man. Some of the lines of that traditional holiday piece are given in the novel. Hardy now filled in the gaps and thus preserved for posterity this amusing relic of the past. After the play was acted, Mrs. Hardy had twenty-five copies of the text printed at the Cambridge University Press, early in 1921.

Two years later Hardy again turned to the drama. In April, 1923, he was at work upon *The Famous Tragedy of the Queen of Cornwall,* and in November of the same year the book was published, with some neatly executed drawings by the eighty-three-year-old poet. His delight in this old story of Tristram and Iseult (as Hardy spelled her name) was, of course, increased by its association with Tintagel in the "Lyonnesse" of his own romantic youth. The play itself is not remarkable as drama or as poetry.

For a long time after the unsatisfactory outcome of Hardy's dramatization of *Far from the Madding Crowd* in 1881 he had very little to do with the theater. In the *Pall Mall Gazette* for August 31, 1892, he explained "Why I Don't Write Plays." Then Barrie suggested that he dramatize "The Three Strangers," and the one-act play "The Three Wayfarers" was the result. It was performed at Terry's Theatre, London, in June, 1893 (and by the Dorchester Dramatic Society[3] in November, 1911). This minor effort somewhat softened Hardy's feeling about the theater, and the phenomenal success of his novel *Tess of the D'Urbervilles* led to another change of mind and attitude. For re-

[3] For a list of the Society's Hardy plays see Appendix 12, p. 277.

quests came from actresses in many countries of Europe to be allowed to act the part of Tess; and this resulted in his making one more attempt to dramatize his fiction. In the midst of his many activities in prose and verse, in that crowded year 1895, he prepared a stage version of his novel. On July 19 Arthur Waugh reported:

Thomas Hardy is busily engaged upon the dramatization of *Tess*. It seems that the task is giving him a deal of trouble, and that Mrs. Patrick Campbell is consulted at every turn in the action. The matter arouses a good deal of interest in literary circles, and there are many surmises as to the course the play is likely to follow. It is clear that, for stage purposes, the development must be considerably rearranged . . . Mrs. Campbell is immensely interested in it.

The possibilities of *Tess of the D'Urbervilles* on the stage were studied in America as well as in London. In 1896 Hardy wrote out a rough draft and some suggestions to send to New York, where plans developed rapidly enough for an opening to be scheduled for March, 1897. Hardy's friends at home urged him to hold at least a "copyright performance" in London on the same day as the American opening. He wrote to Henry Arthur Jones, asking: "Can you tell me how one sets about this sort of thing? . . . Fancy me getting up a play!" He proceeded, however, to discuss terms with a theater, and learned that writing a play, even with all its difficulties, was easier than attending to the business aspects of a theatrical undertaking. On March 15, 1897, he wrote again to Jones, saying, "I am in a hopeless fog on the matter." But once again the divinity that shapes our ends seemed determined to frustrate Hardy's theatrical plans. Just as Pinero's *Squire* had in 1882 popped in between Hardy's writing and his hopes, so in 1897 other more rapid workers had anticipated him with regard to *Tess*. On March 2 a *Tess* by H. A. Kennedy was produced for purposes of copyright at the St. James Theatre (the same one used by Pinero fifteen years earlier). And in America Lorimer Stoddard, a young playwright, wrote an adaptation of the novel which was pronounced "a remarkable achievement." In this play Mrs. Minnie Maddern Fiske began, in the first week of March, 1897, a two-month run at the Fifth Avenue Theatre, New York. Hardy's work had been again rendered useless. Ten years later he wrote stoically of the "unauthorized adaptations of *Tess* done by several people."

His own play had not been produced, and his manuscript had joined other discarded ones in his study at Max Gate. There it had been lying for twenty-seven years, when, in 1924, the amateur players of the Dorchester Dramatic Society proposed a performance of *Tess*. Hardy remembered his own earlier dramatic effort and unearthed his manuscript. Ideas about the theater had in the meantime so changed that his play now seemed hardly suited to the stage. Ibsen's plays were no longer called obscene. But at the age of eighty-four Hardy found himself unable to "get back to the subject close enough to handle it anew." He accordingly submitted his pages without revision to the Dorchester amateurs and contented himself with making suggestions and attending rehearsals. On November 2, 1924, he went to Wool with three of the actors in order to rehearse *Tess* on the spot of the sleepwalking. When the time for the final performance arrived, to the surprise of all, the play proved such a success that it was shortly carried up to London. In September, 1925, Henry Arthur Jones went to see it at the Barnes Theatre, and, remembering his earlier correspondence about the same play, he wrote to Hardy to express his pleasure in the performance. Hardy at the time felt unequal to the exertion of going to London to see his play; but, as a sincere tribute to the author, the play was brought to him. The whole company made a trip to Dorchester, and on December 6, 1925, gave a unique performance in the drawing room at Max Gate. The play was again produced in London in the summer of 1929. Though never so moving as the novel, it offered much reason for thinking that if Hardy's early years had kept him in contact with the theater he might have had as successful a career in writing plays as he enjoyed in writing novels.

It so happened that at the time when the Dorchester amateurs were rehearsing for their 1924 performance of *Tess*, Sir James Barrie was visiting Hardy. At Max Gate Hardy showed his guest a letter from a London firm which had presented the Wessex author with a fine new radio set. The letter stated that the donors were delighted to learn from the author that the radio was giving pleasure at Max Gate, but that they were rather damped to learn from another source that it was not Hardy who listened to the broadcasts but his dog "Wessex"! This was a wire-haired terrier that Hardy had acquired about six months before his second marriage. On that afternoon "Wessex" accompanied Hardy and Barrie to the rehearsal of *Tess*, and all went well until the time came when the "Children's Hour" was due to be broadcast on the radio. Then "Wessex" began to howl. Hardy explained that it was the dog's favorite program, and not even his own drama of *Tess* would induce him to disappoint the terrier. So Barrie and Hardy returned to Max Gate; and while *Tess* went on to its tragic last act, "Wessex" listened to the radio. Barrie later discovered that the dog also enjoyed the early morning weather reports and that Hardy would go downstairs in the cold and turn on the program for him. "Wessex" died two years later (December, 1926) and was memorialized in one of the poems in *Winter Words*.

These last years were serene and happy ones for Hardy. Frail and slight, but with alert bright eyes, he continued to write poems. When it was rumored that Mrs. Hardy also wrote poetry, she admitted the fact, but stated that she had no thought of publication. She was, she explained, satisfied to assist her husband and was "content with his reflected glory. The wife of a genius, unless a genius herself, makes herself appear foolish," by offering her compositions to the public. She took eager delight in Hardy's growing fame. Honors came pleasantly his way. The University of Aberdeen had made him a Doctor of Laws in April, 1905; and after the Order of Merit was received in 1910, Cambridge conferred the degree of Doctor of Letters upon him in 1913. On June 10 of that year Hardy went to Cambridge to receive the degree and startled A. C. Benson by appearing by mistake in an LL.D. gown. Five months later he was again in Cambridge, having been elected an Honorary Fellow of Magdalene College. The ceremony of installation took place on November 2, when Benson was again upset by Hardy's unfamiliarity with academic robes. Benson found the author waiting in the Magdalene library, "in a surplice, with a gown (scarlet) *over* it." He decided to make no comment and accompanied Hardy in the procession to the college chapel, where all the men "stared at the little figure, all ablaze." The Archdeacon of Zanzibar was there, and after some music which Benson called "horrible," the Archdeacon preached a sermon on God being a God of desire, not a mild or impersonal force. Hardy made no comment.

In February, 1920, Oxford decided to forget all about *Jude the Obscure* and voted Hardy a D.Litt. degree, which he went to receive on the tenth of that month. Three years later he again visited Oxford, this time having been elected an honorary fellow of Queen's College. He spent two nights at the college in June, 1923. St. Andrews University in Scotland voted Hardy an LL.D. in May, 1922. This degree was conferred upon him *in absentia.*

More than these public honors Hardy valued his private friendships. His old friend Gosse, now Sir Edmund, delighted his heart one day by writing: "Dearest and most admired of friends: Thank you for the unbroken record of nearly forty-five years of precious intercourse. May we both live to celebrate our jubilee of Friendship." They almost reached that goal. In June, 1927, Gosse visited Hardy at Max Gate, and afterward wrote to a common friend:

He is a wonder, if you like! At 87½ without a deficiency of sight, hearing, mind, or conversation. Very tiny and fragile, but full of spirit and a gaiety not quite consistent in the most pessimistic of poets. He and I collogued merrily of past generations, like two antediluvian animals sporting in the primeval slime.

Gosse survived Hardy by only four months. Mrs. Hardy lived nine years longer. In this period she published a two-volume biography of her husband, *The Early Life of Thomas Hardy* (1928) and *The Later Years of Thomas Hardy* (1930). Later she made arrangements for a Hardy Memorial Room in the Dorset County Museum in Dorchester, but she did not live to see them carried out. The Memorial Room was opened by the poet laureate, John Masefield, on May 10, 1939, but Mrs. Hardy had died at Max Gate on October 17, 1937, at the age of fifty-eight.

With Hardy's growing fame and honors came wealth. From the financial loss of *Desperate Remedies* and the meagerness of the thirty pounds received for *Under the Greenwood Tree* Hardy's fortune improved steadily, until the success of *Tess* placed him in easy circumstances. Before 1891 he asked fifty pounds for a short story; after that date his price was doubled. By the end of the century he was receiving twenty pounds for a single poem. He always retained his simple habits, and not until he became too weak to cycle did he acquire an automobile. He left a fortune of about $450,000.

Thomas Hardy died on January 11, 1928, in the house he had built forty-five years earlier. The trees he had planted around it had grown until they looked almost like a forest. "On the day of Hardy's death," wrote John Macy, "the world knew, that is, everybody but the Nobel Prize Committee knew, that the greatest man of letters in the world had gone and that there was no one quite clearly second to step into his place."

His heart was buried in the grave of his first wife in the Stinsford churchyard, for it was generally felt that, since he was a man whose affections throughout a long life had never left Wessex, his heart should not be carried out of his native region after life had left him. His fame, however, was by this time too great to make it possible to deposit his remains elsewhere than among England's greatest. His ashes were accordingly placed in Poets' Corner, Westminster Abbey, next to those of Charles Dickens. Among the pallbearers were Barrie, Galsworthy, Gosse, A. E. Housman, Kipling, and Shaw.

The Abbey was crowded. From ten o'clock in the morning, long before the doors were opened to admit them, thousands of Hardy's admirers collected in a long queue that stretched from the Abbey past St. Margaret's Church and on toward the Gothic tower of the Houses of Parliament. The cold January rain did not deter them, for they were there without the levity or idle curiosity of ordinary sightseers. While waiting for the hour of the funeral (2 P.M.), they talked of Hardy's works, which were evidently known in every country. English was far from being the only language used in those conversations. Frenchmen and Germans, Dutchmen and Swedes, Italians and Poles mingled in the crowd. Turbaned Hindus stood with solemn patience, and the American accent showed that Hardy was read in Boston, Alabama, and Kansas. The whole assembly belonged to that undistinguished mass of average humanity in which Hardy had taken delight, from which he had himself sprung, and about which he had written. His burial was attended by a concourse of grateful readers. So numerous were they that not all could get into the Abbey when the doors were opened.

There were expressed almost as many reasons for gratitude as there were individual readers in the crowd. One man was grateful for the characters of Tess and Jude. Another rated the famous description of Egdon Heath as the most glorious passage of English prose produced by the nineteenth century and quoted Robert Louis Stevenson's "I would give my hand to write like Hardy." A third preferred the poetry because in it Hardy had given the most specifically personal account of himself. There were those who pleaded the warm humanity of the author, and two of his lines were quoted:

> Whatever his message—glad or grim—
> Two bright-souled women clave to him.

More than one mourner recalled that Hardy "was a man who used to notice such things" as birds on a wintry day, sheep in storms, horses laboring up Ludgate Hill, and the agony of poor animals shot by hunters.

In the crowd on the wet sidewalk there were a few who commented on the irony of Hardy's burial in a Christian church after all that he had written about the blind cosmic force "It," but those that knew him best knew that he had always preserved a truly religious, though unorthodox, spirit. In the *American Student Hymnal*, used in many a college chapel, there is a prayer entitled "The Spirit of Reality":

Thou Source of all good life, enrich and purify our lives and deepen in us our discipleship . . . Make us humble, brave, and loving . . . Lord of sincerity and truth, before whom all that is hollow and unreal shrivels up and is consumed away, give us the spirit of reality; . . . cleanse us from prejudice and partisanship, and purge out from our inmost souls whatever loveth and maketh a lie.

To every word of that prayer Thomas Hardy could have said Amen. His life was one long devotion to the spirit of reality and truth, one long fight against all that is hollow and unreal. No one fully acquainted with his life could find adequate reason for objecting to his burial in Westminster Abbey.

In the brief exchange of quiet conversation among the thousands who were waiting to get into the Abbey on that Monday morning (January 16, 1928), there was little opportunity to express a subtler feeling about Hardy. Though less easy to put into words, it was nonetheless present in the thoughts of some who gathered on that occasion. Somehow or other Thomas Hardy had come to symbolize for them that intense personal human loyalty which was one of the few good results of the World War. In the darkness and gloom of those days, the flame of human loyalty shone the more brightly. Against the challenge of despair first brought by nineteenth-century science and repeated by the chaos of the war, Hardy had steadfastly vindicated the soul of man. He had spoken for all Englishmen when he had placed in Wellington's mouth these words in *The Dynasts*:

> Despite their fierce advantage here, I swear
> By every God that war can call upon
> To hold our present place at any cost.

England had learned to take courage from a man determined

> to hold out unto the last,
> As long as one man stands on one lame leg
> With one ball in his pouch!—then end as I.

St. John Ervine expressed what many would have liked to say to Hardy: "We have learned from you that the proud heart can subdue the hardest fate. In all that you have written you have shown the spirit of man persisting through defeat." For Man was Hardy's great theme. Nature to him was never the all-in-all that it was to William Wordsworth. From the trees Hardy turned back to his kind where he found "life-loyalties." In his novels he had lavished his affection upon men and women of courage, resourcefulness, patience, endurance, tolerance, sympathy, unselfishness, and love. The universe that produced pain and injustice likewise produced all these good things; and in the darkest hour of his life Hardy never forgot these good things. The war generation of 1914-18 which had, like our own, been brought face to face with stern and unlovely reality, found in his so-called pessimism solace and comfort found nowhere else, except in one other poet not unlike him. Hardy agreed perfectly with A. E. Housman that:

> If the smack is sour
> The better for the embittered hour.

Hardy had always declared himself ready to give "a full look at the Worst." No matter how bad it all seemed, he was still ready to exclaim: "Let me enjoy the earth no less!" It is not unnatural, therefore, that among his readers there have been some to insist that at bottom he was an optimist. He found himself like Lear an unwilling prisoner; but he could still say with that fiery ancient monarch:

> Come, let's away to prison:
> We two alone will sing like birds i' the cage:
> And so we'll live, and tell old tales, and laugh
> At gilded butterflies, and hear poor rogues
> Talk of court news; . . . and we'll wear out
> In a wall'd prison, packs and sects of great ones,
> That ebb and flow by the moon.

Obviously "pessimist" is not the right term for Hardy. Melancholy he was, thoughtful, frequently depressed; but courageous ever, with a heart that bled easily because of the pity and tenderness with which it overflowed. Henry W. Nevinson spoke the judgment of many when he declared: "No Englishman since Wordsworth has heard the still sad music of humanity with so fine an ear, and none has regarded the men and women of our country with a compassion so profound and yet so stern, as they pass with tears and laughter between the graves and the stars."

Hardy's soul never quite found its way into the harbor of serenity. He saw so much pain and anguish in the world about him that he was continually pressed with the desire to know why they are there. He tried his best to solve the riddle and failed. Millions of men have made the same attempt and failed likewise, but Hardy found it impossible to accept either FitzGerald's bland resignation or Browning's illogical faith. So he went on brooding over the problem and was often profoundly unhappy because he could not find the answer. But there was nothing of *Job's* curse-God-and-die about Hardy's message, and his life was a concrete illustration of what he believed in. A character such as this raises the morale of all who come into contact with it, and all modern England has drawn virtue from Thomas Hardy. As his ashes were lowered into their resting place in Poets' Corner, a spadeful of Dorset earth was sprinkled on the casket. The soil had been sent to London by a simple Dorset farm laborer who did not wish the poet's remains to lie in alien ground. Kipling, one of the pallbearers, had many years before called Hardy "Lord of the Wessex Coast"; but the mourners in the Abbey knew that his realm had become much more extensive than that. Hardy is one of the great spiritual leaders of the modern world.

> Yes, there at last, eyes opened, did I see
> His whole sincere symmetric history;
> There were his truth, his simple singlemindedness,
> Strained, maybe, by time's storms, but there no less.

"His Heart," from *Moments of Vision*

APPENDICES

I. GENEALOGICAL CHART

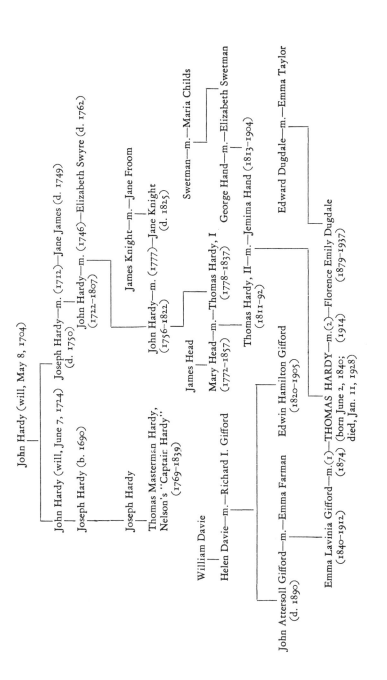

John Hardy (will, May 8, 1704)

John Hardy (will, June 7, 1724) Joseph Hardy—m. (1712)—Jane James (d. 1749)
(d. 1750)

Joseph Hardy (b. 1690) John Hardy—m. (1746)—Elizabeth Swyre (d. 1762)
(1722–1807)

Joseph Hardy

James Knight—m.—Jane Froom

Thomas Masterman Hardy,
Nelson's "Captain Hardy,"
(1769–1839)

John Hardy—m. (1777)—Jane Knight
(1756–1822) (d. 1825)

Swetman—m.—Maria Childs

William Davie

Helen Davie—m.—Richard I. Gifford

James Head

Mary Head—m.—Thomas Hardy, I
(1772–1857) (1778–1837)

George Hand—m.—Elizabeth Swetman

John Attersoll Gifford
(d. 1890)

Edwin Hamilton Gifford
(1820–1905)

Thomas Hardy, II—m.—Jemima Hand (1813–1904)
(1811–92)

Edward Dugdale—m.—Emma Taylor

Emma Lavinia Gifford—m.(1)—THOMAS HARDY—m.(2)—Florence Emily Dugdale
(1840–1912) (1874) (born June 2, 1840; (1914) (1879–1937)
died, Jan. 11, 1928)

2. HARDY'S ESSAYS AND ARTICLES

"HOW I BUILT MYSELF A HOUSE"

In spite of Hardy's veto of the proposal mentioned on page 24, the sketch has been reprinted four times—twice in England and twice in America: in the *Review of Reviews*, London, May 15, 1922, pp. 497-501; in *Chambers's Journal*, London, January 1, 1925, pp. 2-5; in *Life and Art by Thomas Hardy*, New York, 1925, pp. 9-19; and in the *Book League Monthly*, New York, December, 1928, pp. 162-67.

Among Hardy's later prose writings those of particular interest in the list here given are the three titles which deal with his own craft—fiction. His other interests are obvious enough.

1883	"The Dorsetshire Labourer"
1886	"The Rev. William Barnes" (obituary)
1888	"The Profitable Reading of Fiction"
1890	"Some Romano-British Relics Found at Max Gate"
——	"Candour in English Fiction" (cf. p. 118)
1891	"The Science of Fiction"
1892	"Why I Don't Write Plays"
1893	"Ancient Earthworks at Casterbridge"
1902	"Portrait of 'Leader Scott'"
1904	"Laurence Hope" (obituary)
1906	"Memories of Church Restoration"
——	"A Glimpse of John Stuart Mill"
——	"Memories of Henry J. Moule"
——	"Memories of Leslie Stephen"
1908	Preface to *Select Poems of William Barnes*
1920	"William Barnes," in Ward's *English Poets*
1927	"The Preservation of Ancient Cottages"
——	"G.M. [George Meredith]: a Reminiscence"

3. HARDY'S CATALOGUE OF PAINTERS (cf. p. 27)

Giotto (1276-1337)	Raphael (1483-1520)
Angelico (1387-1455)	Sebastiano (1485-1547)
Gozzoli (1420-97)	Del Sarto (1486-1531)
Crivelli (1430-93)	Correggio (1494-1534)
Perugino (1446-1523)	Guido Reni (1575-1642)
Holbein (1460-1524)	Rubens (1577-1640)
Dürer (1471-1528)	Van Alsloot (15??-1626)

Sallaert (1590-1648)
Poussin (1594-1665)
Velasquez (1599-1660)
Rembrandt (1607-69)
Douw (1613-75)
Terburg (1617-81)
Lely (1618-80)
Murillo (1618-87)
Ruysdael (1628-82)
Hobbema (1638-1709)

Kneller (1648-1723)
Greuze (1725-1805)
Romney (1734-1802)
Nollekens (1737-1823)
Flaxman (1755-1826)
Turner (1775-1851)
Wiertz (1806-65)
Danby (1816-75)
Van Beers (1845-?)

4. NOTES ON THE POEMS

POEMS OF 1866 (cf. p. 28)

Published in *Wessex Poems*, 1898

Hap
In Vision I Roamed
At a Bridal
Postponement
A Confession to a Friend in Trouble

Her Dilemma
Revulsion
She to Him (four sonnets)
The Bride-Night Fire
The Two Men

Published in *Poems of Past and Present*, 1902
The Ruined Maid
Published in *Time's Laughingstocks*, 1909
Her Definition
From Her in the Country
A Young Man's Epigram
Published in *Late Lyrics and Earlier*, 1922
Dream of the City Shopwoman

To this list of poems composed while Hardy was under the influence of Swinburne, it may be well to add "A Singer Asleep," a poem written about Swinburne shortly after his death in 1909, in which Hardy recalls

> "that far morning of a summer day
> When, down a terraced street whose pavements lay
> Glassing the sunshine into my bent eyes,
> I walked and read with a quick glad surprise
> New words, in classic guise."

In 1910 Hardy could declare:

> "I still can hear the brabble and the roar
> At those thy tunes, O still one!"

And in August, 1924, he remembered the "official" attitude toward Swinburne, and in "A Refusal" he placed in the mouth of "the grave Dean of Westminster," who was having a hard time keeping infidels out of the Poets' Corner, the exclamation:

> " 'Twill next be expected
> That . . . —what makes my skin burn,
> Yea, forehead to chin burn—
> That I ensconce Swinburne!"

The poems listed above contain seven sonnets. Of these one is Italian, one a Shelleyan experimental mixture, the others Shakespearean. One poem is in elegiac stanzas, one is written in a modification of the Burns stanza, two are in couplets reminiscent of Scott's poems (which Hardy preferred to his novels); and two ballads, one of them in Barnes-like dialect, are written in the anapestic couplet meter of Browning's "How They Brought the Good News from Ghent to Aix." These details clearly indicate Hardy's interest in the technical aspects of verse, and by the end of 1866 Hardy had acquired no little skill in the handling of verse forms. His chief defect lay in his inability to find any poetic subject that would fire his emotions as, for example, the Wye Valley fired Wordsworth's.

POEMS OF 1867 (cf. p. 34)
Published in *Wessex Poems*, 1898
  Neutral Tones
  Heiress and Architect
Published in *Poems of Past and Present*, 1902
  Her Reproach
Published in *Time's Laughingstocks*, 1909
  1967
  Her Confession
  To an Impersonator of Rosalind
  To an Actress
Published in *Late Lyrics and Earlier*, 1922
  A Young Man's Exhortation
Published in *Human Shows*, 1925
  Discouragement

Few though these poems are, they contain *in parvo* everything that Hardy was to publish in the next sixty years. A few are narratives dealing with Dorset characters. Most of the poems are lyrics, "rather of a melancholy turn of mind." We read of "beauty marred," "mournful word," "bitter knowledge," "mockery," "frost," "chill," and "visions ghast and grim."

Winter Words lies sixty years in the future but the poems of 1866-67 are in complete harmony with it. Two subjects recur somewhat frequently— Woman or "that maiden mine," and Nature "racked and wrung by her unfaithful lord," the great all-unknowing, the "crass casualty" of the sonnet "Hap." Already Hardy's mind has been staggered with the imperfections of the universe. His own personal disappointment he could get over; he was still young. But wherever he looked he found "hopes dismayed" and "plans marred"; and Society as he had observed it in London was not likely to help the situation. His sonnet "Discouragement" speaks of a whole life's circumstance being dependent "on hap of birth," and prospects for the future seemed to him to blast all thought "of heroism and worth." Even at this early date the sober philosophy of Hardy's later years had made its appearance, only it remained unpublished. And similarly two characteristic alleviations were already present—delight in nature and delight in human loyalty. In "Postponement," the song of a bird "snow-bound in woodland" "reached me on wind-wafts," and we recognize the hand that was later to write of the robin, the thrush, the love-birds, the gold-finch, the blinded bird, and the bullfinches. The theme of "Neutral Tones" is, negatively, the same loyalty of which Hardy was to sing in one of his most successful dactylics, "In a Wood." R. W. King calls "Neutral Tones" the best of Hardy's early poems, and J. Middleton Murry has declared: "That is, I think, a fine poem." It is a striking poem, but not a great one. None of these poems are great. If all the manuscripts that Hardy left behind in London in 1867 had been destroyed, it would not have lowered his future reputation as a poet. But we should then have been lacking this evidence of the maturity of Hardy's mind and of the degree to which he had developed in technical skill by the age of twenty-seven.

POEMS OF 1887 (cf. p. 115)

1. Genoa and the Mediterranean
2. Shelley's Skylark
3. In the Old Theatre, Fiesole
4. On the Palatine
5. Building a New Street in the Ancient Quarter
6. The Vatican
7. At the Pyramid of Cestius near the Graves of Shelley and Keats
8. The Bridge of Lodi

"SATIRES OF CIRCUMSTANCE" (cf. pp. 171-72)

There were originally twelve "Satires," and in place of the phrase "In Fifteen Glimpses," now printed in the *Collected Poems*, the *Fortnightly*

Review published the "Satires" "In Twelve Scenes." One of these, "On the Doorstep," was later removed from the group of "Satires" and given separate publication in *Moments of Vision* in 1917. Four other poems were added to the original list, to make up the fifteen "Satires" which appear today in the *Collected Poems*. The four which did not appear in the *Fortnightly* are: "In the Study," "At the Draper's," "On the Death-Bed," and "In the Moonlight."

"VETERIS VESTIGIA FLAMMAE" (cf. p. 173)

The nineteen poems which supplement the "Poems of 1912-13" are:

From *Moments of Vision* (1917)

1. The Peace-Offering
2. Something Tapped
3. The Last Performance
4. It Never Looks Like Summer
5. An Upbraiding

From *Late Lyrics* (1922)

1. The West-of-Wessex Girl
2. A Man Was Drawing Near to Me.
3. The Old Gown
4. The Dream Is—Which?
5. The Marble Tablet
6. On a Discovered Curl of Hair
7. A Woman Driving
8. The Last Time

From *Human Shows* (1925)

1. When Dead
2. Ten Years Since
3. Two Lips
4. When Oats Were Reaped
5. The Frozen Greenhouse
6. She Opened the Door

5. HARDY'S QUOTATIONS FROM ENGLISH LITERATURE

This is not a list of Hardy's readings, but merely a tabulation of those English authors whom he alludes to or quotes. They are arranged, approximately, in chronological order.

BEDE: The *Ecclesiastical History* is mentioned in *Jude the Obscure*.

SIR THOMAS WYATT: "The Lover's Appeal" (in the *Golden Treasury*) is quoted in *A Pair of Blue Eyes*, and six lines from "Since Love Will Needs That I Shall Love" are quoted in *The Well-Beloved*.

ROGER ASCHAM: *The Schoolmaster* is quoted in *Tess of the D'Urbervilles*.

WILLIAM SHAKESPEARE: Hardy's use of Shakespeare is so extensive that a separate appendix is devoted to this subject. See pp. 246-57.

BIBLE (King James): Hardy's knowledge and use of the Bible are almost as extensive as is his use of Shakespeare. He turns to the Old Testament more frequently than to the New; and his later works are more crowded with Biblical echoes than the earlier. In *Under the Greenwood Tree* the following books in the Bible are each quoted or alluded to once: I Samuel, Ecclesiastes, Jeremiah, Matthew, and Revelation. In the dictated novel *A Laodicean* Leviticus, Job, Psalms, Luke, John, and Romans each figure once. Details about the use of the Bible in *Far from the Madding Crowd* are given in Carl J. Weber's edition of that novel, published in 1937 by the Oxford University Press, New York. Similar information with regard to *Tess of the D'Urbervilles* is available in the same editor's annotation of this novel, published by Harper & Brothers, New York, 1935.

FRANCIS BACON: *Novum Organum* is quoted in the General Preface of 1911, and the "argumentum ad verecundiam" is quoted in *Jude the Obscure*.

LODGE, NASH, and CONSTABLE: mentioned in *A Laodicean*.

EDWARD DYER: "My Mind to Me a Kingdom Is" is quoted in *The Return of the Native*.

BEAUMONT and FLETCHER: *The Maid's Tragedy* is mentioned in *Far from the Madding Crowd*.

THOMAS CAMPION: "Cherry Ripe" is alluded to in *Tess of the D'Urbervilles*.

ROBERT HERRICK: "The Poetry of Dress" (in the *Golden Treasury*) is quoted in Hardy's notes for March, 1875.

MICHAEL DRAYTON: *Polyolbion* and "Where Stour Receives Her Strength" are quoted in *Jude the Obscure*.

EDMUND WALLER: "Go, Lovely Rose" is quoted in "An Indiscretion in the Life of an Heiress."

GEORGE HERBERT: "Vanity" (a poem in *The Church*) is quoted in *The Woodlanders*.

RICHARD CRASHAW: "Love's Horoscope" is quoted on the title page of *Two on a Tower*, and "Wishes for the Supposed Mistress" in *The Well-Beloved*.

THOMAS FULLER: *The Holy State* is quoted in *Jude the Obscure*.

JEREMY TAYLOR: *Holy Dying* is quoted in *Tess of the D'Urbervilles* and referred to in *Jude the Obscure*.

JOHN BUNYAN: *Pilgrim's Progress* is mentioned in *Far from the Madding Crowd* and is alluded to in *The Woodlanders* and in *Tess of the D'Urbervilles*.

JOHN MILTON: "L'Allegro" is quoted in *A Pair of Blue Eyes* and in *A Group of Noble Dames*. "Comus" is alluded to in *The Mayor of Casterbridge,* and the Divorce Tract is twice quoted—once in *Jude the Obscure* and once in the poem "In Gibbon's Old Garden." "Lycidas" is quoted in *Far from the Madding Crowd. Paradise Lost* figures frequently; allusions to it are found in *A Pair of Blue Eyes, Far from the Madding*

Crowd, The Return of the Native, and Hardy's notes for July 8, 1888.
Quotations from the epic occur in *The Return of the Native* and in
Tess of the D'Urbervilles.

ROBERT BURTON: *The Anatomy of Melancholy* is referred to in *Jude the
Obscure.*

ROBERT SOUTH: *Sermons* (as reprinted in 1842) are quoted in *Tess of the
D'Urbervilles.*

JOHN DRYDEN: "Alexander's Feast" is quoted in *The Return of the Native,*
and "Absalom and Achitophel" is quoted in *A Laodicean.* The translation from the *Aeniad* (Hardy's mother gave him a copy about 1850) is
quoted in *Desperate Remedies* and in *An Indiscretion* (II,i).

WILLIAM CONGREVE: "The Mourning Bride" is mentioned in *Far from the
Madding Crowd,* and "The Way of the World" is quoted in *The Woodlanders.*

JOSEPH ADDISON: *The Spectator* is mentioned, referred to, and quoted in
Far from the Madding Crowd and *Jude the Obscure.*

DANIEL DEFOE: *Robinson Crusoe* is mentioned in *Far from the Madding
Crowd* and *Jude the Obscure,* is alluded to in *The Woodlanders,* and is
quoted in *A Laodicean.*

JOHN GAY: *The Beggar's Opera* is mentioned in *The Return of the Native,*
and Polly is referred to in the same novel. "Black-eyed Susan" is quoted
in *A Pair of Blue Eyes.*

JAMES THOMSON: "Winter" is echoed in *Far from the Madding Crowd,*
and "The Castle of Indolence" is alluded to in *The Return of the Native*
and quoted in Hardy's notes in May, 1887.

EDWARD YOUNG: *Night Thoughts* is mentioned in *Far from the Madding
Crowd.*

HENRY FIELDING and TOBIAS SMOLLETT are both mentioned in *Jude the
Obscure.*

LAURENCE STERNE is also mentioned in *Jude the Obscure; Tristram Shandy*
is alluded to in *A Laodicean;* and *A Sentimental Journey,* in *The Woodlanders.*

THOMAS GRAY: "Ode on the Spring" (in *Golden Treasury*) is quoted in
A Pair of Blue Eyes. "Ode on a Distant Prospect of Eton College" is also
quoted; and lines from the *Elegy* appear both in *Far from the Madding
Crowd* and in *A Pair of Blue Eyes.*

RICHARD B. SHERIDAN: *The Rivals:* Lydia is referred to in *The Return of
the Native,* and in the same novel occurs an allusion to the Speech against
Warren Hastings.

EDWARD GIBBON: mentioned in *Jude the Obscure;* and the *Decline and Fall* figures at least six times: five times it is quoted or referred to in *Jude*, and another allusion is found in the 1895 Preface to *The Woodlanders*.

ISAAC BICKERSTAFF: *Love in a Village* (1763) and *Maid of the Mill* (1765) are both mentioned in *Far from the Madding Crowd*.

SAMUEL JOHNSON: "The Vanity of Human Wishes" is mentioned in *Far from the Madding Crowd*, and *Rasselas* is both alluded to and mentioned in *The Return of the Native*.

JAMES BOSWELL: *The Life of Johnson* is referred to or quoted in *Far from the Madding Crowd*, *Jude the Obscure*, and the General Preface of 1911.

THOMAS CHATTERTON: the "Minstrel's Song" (in *Aella*) is quoted in a modernized form in *The Woodlanders*, and "The Whore of Babylon" is echoed in *Jude the Obscure*.

WILLIAM COWPER: "John Gilpin's Ride" is alluded to in *The Mayor of Casterbridge*, and the apocryphal Gospels are mentioned in *Jude the Obscure*.

ROBERT BURNS: "Bonnie Peg" is quoted in *The Mayor of Casterbridge*, and "Auld Lang Syne" in *A Pair of Blue Eyes*.

THOMAS R. MALTHUS: the Essay on the Principle of Population is referred to in *Tess of the D'Urbervilles*.

WILLIAM WORDSWORTH: "Lines Written in Early Spring" is quoted in *Tess*; "Resolution and Independence" is quoted in *The Woodlanders* and cited in Hardy's notes for July, 1868; and the Ode on Immortality is quoted in *Tess of the D'Urbervilles*. Hardy referred to Wordsworth in *Tess* as a "breezy" poet; and mentioned his "Two April Mornings" in a letter written February 2, 1880. It is obvious that Hardy liked Wordsworth's style, but distrusted his philosophy.

SAMUEL TAYLOR COLERIDGE: "The Ancient Mariner" is referred to in *Desperate Remedies* and "The Three Graves" is mentioned in *A Pair of Blue Eyes*.

SIR WALTER SCOTT: Mrs. Hardy's biography records that Hardy preferred Scott's poetry to his novels. It is surprising, therefore, to observe that not a line of his poetry is quoted and that there is only one passing allusion to one of the poems. The "goblin page" of "The Lay of the Last Minstrel" is referred to in *The Mayor of Casterbridge*. On the other hand, at least four of the novels appear. *The Antiquary* is quoted in *The Mayor of Casterbridge*, and in the same novel *The Bride of Lammermoor* is referred to, and Gurth in *Ivanhoe* is mentioned. From *Kenilworth* Amy Robsart is mentioned in *The Woodlanders*.

THOMAS CAMPBELL: The song "Can you keep the bee from ranging" is quoted in *Under the Greenwood Tree*.

WILLIAM COMBE: *Doctor Syntax* (1812) is mentioned in the *Madding Crowd*.

LORD BYRON: "When we two parted" is quoted in *Blue Eyes*. "Childe Harold" is mentioned in "An Indiscretion" and quoted in *Jude*. Two stanzas from "Don Juan" are quoted in *A Laodicean*.

MARY WOLLSTONECRAFT SHELLEY: *Frankenstein* is mentioned in *A Laodicean*.

PERCY BYSSHE SHELLEY: mentioned in *Jude*. "Laon and Cythna" is quoted in *The Mayor of Casterbridge*. "The Revolt of Islam" is quoted in *The Woodlanders* and on the title page of *The Well-Beloved*. "Alastor" is alluded to in *The Mayor of Casterbridge*. "When the lamp is shattered" is mentioned in *A Pair of Blue Eyes* and quoted in "An Indiscretion" and in *Desperate Remedies*. Two lines from "One Word is Too Often Profaned" appear in *Desperate Remedies*. The "Ode to the West Wind" is quoted in *Far from the Madding Crowd*; "Adonais" in *The Hand of Ethelberta*; and "Prometheus Unbound" in *The Well-Beloved*. Hardy's favorite, dating from the time when as a twenty-two-year-old young man in London he had bought a two-volume edition of Shelley's poems, was apparently "Epipsychidion," which is quoted in four of his novels, "An Indiscretion," *The Mayor of Casterbridge, The Woodlanders*, and *Jude the Obscure*.

JOHN KEATS: "On First Looking into Chapman's Homer" is paraphrased in *Far from the Madding Crowd*. "La Belle Dame Sans Merci" is mentioned and quoted in two chapters of *A Pair of Blue Eyes*. Three lines of the "Ode to a Nightingale" are quoted in *A Laodicean*, and the "Ode to Autumn" is echoed in *The Woodlanders*. "The Eve of St. Agnes" is quoted in the *Madding Crowd*, and Keats is mentioned in *The Return of the Native*.

SAMUEL ROGERS is alluded to in *The Return of the Native*.

THOMAS CARLYLE: the Essay on Goethe is paraphrased in *The Mayor of Casterbridge*, and "Jean Paul Richter" is cited in Hardy's notebook for 1868.

THOMAS BILBY: "Joyful" (hymn) is quoted in *Tess of the D'Urbervilles*.

J. H. NEWMAN: "Lead Kindly Light" is quoted in *Far from the Madding Crowd* and alluded to in *Jude the Obscure*. The *Apologia* is both quoted and referred to in *Jude*.

ALLAN CUNNINGHAM: "It's hame, and it's hame" is quoted in *The Mayor of Casterbridge*.

THOMAS HOOD: "The Bridge of Sighs," "pure womanly," is echoed on the title page of *Tess of the D'Urbervilles*.

CAROLINE NAIRNE: "The Lass of Gowrie" is quoted in *The Mayor of Casterbridge*.

ALFRED TENNYSON: "In Memoriam" is quoted in *A Pair of Blue Eyes*, in

Tess of the D'Urbervilles, and in the Apology prefixed to *Late Lyrics*. "Break break break" is quoted in *A Pair of Blue Eyes*, and "Princess Ida" in *The Mayor of Casterbridge*.

ROBERT BROWNING: Hardy's debt to Browning is given separate consideration. See pages 269-276.

JOHN KEBLE: "Why should we faint" is quoted in *Jude the Obscure*.

WILLIAM MAKEPEACE THACKERAY: "Book of Snobs" is quoted in "An Indiscretion."

MATTHEW ARNOLD: the "home of lost causes" is quoted in *Jude the Obscure*, and in the same novel Arnold is referred to and also mentioned by name. "Hebraism and Hellenism" is paraphrased in *Tess of the D'Urbervilles*, and the "Function of Criticism" is quoted in the Apology to *Late Lyrics*. Arnold, like Browning and Wordsworth, is quoted for his ideas. Tennyson, like Shelley and Keats, is quoted for his poetic phrasing.

JOHN STUART MILL: "On Liberty" is cited in Hardy's notes for 1868, is mentioned in one chapter of *Jude the Obscure*, and quoted in another.

HERBERT SPENCER: *First Principles* is quoted in the General Preface.

ALGERNON CHARLES SWINBURNE: in the serial version of *Tess of the D'Urbervilles*, "The Garden of Proserpine" and "Behold, When Thy Face Is Made Bare" are quoted. In *Jude* the "Prelude" to "Songs before Sunrise" and the "Hymn to Proserpine" are quoted. "Aholibah" is mentioned in *Tess*, and "Tristram of Lyonnesse" is echoed in poems about Lyonnesse and in Hardy's play *The Queen of Cornwall*. Swinburne is eulogized in Hardy's poem "A Singer Asleep."

DANTE GABRIEL ROSSETTI: "The Blessed Damozel" is mentioned in *Desperate Remedies*.

EDMUND GOSSE: "Two Points of View" is paraphrased in *The Return of the Native* and quoted in *The Woodlanders*.

No great omission is involved in confining the above list to English authors. Hardy was satisfied with native products. Among French authors he mentioned Rochefoucauld and George Sand; among German authors, Heine and Schopenhauer.

Only three American authors were quoted by him. Walt Whitman, whose "I foresee too much" was quoted in *Desperate Remedies*, replaced Swinburne in the final version of *Tess of the D'Urbervilles*. Longfellow's "Excelsior" was mentioned in *Jude the Obscure*, and in that same novel Poe's "Raven" was quoted. J. C. Powys has reported: "In my own youth Thomas Hardy pointed out to me, with more passionate appreciation than I ever heard him display for any other author, the power and beauty of

Poe's *Ulalume*. . . . Hardy it was, the very first time I saw him, who introduced me to that most startling and characteristic of all Poe's poems." In 1909 Hardy wrote a letter in which he spoke of Poe as "that fantastic and romantic genius" who was "the first to realize to the full the possibilities of the English language in rhyme and alliteration."

For a man who "took no courses," who never attended a university (if we disregard the night classes in French, attended for a short while at the University of London), Hardy's mastery of English literature is astounding. "How knoweth this man letters, having never learned?" Hardy's list of quotations is more than ordinarily important because it tells the reader a great deal about how Hardy learned to write. In this list there are very few serious omissions. It is evident that Pope had little to say to Hardy. More surprising is the absence of Huxley and of Fitzgerald. The latter's name does not appear, but Hardy knew the *Rubaiyat* and asked to have some of it read to him only a few hours before he died. The library of Colby College now owns the textbook used by Hardy in his study of English authors. It was Thomas Arnold's *A Manual of English Literature* (London, 1867). [Thomas Arnold (1823-1900), M.A. (1865) of University College, Oxford, was the younger brother of Matthew Arnold and the father of Mrs. Humphrey Ward.]

6. HARDY'S DEBT TO SHAKESPEARE

One book which Hardy acquired before he left Dorchester was Walter Bagehot's *Estimates of Some Englishmen and Scotchmen*, published in 1658. One of the chapters in this book deals with Shakespeare, the poet on whose works Hardy lavished a lifetime of study. "No lists are needed to establish this," declares one of Hardy's critics, "nor the placing of quotations side by side." But without detailed lists no reader can possibly know the intensity and the persistence with which Thomas Hardy studied his Shakespeare.

The results of a preliminary examination of Hardy's indebtedness to Shakespeare were published in the *Shakespeare Association Bulletin* (IX, 91-97, 162-63), April and July, 1934. After reading this article the second Mrs. Hardy wrote to the author: "I consider this article one of the best that has been written about my late husband. I don't think even you would realize how truly you have written. Only a few hours before his death Mr. Hardy spoke of Shakespeare."

Since this important formative influence of Shakespeare upon Hardy was thus one not confined merely to his early years, it will help the concentration of the reader's attention upon this point, if Hardy's long-continued devotion to Shakespeare is here summarized. When he was twenty-eight he re-read various Shakespearean plays, while making his own first attempts at writing fiction, with results hereafter to be disclosed. At the age of thirty, while keeping up a regular correspondence with Miss Gifford, he continued to read Shakespeare. In the margin of his copy of *Hamlet* he marked with the date "December 15, 1870" the passage, "Thou wouldst not think how ill all's here about my heart." And he recorded "July 1871" in his copy of *Macbeth* beside the passage that runs, "Things at their worst will cease or else climb upward." After his marriage he lived for a while at Wimborne and was there invited to share Shakespearean "readings." On February 4 and again on February 11, 1882, he attended readings of *The Tempest.* Two years later Hardy went (August 14, 1884) to see a performance of *Othello* given by strolling players at Dorchester, and afterward he wrote up an amusing account of it. In 1888 he was greatly interested in the Shakespearean plays given by Ada Rehan, and on July 9 of this year he saw her and Drew in *The Taming of the Shrew.* Just after he had passed his fiftieth birthday he went again to see her in *As You Like It,* and it is possible that his poem "The Two Rosalinds" was suggested by this performance of July 2, 1890. A year later he recorded Shakespeare quotations heard at the dinner table in a London hotel and incorporated Shakespearean words and phrases in his own writing. When Hardy's father died on July 20, 1892, the novelist summarized his life by recalling four lines of *Hamlet*:

> "Thou hast been
> As one, in suffering all, that suffers nothing,
> A man that fortune's buffets and rewards
> Hast ta'en with equal thanks."

In December, 1895, he saw Forbes-Robertson and Mrs. Patrick Campbell do *Romeo and Juliet.* In 1896 Hardy and his wife went to Stratford-on-Avon and took lodgings there for a week in August. He visited the places associated with Shakespeare and there began a careful re-reading of *King Lear.* He finished the play September 6, 1896, while at Dover, and wrote out some observations on it in which he disagreed with the "commentators." On June 26, 1905, when he was sixty-five, he wrote to the Shakespeare Memorial Committee, and three years later he wrote another letter in which he expressed his view of Shakespeare's chief distinction. In April, 1916, he wrote his poem "To Shakespeare after Three Hundred Years," printed in the Shakespeare Memorial volume of that year. When he was seventy-eight he again recorded his views of Shakespeare. In 1922 he reached the age of eighty-two, but even then was not too old to like still to recall those early London days when he would carry a text of Shakespeare to a Phelps performance and sit in the front row and follow the printed dialogue by the stage lights. In July of that year he attended an outdoor performance of *A Midsummer Night's Dream* given by amateurs. When eighty-six years old Hardy read an editorial in the London *Times*, discussing the "dram of eale" passage in *Hamlet*, and he was still zealous enough in the service of Shakespeare to write the following letter, which appeared in the *Times* on June 17, 1926:

"Your leading article on the famous passage with which Shakespeare's printers have tantalized the poet's readers for the last 300 years reminds me that in the 1860s I worked at elucidating it and marked in the margin of a copy I used my own conjectural reading. I give it here, since it may pass in the crowd of conjectures on what Shakespeare really did write, as being not much worse than the rest:

'The dram of ill
Doth all the noble substance leaven down
To his own scandal.'"

Hardy lived to pass only one more birthday after this contribution to textual emendation. For eighty years the Bard of Avon had been his guide and friend. More than any other English author, Hardy saturated his mind with Shakespearean words, Shakespearean thoughts, Shakespearean characters, Shakespearean attitudes, Shakespearean situations, Shakespearean humor, Shakespearean tragedy.

That part of Hardy's debt which is most easily recognized consists of direct borrowings from the plays. *Hamlet* is the one most frequently quoted, but Hardy knew them all, from the earliest to the latest. He knew the lines that everyone knows, but he quotes unusual and little-known lines as well. He began to quote Shakespeare before he was thirty, and he was still at it when he was nearing ninety. The list of his direct quotations from Shakespeare cannot be paralleled in the work of any other novelist.

It will help us to understand Hardy's instinctive and lifelong appreciation of Shakespeare, if the careers of the two are for a moment placed side by side. Both were born in or near a small town, a little more than one hundred miles from London, in days when that meant comparative isolation in a quiet sheep-raising countryside. Both were born in small thatched houses which are still standing. Both had as mothers women of marked character, and both had fathers engaged in business. Both received only a limited schooling, and that chiefly in the classics. Neither went to the university. Both read widely, and both went up to London before they were twenty-five. Both began with crude and imitative work as writers, both wrote anonymously, and both brought to their work their fathers' sense of humor. Both attained success before the age of thirty-five, and both aroused the jealousy of other writers. Both appealed to ordinary readers, but good critics and royalty joined in acclaiming both men. The writings of both men include some excellent rural portraits—of clownish characters who have become famous. Both knew the folklore and the superstitions, the songs and the dances, the accent and the idiom of the rustic. Both men were patriotic Englishmen, and wrote in celebration of England's wars, of English heroes, of the English countryside. Both men had a tender sympathy for mankind, a hatred of hypocrisy and injustice, and an intense love of loyalty. Both returned from London to their place of birth, and built themselves large houses in which they died. And the hearts of both are buried in or near the church of their boyhood. Both men have given their names to their own sections of England. This list might be greatly lengthened, but enough has been said to explain how perfectly natural, one might almost say inevitable, it was for Hardy to single Shakespeare out as his guide. Once this native sympathy is fully understood, the amazing extent of Hardy's indebtedness to the earlier poet will seem less artificial and labored.

Twice in *Jude the Obscure* and once in *The Hand of Ethelberta* Hardy mentions by name the author to whom he was indebted more than to any other. The extent of that debt is not confined merely to the words or lines quoted, but includes characters, themes, situations, plots, moods, ideas, and philosophies as well. An entire book might easily be filled on this subject alone. All that can be attempted here is to indicate Hardy's acquaintance with individual plays and poems. In this list references to the plays are by act, scene, and line; thus, "5,2,347" means "Act V, scene ii, line 347." References to Hardy's novels are by chapters; thus "Mayor (33)" means Chapter XXXIII in *The Mayor of Casterbridge*, and "Jude (6,3)" means Part VI, chapter iii, in *Jude the Obscure*.

TITUS ANDRONICUS

"Integer vitae . . . oh, 'tis a verse in Horace" (4,2,22) is echoed in *Tess of the D'Urbervilles* (34): "'Integer vitae' says a Roman poet."

LOVE'S LABOUR'S LOST

The title of the play is quoted in *A Laodicean* (3,6), and in the same novel (3,8) "Armado the braggart" is mentioned, and "good Lord Boyet" (2,1,13), "Fair Princess, welcome to the court of Navarre" (2,1,90), and "Rebuke me not" (5,2,347) are quoted.

"The dancing horse" (1,2,56) has his Wessex counterpart among the "inspired monsters" of *The Mayor of Casterbridge* (1).

TWO GENTLEMEN OF VERONA

"Poor wounded name . . ." (1,2,3) is quoted on the title page of *Tess of the D'Urbervilles.*

THE COMEDY OF ERRORS

The two Dromios are mentioned in *The Trumpet-Major* (39).

KING JOHN

"When fortune means to men most good . . ." (3,4,119) is quoted in *A Laodicean.*

A MIDSUMMER NIGHT'S DREAM

Hermia and Helena are mentioned in *A Laodicean* (3,6).

"The course of true love . . ." (1,1,134) is twice paraphrased in *Under the Greenwood Tree* and once in *A Laodicean.*

"A fair vestal throned . . ." (2,1,150) is quoted in *A Pair of Blue Eyes* (1).

"Puck . . . Hermia . . . Demetrius" (3,2) are alluded to in *Two on a Tower* (39).

"—local habitation . . ." (5,1,12) is quoted in *A Laodicean.*

At the age of 82 Hardy went to an outdoor amateur performance of *A Midsummer Night's Dream.*

THE TAMING OF THE SHREW

"Our cake's dough" (1,1,109) is quoted in *Far from the Madding Crowd* (33) and in *The Mayor of Casterbridge* (13).

"Thereby hangs a tale" (4,1,60) is quoted in "An Indiscretion in the Life of an Heiress" (2,1).

Hardy saw Ada Rehan and Drew in *The Taming of the Shrew* on July 9, 1888.

THE MERCHANT OF VENICE

"I hold the world but as the world . . ." (1,1,76) is quoted in *The Trumpet-Major.*

"The devil can cite Scripture for his purpose" (1,3,99) is echoed in *The Hand of Ethelberta.*

"How all the other passions . . ." (3,2,108) is quoted in "An Indiscretion in the Life of an Heiress" (2,5).

"Still quiring to the young-eyed cherubim" (5,1,58) is quoted in *A Laodicean* (1,2).

ROMEO AND JULIET

The title of this play is mentioned in *Ethelberta* and in *A Laodicean* (3,8). Romeo is mentioned in *The Mayor* (17). Rosaline, Romeo, and Juliet are mentioned in *The Well-Beloved* (1,8), together with an allusion to the "son of the Montagues" and to "this daughter of the Capulets." Juliet is referred to in *Desperate Remedies*.

"If I profane . . ." (1,5,95) is quoted in *A Laodicean* (3,8).

"Too rash, too unadvised . . ." (2,2,118) is quoted in *The Well-Beloved* (1,8).

"Hence will I to my ghostly father's cell" (2,2,189) is quoted in "An Indiscretion in the Life of an Heiress" (2,6).

"Violent delights . . . violent ends" (2,6,9) is quoted in *Tess of the D'Urbervilles* (33).

Romeo eloping with Juliet is mentioned in *The Well-Beloved*.

"O! what learning is!" (3,3,160) is echoed in *Under the Greenwood Tree* (3).

"It was the nightingale" (3,5,2) is echoed in *Under the Greenwood Tree* (5,2).

RICHARD II

"Fear and be slain" (3,2,183) is quoted in *A Pair of Blue Eyes* (18).

"What sport shall we devise" (3,4,1) and "We'll play at bowls" (3,4,3) are quoted in *Two on a Tower* (27).

HENRY IV, Part I

"Thou wilt not utter what thou dost not know . . ." (2,3,114) is quoted in *A Pair of Blue Eyes*.

"Enfeoffed herself to popularity . . ." (3,1,69-73) is quoted in *The Hand of Ethelberta* (24).

"Thought's the slave of life . . ." (5,4,81) is quoted in the General Preface written in 1911.

HENRY IV, Part II

"Shallow and Silence themselves" step from Act V, scene 3, to appear in Chapter XXVIII of *The Mayor of Casterbridge*.

HENRY V

"Tombless with no remembrance" (1,2,229) is quoted in the "Sapphic Fragment" of *Poems of Past and Present*.

"Falstaff . . . talked of the whore of Babylon"; this is imitated in *Jude the Obscure* (6,7).

"Piece out my imperfections with your thoughts," from line 23 of the Prologue, is quoted in an unpublished letter written by Hardy on January 31, 1904, and repeated in another letter written March 13, 1904, in which Hardy calls this "a line which often occurs to me."

THE MERRY WIVES OF WINDSOR

The Hostess of the *Garter* is referred to in *A Laodicean* and "Thereby hangs a tale" (1,4,155) is quoted in "An Indiscretion in the Life of an Heiress" (2,1).

AS YOU LIKE IT

On July 2, 1890, Hardy saw Ada Rehan play the part of Rosalind. He wrote a poem entitled "The Two Rosalinds." Rosalind is referred to in *A Group of Noble Dames*.

"Sermons in stone . . ." (2,1,17) is quoted in *Tess of the D'Urbervilles* (23).

"Under the greenwood tree" (2,5,1) was used as the title of one of the novels.

"Come hither, come hither" (2,5,5) is quoted on the last page of *the Greenwood Tree*.

"Thereby hangs a tale" (2,7,28) is quoted in "An Indiscretion" (2,1) and in *A Laodicean*.

"Why, if thou never wast at court . . ." (3,1,41-46) is echoed in *Tess of the D'Urbervilles*.

"Cat will after kind" (3,2,110) is quoted in *A Laodicean* (6,4).

"Thank Heaven fasting for a good man's love" (3,5,58) is quoted in *The Mayor of Casterbridge* (33).

TWELFTH NIGHT

"Journeys end in lovers meeting" (2,3,44) and "Sweet-and-twenty" (2,3,52) are quoted in *A Pair of Blue Eyes* (11).

"No cakes and ale" (2,3,125) is quoted in Hardy's correspondence.

"Worm in the bud" (2,4,114) is quoted in *A Pair of Blue Eyes* (31) and in *The Mayor of Casterbridge* (34).

"Patience on a monument" (2,4,117) is quoted in *Tess of the D'Urbervilles* (9).

"—Time brings in his revenges" (5,1,389) is loosely quoted in *Two on a Tower* (41).

ALL'S WELL THAT ENDS WELL

The title (repeated in 5,2,25) is quoted at least five times: in *A Laodicean* (6,4), in "The Romantic Adventures of a Milkmaid" (5), in "The Waiting Supper" (4), in *The Woodlanders* (29), and in *Jude the Obscure* (6,5).

MEASURE FOR MEASURE

"When I would pray and think . . ." (2,4,1-4) is quoted in "An Indiscretion in the Life of an Heiress" (1,1).

"Love talks with better knowledge" (3,2,163) is quoted in *The Woodlanders* (45).

"Take, O take those lips away" (4,1) is quoted in *Tess of the D'Urbervilles* (9).

JULIUS CAESAR

"Calpurnia's cheek is pale" (1,2,184) is quoted in *The Mayor of Casterbridge* (37).

"When beggars die . . . comets seen . . ." (2,2,30-31) is echoed in *Two on a Tower* (13).

"A plain blunt man who" (3,2,222) is quoted in *Far from the Madding Crowd* (26).

"All his faults . . . conn'd by rote" (4,3,96-97) is quoted in a note on Edmund Kean which Hardy inserted in the *Dorset County Chronicle* in June, 1902.

"a tide in the affairs of men" (4,3,218) is loosely quoted in *A Laodicean*.

HAMLET

There are references to Hamlet in *The Hand of Ethelberta*, to Guildenstern in *Far from the Madding Crowd*, and to Horatio in *The Woodlanders*.

"A violet in the youth . . ." (1,3,7) is quoted on the title page of *A Pair of Blue Eyes*.

"—show the steep and thorny way" (1,3,48) and "reck'd not his own rede" (1,3,51) are quoted in *Far from the Madding Crowd* (29).

"To the manner born" (1,4,15) is quoted in *Far from the Madding Crowd*.

The famous "dram of eale" passage (1,4,36) was emended by Hardy in the *Times*, June 17, 1926.

"Bias," as in "assays of bias" (2,1,65), was used by Hardy to describe John Durbeyfield's gait. Richard Le Gallienne asked: "Who else [other than Hardy] would describe the unsteadiness in the walk of an aged tippler as 'a bias in his gait'?" The answer is: William Shakespeare.

"—happy in that . . . not over happy" (2,2,232) is quoted in *Far from the Madding Crowd* (22).

"There is nothing either good or bad . . ." (2,2,256) is quoted in *Two on a Tower*.

"Sigh gratis" (2,2,338) is quoted in *Tess of the D'Urbervilles* (28).

"Exclaim against their own succession" (2,2,367) is quoted in *Tess* (26).

"Is it not monstrous" (2,2,585) is quoted in *Jude the Obscure* (6,3).

"Sea of troubles" (3,1,59) is quoted in *The Woodlanders* (4).

"Endure the ills we have . . ." (3,1,81) is quoted in *Tess of the D'Urbervilles* (36).

"Sicklied o'er with the pale cast of thought" (3,1,85) is echoed in *A Pair of Blue Eyes*.

"Out-herods Herod" (3,2,16) is echoed in *A Pair of Blue Eyes*.

"Thou . . . hast ta'en with equal thanks" (3,2,66-69): these four lines Hardy quoted upon the death of his father, July 20, 1892, as describing his parent's character.

"As one, in suffering all" (3,2,67) is quoted in *The Woodlanders* (3).

"Where love is great . . ." (3,2,181) is quoted in *A Pair of Blue Eyes* (27).

"Can one be pardoned and retain the offence" (3,3,56) is quoted in *A Pair of Blue Eyes*.

"I must be cruel only to be kind" (3,4,178) is echoed in *The Trumpet-Major*.

"Nature is fine in love . . ." (4,5,161-163) is quoted in *The Woodlanders* (45).

"—dog will have his day" (5,1,315) is echoed in *A Laodicean*.

"Let a beast be lord of beasts . . ." (5,2,88) is quoted in *A Pair of Blue Eyes* (9).

"If it be not now, yet it will come" (5,2,225) is echoed in *Under the Greenwood Tree*.

"Ever 'gainst that season . . . wherein our Savior's birth . . . they say no spirit can walk" (1,1,158-162) finds an echo in the poem "Her Late Husband": "some Christmas night, when angels walk, they say."

Ophelia's "ground unsanctified" (5,1,249) is like Tess's baby's "shabby corner," in *Tess of the D'Urbervilles* (14).

"—a divinity that shapes our ends" (5,2,10) is echoed in *The Wood-landers.*

OTHELLO

Othello and "his Ancient" are mentioned in *Ethelberta* (7).
"She has deceived her father and may thee" (1,3,294) is quoted in *A Group of Noble Dames.*
"Thereby hangs a tale" (3,1,8) is quoted in "An Indiscretion in the Life of an Heiress."
"Not poppy nor mandragora" (3,3,330) is quoted in *The Woodlanders* (36) and also in *Wessex Tales.*
"Men are not gods" (3,4,148) is quoted in *The Woodlanders* (39).
Desdemona and "the black man" are mentioned in *Far from the Madding Crowd* (44).
On August 14, 1884, Hardy attended a performance of *Othello* given by strolling players at Dorchester.

KING LEAR

"More sinned against than sinning" (3,2,60) is quoted in *Tess of the D'Urbervilles* (35).
"As flies to wanton boys . . ." (4,1,38-39) is quoted in the 1892 Preface to *Tess.*
Lear on the Heath (3,3) is referred to in the 1895 Preface to *The Return of the Native.*
"An excellent thing in woman" (5,3,273) is echoed in *A Pair of Blue Eyes.*
In 1896 Hardy began to read *King Lear* anew at Stratford, and completed his reading on September 6, 1896, at Dover.

MACBETH

"Incarnadined" (2,2,62) is quoted in *Far from the Madding Crowd* (57) and in *A Laodicean.*
"To be thus is nothing; but to be safely thus" (3,1,48) is quoted in *The Hand of Ethelberta* (31).
"Cabined, cribbed" (3,4,24) is paraphrased in *Tess of the D'Urbervilles* (2).
"What's done cannot be undone" (5,1,75) is quoted in *The Return of the Native.*
"The sear, the yellow leaf" (5,2,23) is echoed in *Wessex Tales.*
"To-morrow and to-morrow and to-morrow" (5,5,19) is paraphrased in

Tess of the D'Urbervilles (19), and quoted in a letter written February 11, 1880.

". . . tale told by an idiot" (5,5,26) is quoted in *Tess of the D'Urbervilles* (53).

"—full of sound and fury . . . " (5,5,31-32) is quoted in *Far from the Madding Crowd* (4).

ANTONY AND CLEOPATRA

"Is she as tall as me" (3,3,14) and "Dwarfish" (3,3,19) are echoed in "The Withered Arm."

"Kissed away kingdoms and provinces" (3,10,7-8) is quoted in *A Pair of Blue Eyes.*

In a French railway carriage, in August, 1890, Hardy saw "a Cleopatra . . . a good-natured amative creature by her voice, and her heavy moist lips."

CYMBELINE

"The two mourners in *Cymbeline*" are referred to in *The Woodlanders* (45).

"The country base" (5,3,19) is the same game that re-appears in *Under the Greenwood Tree* (1,9) and in *Far from the Madding Crowd* (44).

The verb "to false" (2,3,74) is found in Hardy's poem "The Inscription."

THE TEMPEST

Ariel is mentioned in *A Laodicean.* Miranda is referred to in *A Pair of Blue Eyes,* and Caliban in *Two on a Tower.*

Gonzalo's desire to "die a dry death" (1,1,71) is quoted in *Far from the Madding Crowd* (47).

". . . this moon-calf" (2,2,114) is perhaps echoed in "no moon, no man" in *The Return of the Native* (1,3).

"We are such stuff . . ." (4,1,156) is echoed in *Far from the Madding Crowd* (54) and quoted in the Apology prefixed to *Late Lyrics.*

SONNETS

"Oh, for my sake . . ." (3,1-3) is quoted in "An Indiscretion in the Life of an Heiress" (1,4).

"Unbless" (3,4) is echoed in the "unbloom" of the poem "Hap."

"In me thou seest . . ." (73) is quoted in *The Well-Beloved* (3,1).

"Farewell! thou art too dear . . ." (87,1-2) is quoted in *The Hand of Ethelberta* (24).

"Love . . . which alters when . . . finds" (116,2-3) is quoted in *Desperate Remedies* (11,4) and in *Tess of the D'Urbervilles* (53).

7. NOTES ON THE WESSEX NOVELS

DESPERATE REMEDIES

Published by Tinsley Brothers, 1871; 3 vols., red cloth. This is the only book for which Hardy himself paid the cost of publication.

UNDER THE GREENWOOD TREE

Tinsley Brothers, 1872; 2 vols., green cloth. This novel and *Desperate Remedies* are the only books which Hardy published anonymously, and the only ones which were not serialized.

Had Tinsley been patient for a few years more, he would have had less cause for complaint. The "best little prose idyll" did not die after Tinsley's three editions. Among those into whose hands a copy fell was Henry Holt, a young American publisher. He carried a copy of the idyll back to the United States, and in the following year he printed it. Published on May 10, 1873, under the imprint of Holt & Williams, *Under the Greenwood Tree* has the distinction of being not only the first of Hardy's work to be offered to American readers but also the first book to appear on either side of the ocean with his name on it. The English *A Pair of Blue Eyes* was published May 17, and the American *Blue Eyes* on July 26, 1873. *Under the Greenwood Tree* also has the invidious distinction of being the first of numerous American piracies of Hardy. It was printed by George Munro in 1877. Hardy's sale of the copyright in this novel to Tinsley resulted in an unusual publishing record for this title. Tinsley Brothers disposed of their rights to Chatto & Windus. This firm republished the novel and also licensed editions by J. M. Dent, by William Collins Sons & Co., and by Eveleigh Nash & Grayson (now Grayson & Grayson). Eventually the copyright reverted to Hardy and Macmillan & Co. became the sole authorized British publishers. They, however, made no attempt to stop the sale of the previously published editions, and later allowed G. G. Harrap & Co. to buy the sheets of the Macmillan edition to use in a Hardy publication of their own. At the time of Hardy's death in 1928 there were six British editions of the *Greenwood Tree* simultaneously on the market—Chatto, Collins, Dent, Harrap, Macmillan, and Nash & Grayson. In America there were authorized editions by Holt and by Harpers, two imported editions (E. P. Dutton & Co. imported the Dent edition, and G. P. Putnam's Sons imported the Chatto & Windus edition), and at least six unauthorized editions. In 1924 the novel was translated into French by Eve Paul-

Margueritte (*Sous la verte feuillé*). In 1937 it was published in Toronto, Canada.

A PAIR OF BLUE EYES

Serialized in *Tinsley's Magazine*, September, 1872 to July, 1873; published by Tinsley Brothers, 1873, 3 vols., green (and blue) cloth. A second edition, in one volume, for six shillings was issued in September, 1877, by H. S. King & Co., and later reprinted. A third edition was published in 1880 by Kegan Paul & Co., and a fourth appeared in May, 1884, published by Sampson Low, Marston, Searle & Rivington; reprinted in 1886 and 1890. In 1913 a French translation by Eve Paul-Margueritte appeared under the title *Deux yeux bleus.*

FAR FROM THE MADDING CROWD

The immediate success of this novel is indicated by the fact that it was published seven times during the year 1874:

1. *Cornhill Magazine*, London, January to December.
2. *Living Age*, Boston, January 31, 1873, to January 9, 1875.
3. *Every Saturday*, Boston, January 31 to October 24 (then merged with the *Living Age*).
4. *Eclectic Magazine*, New York, March, 1874, to February, 1875.
5. *Semi-Weekly Tribune*, New York, June 26 to December 15; reprinted in 1875 as a 20¢ book.
6. Henry Holt, New York: first edition, November 17; one volume, light-tan cloth.
7. Smith, Elder & Co., London: first English edition, November 28; 2 vols., green cloth.

Next to *Tess of the D'Urbervilles* this novel was Hardy's best seller. It was pirated in New York in 1879, in Chicago in 1880, and in Philadelphia about 1900. In 1878 it was published at Leipzig, and in 1901 a French translation appeared in Paris. In England Smith, Elder issued a second edition in 1875, and a one-volume edition at 7/6 in 1877; and in 1882 Sampson Low, Marston Searle & Rivington published a six-shilling edition, reprinted in 1889. Modern edited publications of the novel include one by William T. Brewster (New York, Harpers, 1918), one by Cyril Aldred (London, Macmillan, 1935), and one by Carl J. Weber (New York, Oxford University Press, 1937).

THE HAND OF ETHELBERTA

Serialized in *Cornhill Magazine*, July 1875, to May, 1876, and published by Smith, Elder & Co., 1876, 2 vols., brown cloth.

A second (one-volume) edition at 7/6 was published by Smith, Elder in June, 1877, reprinted in 1878. A third edition at 6/- was issued by Sampson Low in 1882, reprinted in 1888, 1890, and 1891. In America the novel was serialized in the New York *Times* from June 20, 1875, to April 9, 1876. In May, 1876, it was published in one volume by Henry Holt.

THE RETURN OF THE NATIVE

Serialized in *Belgravia*, January to December, 1878; published by Smith, Elder & Co., 1878; 3 vols., brown cloth.

After their initial edition, Smith, Elder & Co. had nothing more to do with the *Native*. The novel was issued in one volume at six shillings in December, 1879, by Kegan, Paul & Co., and in May, 1884, a third edition was published in London by Sampson Low & Co. Tauchnitz issued an edition in two volumes at Leipzig in 1879, and there have been two French translations, one of them greatly abridged.

Editorial discussion and annotation have been provided in the following editions: by J. W. Cunliffe (New York, Scribners, 1917), by Warner Taylor (New York, Harpers, 1922), by Albert C. Baugh (New York, Macmillan, 1928), by Irene M. Haworth (Boston, Ginn & Co., 1931), by Carl Van Doren (New York, Literary Guild, 1931), and by Cyril Aldred (London, Macmillan, 1935).

For the text of the entire Mummers' Play, as Hardy late in life wrote it down from memory, see *The Play of Saint George*, by Roger S. Loomis, New York, Samuel French, 1928.

For a detailed study of the folklore in this and in other books by Hardy see Ruth A. Firor's *Folkways in Thomas Hardy*, Philadelphia, University of Pennsylvania Press, 1931.

For a discussion of Hardy's use of a time chart in the novel see "Chronology in Hardy's *Return of the Native*," by John P. Emery, in *Publications of the Modern Language Association* (LIV, 618-20), New York, June, 1939. Detailed evidence gathered from other Wessex Novels regarding this aspect of Hardy's workmanship is presented in "Chronology in Thomas Hardy" by Carl J. Weber, also in *P.M.L.A.* (LIII, 314-20), New York, March, 1938.

Hardy once confessed that in Mrs. Yeobright he had drawn something of the character of his own mother. She died April 3, 1904.

THE "LOST" NOVEL

"An Indiscretion in the Life of an Heiress" was reprinted in the *Living Age*, Boston, October 5 and 12, 1878. In 1934 Mrs. Hardy reprinted the story for private circulation only. In 1935 it was published, with an introduction by Carl J. Weber on "Hardy's 'Lost' Novel," with notes and a map, by the Johns Hopkins Press, Baltimore, Maryland. A more detailed examination of the "lost" novel was given by William R. Rutland in *Thomas Hardy: a Study of His Writings and Their Background* (Oxford, Blackwell, 1938), pp. 111-33, where objections are raised to some of the points made in the Johns Hopkins volume. A summary of Rutland's view appeared in *Thomas Hardy*, by William R. Rutland (London, Blackie & Son, 1938), pp. 46-48.

THE TRUMPET-MAJOR

Serialized in *Good Words*, January to December, 1880; published by Smith, Elder & Co., 1880, 3 vols., red cloth.

On January 19, 1882, the New York *Nation* pointed out Hardy's appropriation of Apperley's words in the *Quarterly Review*, and on January 28, 1882, *The Critic* (New York) accused Hardy of plagiarizing in *The Trumpet-Major* from the American author A. B. Longstreet.

For a parallel printing of Hardy's militia-drill scene and the original sketch by O. H. Prince and for a history of the affair see "A Connecticut Yankee in King Alfred's Country," by Carl J. Weber, *The Colophon* (n.s., I:525-35), New York, June, 1936.

For information about the production of Pinero's play *The Squire* in New York theaters (first in October, 1882, and again in 1889, 1890, and 1892), see T. Allston Brown's *History of the New York Stage*, 1903.

On the day Hardy's play opened in London, another dramatization of *Far from the Madding Crowd* ended a two-weeks' run at the Union Square Theater in New York. This American play was the work of A. R. Cazauran, and in it Clara Morris played the part of Bathsheba. For information about this dramatization see Vera Liebert's article in *The Colophon* (n.s., III, 377-82), New York, September, 1938.

The charges of plagiarism did not affect the sale of *The Trumpet-Major* in any way. In October, 1881, a second (one-volume) edition at 6/- was published by Sampson Low, Marston, Searle & Rivington. This was reprinted in 1887, 1890, 1892, and 1893.

A LAODICEAN

Serialized in *Harper's Magazine*, December, 1880, to December, 1881; published by Sampson Low, Marston, Searle & Rivington, 3 vols., slate-green cloth. For details regarding Hardy's unacknowledged borrowing see "Plagiarism and Thomas Hardy," by Carl J. Weber, in *The Colophon* (n.s., II, 433-54), July, 1937.

TWO ON A TOWER

Serialized in the *Atlantic Monthly*, May to December, 1882, the only one of the Wessex Novels to be serialized in America but not in England. Published by Sampson Low, Marston, Searle & Rivington, 1882, 3 vols., green cloth. The same firm reprinted the novel early in 1883; and in May issued a one-volume edition at six shillings; reprinted in 1888, 1890, 1891, and 1893.

THE ROMANTIC ADVENTURES OF A MILKMAID

Of the following ten American imprints, all except the last were published in New York:

1. Harper & Brothers, June 29, 1883; first edition. No. 322 in Franklin Square Library, 10 cts.
2. George Munro, July 14, 1883. No. 1686 in Seaside Library, 10 cts.
3. J. W. Lovell Co., August 7, 1883. No. 157 in Lovell's Library, 20 cts.
4. George Munro, December 15, 1883. No. 139 in Seaside Library, Pocket Edition, 20 cts.
5. Norman L. Munro; no date; probably late in 1883. No. 30 in Munro's Library, 10 cts.
6. George Munro, January 25, 1884. A reprint of the December issue.
7. F. M. Lupton, 1886. No. 80 in Leisure Hour Library, 3 cts.
8. George Munro's Sons, 1896. No. 451 in Majestic Series, 25 cts.
9. George Munro's Sons (?1896). No. 83 in Library of Popular Novels, 50 cts.
10. Max Stein & Co., Chicago (?1911).

In March, 1912, the manuscript of this story was bought by Pierpont Morgan; it is now in the Morgan Library in New York City. In 1913 the story was "collected" in *A Changed Man*, published by Harpers.

THE MAYOR OF CASTERBRIDGE

Serialized in *The Graphic*, London, January to May, 1886; published by Smith, Elder & Co., 1886, 2 vols., blue cloth. Second edition by Sampson Low, Marston, Searle & Rivington, 1887, one volume, red cloth.

Some of the important features of this novel are treated in an excellent text edition, prepared by Ernest F. Amy, published in 1933 by Thomas Nelson & Sons, New York.

For a detailed account of the Lowell-Hawthorne-Hardy-Gosse episode see "Lowell's 'Dead Rat in the Wall,' " by Carl J. Weber, in the *New England Quarterly* (IX, 468-72, 686-88), Boston, September and December, 1936.

For a detailed account of Hardy's suppression of nearly a chapter in the novel and of Rebekah Owen's success in getting him to put it back see "The Restoration of Hardy's Starved Goldfinch," *Publications of the Modern Language Association* (LV), New York, 1940. Further information about the Owen sisters, Rebekah and Catharine, and their long friendship with Hardy and their interest in and connection with his novels may be found in *Rebekah Owen and Thomas Hardy*, by Carl J. Weber, Colby College Monograph No. 8, Waterville, Maine, 1939. The change in Henchard's name is an example of Hardy's tentative naming of his characters and places. Further information about this matter may be found in an article based on a study of the author's manuscripts, "The Manuscript Names of Hardy's Characters," by Carl J. Weber, in the *Review of English Studies* (X, 456-59), London, October, 1934.

THE WOODLANDERS

Serialized in *Macmillan's Magazine*, London, May, 1886, to April, 1887. Published by Macmillan & Co., 1887, 3 vols., green cloth. Second edition by the same firm, 1887, one volume, red pebbled cloth.

Rebekah Owen's interesting report of Hardy's surprising remarks about *The Woodlanders* has been presented in detail in an article, "Hardy and *The Woodlanders*," by Carl J. Weber, in the *Review of English Studies* (XV, 330-33), London, July, 1939. Hardy is reported as saying that Grace Melbury never interested him much. "He was provoked with her all along."

A detailed account of "Hardy's 'Song in *The Woodlanders*' " was given by Carl J. Weber, in *ELH, a Journal of English Literary History* (II, 242-45), Baltimore, Maryland, November, 1935.

The Woodlanders offers an interesting illustration of the publishing situation in America in 1887. At the very time that Macmillan was offering the novel to English readers in three volumes at a price of 31/6 ($7.50), Harpers offered American readers the same story in a cloth-bound single volume for seventy-five cents. Being fully aware of the results of the lack of international copyright protection, Harpers were not satisfied with this bargain offer, and on March 25, 1887, they published the novel for twenty cents as No. 572 in their "Franklin Square Library." On April 16 they announced a one-volume edition in boards. But before the year was over, three unauthorized editions were added to the list. George Munro issued *The Woodlanders* as No. 957 in his "Seaside Library"—"a $1.50 Book for 10 Cents"; Norman L. Munro did the same, as No. 725 in "Munro's Library"; and the J. W. Lovell Company issued *The Woodlanders* as No. 956 in "Lovell's Library." Thus there were six American editions in 1887, from half of which Hardy received nothing and from the other half very little. But even these six did not exhaust the power of Hardy's name to attract piratical activity. During the succeeding decade A. L. Burt & Co. published *The Woodlanders* anew as No. 109 of "The Manhattan Library"; and in Chicago, Rand McNally issued the novel as No. 235 of the "Globe Library." This plethora of editions at ten, twenty, and twenty-five cents makes it obvious why Henry Holt had not been eager to continue as Hardy's publisher. After fourteen years of activity of making him known to American readers, Holt gave up the contest. The history of Hardy's novels in the United States thus differs greatly from their history in England. An extensive examination of the cause of this situation in America and a detailed bibliography of the numerous imprints under which the Wessex writings have gained American publication have been presented in "Thomas Hardy in America," by Carl J. Weber, in *The Colophon* (n.s., III, 383-405; n.g.s., I, 95-96), New York, September, 1938, and March, 1939.

In 1932 *The Woodlanders* was translated by Antoinette Six into French under the title *Les Forestiers*.

TESS OF THE D'URBERVILLES

Serialized in *The Graphic*, London, July to December, 1891; published by J. R. Osgood, McIlvaine & Co., 1891, 3 vols., tan cloth; one-volume edition by the same firm, September, 1892.

In preparing a time chart for his guidance in writing the novel Hardy began by fixing his characters definitely in time.

1860	Alec D'Urberville born.	1875	Abraham Durbeyfield born.
1861	Angel Clare born.	1877	Hope Durbeyfield born.
1867	Tess born in November.	1879	Modesty Durbeyfield born.
1868	A Durbeyfield baby born and died.	1881	Angel Clare decides to "do without Cambridge."
1869	Another Durbeyfield baby born and died.	1883	Another Durbeyfield baby born.
1871	Elizabeth-Louisa born in December.		

Thus the actors are all ready for the curtain to rise in 1884. Hardy, writing in 1889, planned the action to fall within the preceding five years. If arranged, for convenience, in the five-act divisional scheme of a Shakespearean play, the calendar would appear as follows:

Act I. The Betrayal, 1884.

May 30: John Durbeyfield learns that he is "Sir John."

May 31: Death of Prince, the horse.

June 1: Tess, now sixteen, visits Trantridge.
June 9: Alec calls at Marnhull.
June 15: Tess moves to Trantridge.
September 27: The seduction on The Chase.
October 26: Tess returns home.

June 1885: "Sorrow" is born.
August 1885: The baby dies and is buried.

Act II. Courtship and Marriage, 1887.
May: Tess goes to Talbothays dairy.
August: The first embrace.
November 30: The wedding day is set.
December 24: Tess and Angel go shopping in Dorchester.
December 31: The marriage; the ride to Wool.

January 1, 1888: The estrangement.
January 2: The sleep walking.
January 3: The separation; Tess returns home.
January 21: Clare sails for Brazil.

Act III. The Forsaken Wife, 1888.
November: Tess arrives at Flintcomb-Ash.
December 30: Tess walks to Beaminster, meets Alec.
March 10, 1889: John Durbeyfield dies; Tess returns home.

Act IV. Despair and Murder, 1889.
April 6: The Durbeyfields have to leave Marnhull.
May: Clare returns from Brazil, finds Tess at Bournemouth.

Act V. "Justice," 1889.
May 24: Tess and Angel hide at Bramshurst Court.
May 31: They flee through Salisbury at night.
June 1: Tess is arrested at Stonehenge, just five years to a day since she
set out to visit Trantridge.
July: Tess is executed at Winchester; age 21. Sir Frederick Pollock wrote
Hardy that no jury would have convicted Tess.

Hardy thus planned to have the curtain fall at the end of his drama in the
very month in which he began to write.

Details regarding the publication of this novel and its bibliographical
history are supplied in the Harper's Modern Classics edition, New York,
1935, edited by Carl J. Weber. Numerous critical observations and judg-
ments are therein assembled. This novel has never received the editorial
attention given Hardy's other works, and the annotation just referred to

remains the only edited *Tess* ever published. Next year will mark the fiftieth anniversary of the first appearance of this novel.

JUDE THE OBSCURE

Began as "The Simpletons" in *Harper's Magazine*, December, 1894; continued (serialized) as "Hearts Insurgent," January to December, 1895; published by Osgood, McIlvaine & Co., 1896, 1 vol., blue-green cloth. This was the first time a first edition of one of the Wessex Novels appeared in one volume.

THE WELL-BELOVED

Serialized in the *Illustrated London News*, October to December, 1892; published by Osgood, McIlvaine & Co., 1897, 1 vol., blue-green cloth.

8. THE SHORT STORIES OF THOMAS HARDY
(cf. p. 81)

The titles in the following list are arranged not in the order in which they appeared in the four books into which Hardy collected them, since that order is often misleading (for instance, one of the earliest stories, "What the Shepherd Saw," 1881, was not collected until Hardy published his very last prose volume in 1913), but in the order of serial publication or of composition. Of these forty-four stories all except those numbered 1, 2, 10, 28, 35, 37, and 44 were published in one posthumous volume, *The Short Stories of Thomas Hardy,* London, Macmillan, 1928; pp. 1078.

Title	Magazine or Newspaper in Which the Story First Appeared	Title of Book in Which the Story Was Collected
1. "Destiny and a Blue Cloak"	New York *Times*, Oct. 4, 1874	Never reprinted by Hardy; collected posthumously in *Revenge Is Sweet*, 1940
2. "An Indiscretion in the Life of an Heiress"	*New Quarterly Magazine,* July, 1878	Privately printed by Mrs. Hardy in 1934; first published separately by the Johns Hopkins Press, 1935
3. "The Distracted Young Preacher"	*New Quarterly Magazine,* April, 1879	*Wessex Tales,* 1888
4. "Fellow-Townsmen"	*New Quarterly Magazine,* April, 1880	*Wessex Tales,* 1888

Title	Magazine or Newspaper in Which the Story First Appeared	Title of Book in Which the Story Was Collected
5. "What the Shepherd Saw"	*Illus. London News,* Christmas, 1881	*A Changed Man,* 1913
6. "The Honorable Laura"	Unidentified English newspaper	*A Group of Noble Dames,* 1891
7. "A Tradition of Eighteen Hundred and Four"	Written about Christmas, 1882; magazine publication uncertain	*Life's Little Ironies,* 1894; transferred to *Wessex Tales* in 1912
8. "The Three Strangers"	*Longman's Magazine,* March, 1883	*Wessex Tales,* 1888
9. "The Romantic Adventures of a Milkmaid"	*The Graphic,* June, 1883	*A Changed Man,* 1913
10. "Our Exploits at West Poley"	Advertised in *Youth's Companion,* Nov. 22, 1883; never printed	Not published
11. "The Duchess of Hamptonshire"	*The Independent,* Feb. 7, 1884	*A Group of Noble Dames,* 1891
12. "Interlopers at the Knap"	*English Illustrated Magazine,* May 1884	*Wessex Tales,* 1888
13. "A Tryst at an Ancient Earthwork"	*Detroit Post,* March 15, 1885	*A Changed Man,* 1913
14. "A Mere Interlude"	*Bolton Weekly Journal,* Oct. 17, 1885	*A Changed Man,* 1913
15. "Alicia's Diary"	*Bolton Weekly Journal,* Oct. 15, 1887	*A Changed Man,* 1913
16. "The Withered Arm"	*Blackwood's Magazine,* Jan., 1888	*Wessex Tales,* 1888
17. "The Waiting Supper"	*Murray's Magazine,* Jan.-Feb., 1888	*A Changed Man,* 1913
18. "A Tragedy of Two Ambitions"	*Universal Magazine,* Dec., 1888	*Life's Little Ironies,* 1894
19. "The First Countess of Wessex"	*Harper's Magazine,* Dec., 1889	*A Group of Noble Dames,* 1891

Title	Magazine or Newspaper in Which the Story First Appeared	Title of Book in Which the Story Was Collected
20. "The Lady Penelope"	*Longman's Magazine*, Jan., 1890	*A Group of Noble Dames*, 1891
21. "The Melancholy Hussar"	*Three Notable Stories* (book), 1890; no magazine publication	*Life's Little Ironies*, 1894; transferred to *Wessex Tales* in 1912
22. "Barbara of the House of Grebe"	*The Graphic*, Christmas, 1890	*A Group of Noble Dames*, 1891
23. "The Marchioness of Stonehenge"	*The Graphic*, Christmas, 1890	*A Group of Noble Dames*, 1891
24. "Lady Mottisfont"	*The Graphic*, Christmas, 1890	*A Group of Noble Dames*, 1891
25. "The Lady Icenway"	*The Graphic*, Christmas, 1890	*A Group of Noble Dames*, 1891
26. "Squire Petrick's Lady"	*The Graphic*, Christmas, 1890	*A Group of Noble Dames*, 1891
27. "Anna, Lady Bixby"	*The Graphic*, Christmas, 1890	*A Group of Noble Dames*, 1891
28. "The Doctor's Legend"	*The Independent*, March 26, 1891	Never reprinted by Hardy, collected posthumously in *Revenge Is Sweet*, 1940
29. "Wessex Folk" (title later changed to "A Few Crusted Characters")	*Harper's Magazine*, March-June, 1891	*Life's Little Ironies*, 1894
30. "For Conscience Sake"	*Fortnightly Review*, March, 1891	*Life's Little Ironies*, 1894
31. "To Please His Wife"	*Black and White*, June 27, 1891	*Life's Little Ironies*, 1894
32. "On the Western Circuit" (originally called "The Writer of the Letters")	*English Illustrated Magazine*, Dec., 1891	*Life's Little Ironies*, 1894
33. "The Son's Veto"	*Illustrated London News*, Christmas, 1891	*Life's Little Ironies*, 1894

Title	Magazine or Newspaper in Which the Story First Appeared	Title of Book in Which the Story Was Collected
34. "Master John Horseleigh, Knight"	McClure's Magazine, July, 1893	A Changed Man, 1913
35. "The Intruder"	Dorset County Chronicle, Dec. 25, 1890	Not collected by Hardy; published separately, Fairfield, Maine, 1938
36. "The Fiddler of the Reels"	Scribner's Magazine, May, 1893	Life's Little Ironies, 1894
37. "The Spectre of the Real" (with Florence Henniker)	To-Day, March, 1894	In Scarlet and Gray, 1896
38. "An Imaginative Woman"	Pall Mall Magazine, April, 1894	Wessex Tales, 3d ed., 1896; transferred to Life's Little Ironies in 1912
39. "A Committee Man of 'The Terror'"	Illustrated London News, Christmas, 1896	A Changed Man, 1913
40. "The Duke's Reappearance"	Saturday Review, Dec. 14, 1896	A Changed Man, 1913
41. "The Grave by the Handpost"	St. James's Budget, Christmas, 1897	A Changed Man, 1913
42. "A Changed Man"	The Sphere, April 21, 1900	A Changed Man, 1913
43. "Enter a Dragoon"	Harper's Magazine, Dec., 1900	A Changed Man, 1913
44. "Old Mrs. Chundle"	Ladies' Home Journal, Feb., 1929	Published separately, New York, 1929

9. MRS. HARDY'S PHILOSOPHY

The easiest way to give the reader some conception of Mrs. Emma Hardy's "philosophy and mysticism" (cf. p. 163) is to quote a few passages from her little-known book, *Spaces* (Dorchester, Cornhill Press, 1912), which offers the reader "an exposition of Great Truths by a new treatment." The book is divided into four parts.

Part 1 deals with "The High Delights of Heaven." In Heaven, the reader is assured, "pleasures will be in every way exhilarating and in full measure. No vice, lust, evil act, or evil desires of any kind . . . Lightness of body and ease of locomotion—whether by wings or otherwise—no weight, no trouble of the flesh; the same body, yet transfigured as Christ's—lovely to behold, with an effulgent light shining in Heaven's translucent atmosphere . . . However, Heaven will not be the same for all saved ones. Those who have accepted late . . . will have happiness made for them of the kind they most like, more material than those who have had life-long communication with God on earth.'

Part 2 is about "The Acceptors and Non-Acceptors." It begins with an account of the revolt of the angels "and the casting out of heaven" and proceeds to explain the "plan of Salvation prepared to rescue many . . . from Satan's power in the end of time." Mrs. Hardy then continues: "We are now either *acceptors* or *non-acceptors* of His Salvation . . . If we are non-acceptors then we remain Satan's followers,—unredeemable, revolted still—with evil natures retained . . . Christ's . . . sacrifice for offenders can only be of use if *accepted* . . . through prayer . . . , prayer being as it may be said, a kind of electrical communication with God our Creator."

Part 3 is about Hell; it is entitled "New Element of Fire." The author has a vivid idea of what is going to happen at 4 A.M. on the Last Day. She writes: "Fires of Hell will not resemble fire here on earth, nor cause the same kind of misery and pain, precisely, for it will be our element to breathe in or live in, somehow . . . The fire of Hell keeps alive in pain and wretchedness all who come into it . . . The doomed, probably, *certainly* are not in hell immediately after death as their bodies are not changed, and soul and body must go together at last . . . The Last Day must not be considered as literally a day of twenty-four hours more or less, but as any prolongation . . . And then will occur the general darkening of the sun, moon, and stars by blackest clouds, . . . when suddenly a spot of light will appear in the East at 4 o'clock A.M. according to western time—and dark night of Eastern time or about that hour, varying at distances . . . And whilst bodies will be seen rising and floating in the phosphorescent great oceans, . . . the graveyards will be crowded with strange moving figures seen dimly in the darkness . . . Peoples everywhere will prostrate themselves, the electric lights of the world will shine forth again, not *lit* by mortal hands which will have failed to set them aglow through the darkness."

Part 4 is entitled "Retrospect."

10. HARDY'S DEBT TO ROBERT BROWNING

Hardy's letter (cf. p. 190) was printed by T. J. Wise in *A Browning Library*, 1929, p. 118. There Wise incorrectly gave the date as March 3, and he was also in error in printing "leading" for "literary" in the first sentence of the letter.

A detailed criticism of Hardy's poetry (and of his novels) may be found in *Thomas Hardy*, By H. C. Duffin, University of Manchester, 3d ed., 1937. In this work Duffin declares: "A closer analogy may indeed be drawn between Hardy and Browning than with any other among the poets."

The subsequent history of Hardy's birthday gift to Browning and of the letter that was sent with the books has been told in a semicentennial notice, "Pessimist to Optimist," by Carl J. Weber, in the *Saturday Review of Literature*, New York, May 7, 1938, p. 21.

Further evidence of Hardy's acknowledgment of his indebtedness to Browning is given in the pages that follow. This evidence is arranged chronologically under the titles of Browning's poems. The list dates from almost the very beginning of Hardy's residence in London. In this list references to Hardy's novels are by chapters or by parts and chapters in case two numbers are given.

SORDELLO

In 1863 Browning reprinted *Sordello*, adding a Dedication from which Hardy quoted three times.

"Incidents in the development of a soul: little else is worth study:" this Hardy wrote into his notebook on December 13, 1889, on learning of Browning's death. This same passage is echoed in Hardy's remarks on steps "towards the soul's betterment" in the "Apology" prefixed to *Late Lyrics*.

"My own faults of expression were many; but with care . . ."; this Hardy copied into his notes in November, 1917.

PIPPA PASSES

In *Tess of the D'Urbervilles* (37) Hardy quoted two lines from Pippa's well-known song. Hardy quoted from memory and thought the two lines were only one line. He wrote that Angel Clare "quoted the line of the poet in a peculiar tone of his own." A year later Hardy revised the sentence, to read: he "quoted the line of the poet, with a few improvements of his own." In 1912, while revising *Tess* for the definitive edition, the passage was once more emended, to read: "quoted a line from a poet, with peculiar emendations of his own."

HOW THEY BROUGHT THE GOOD NEWS FROM GHENT TO AIX

Hardy imitated the theme, mood, words, and meter of this poem in "My Cicely." Using the same rapid anapestic rhythm, the poem describes how

"I mounted a steed in the dawning" in London, and "made for the ancient West Highway." A decade after the publication of the poem Hardy wrote to a public reader who was planning a Hardy program: "The poem *My Cicely* would afford a capital panoramic treatment of the Great Western Road from London to Exeter, accompanied by your recitation of the journey with the galloping movement of the verses."

THE LABORATORY

The idea of a young girl, planning to make use of poison, speaking a monologue, is used by Hardy in "The Chapel-Organist." Both poems use the anapestic rhythm.

CRISTINA

The incident and its result,

"She should never have looked at me
If she meant I should not love her! . . .
What? To fix me thus meant nothing?"

are reproduced in Hardy's poem "A Church Romance," where

"her sight
Swept the west gallery and caught its row
Of music-men . . .
. . . said: 'I claim thee as my own forthright!' "

Similarly the concept of "moments when the spirit's true endowment stands out plainly" and the statement that "in some such moment Mine and her souls rushed together" are reproduced in Hardy's "At Castle Boterel":

"It filled but a minute. But was there ever
A time of such quality . . ."

A WOMAN'S LAST WORD

The short lines, the feminine rhymes of the odd-numbered lines, the masculine rhymes of the even-numbered ones, the quatrain divisions, are all reproduced in Hardy's poem "The Pine Planters." In addition to these metrical echoes, Browning's theme

"What so wild as words are?
I and thou
In debate, as birds are,
Hawk on bough,"

is echoed in Hardy's lines

> "I have helped him so many,
> So many days,
> But never win any
> Small word of praise!"

LOVE AMONG THE RUINS

The unusual alternation of pentameter with initially truncated dimeter lines, which is one of the marked features of this poem, is reproduced in *The Dynasts*:

> "Ere the concussion hurtle, draw abreast
> Of the sea
> Where Nelson's hulls are rising from the west
> Silently."

The rhyme scheme here employed by Hardy is that of another equally unusual pentameter-and-dimeter alternation—found in Browning's "A Grammarian's Funeral."

SAUL

One of Hardy's most frequently repeated ideas, that of man's moral superiority to an indifferent god, is found in David's thought in this poem. "Man with his struggling consciousness seems to have an unhappy superiority to the Higher Powers. It is almost parallel to Browning's suggestion in *Saul*. There David, with his power of love, feels that in this respect man is somehow superior to his Creator."—H. M. Margoliouth.

Hardy expresses this idea in "Nature's Questioning," "God-Forgotten," in *The Dynasts*, and particularly in "God's Education":

> "Said I: 'We call that cruelty.'
> He mused: 'The thought is new to me.' "

BY THE FIRESIDE

Of the two lines (191-192) which Tennyson so much admired Hardy quotes one in *Tess of the D'Urbervilles* (35). Line 248 is quoted in *Jude the Obscure* (2,1). The thought that

> "Had she willed it, still had stood the screen
> So slight, so sure, 'twixt my love and her"

is echoed in Hardy's poem "At the Word 'Farewell' ":

> "Even then the scale might have been turned
> Against love by a feather."

ANY WIFE TO ANY HUSBAND

Lines 43-97 ("We meet and part . . . Because thou once hast loved me . . . Only why . . . ?") are possibly echoed in Hardy's "On the Departure Platform," with its similar concern with the transitory nature of human happiness, "and why . . . ? why, I cannot tell!"

TWO IN THE CAMPAGNA

The thought of lines 1-37,

"I wonder do you feel to-day . . .
I would that you were all to me,
You that are just so much, no more,"

is echoed in Hardy's poem "Between Us Now":—

"Between us now and here— . . .
Is your heart far away,
Or with mine beating."

MEMORABILIA

The "moulted feather" which Browning "picked up on the heather" and "put inside his breast" in his poem about Shelley has a counterpart in Hardy's poem "Shelley's Skylark," with its lines about "a little ball of feather" which "we will lay safe."

IN A YEAR

Browning's "Never any more . . . need I hope to see his face As before" is echoed in Hardy's "On the Departure Platform": ". . . never as then! . . . nought happens twice thus."

INSTANS TYRANNUS

Line 53 is quoted in "An Indiscretion in the Life of an Heiress" (1,5).

THE LAST RIDE TOGETHER

Line 53 is quoted in the General Preface which Hardy wrote in October, 1911.

The thought of lines 56-59, beginning

"What hand and brain went ever paired?
What heart alike conceived and dared?"

is expressed in Hardy's "The Temporary the All," with its similar lament, "lo, me!" about the inability of hand to keep up with brain.

A GRAMMARIAN'S FUNERAL

The lines about the high man and the low man, quoted on page 194, were paraphrased by Hardy, in his comment on the strong man and the weak man, quoted on page 204.

Rhyme and metrical echoes from this poem are to be heard in *The Dynasts:* see above, p. 272.

THE STATUE AND THE BUST

This was Hardy's favorite among Browning's poems. He quoted from it seven times:

Lines 51-53 in *Desperate Remedies* (3,2).

Line 138 in "An Indiscretion" (1,8).

Lines 160-62 in *Desperate Remedies* (13,4) and again in "The Waiting Supper" (4).

Lines 214-18 in *Far From the Madding Crowd* (49).

Lines 222-23 in *Jude the Obscure* (4,5).

Line 246 in *The Woodlanders* (46).

In 1887 Hardy visited the scene of this poem in Florence. In May of the same year he told Browning of his visit and learned from the poet that he had "invented" the bust.

In his poem "George Meredith" Hardy used the *terza rima* of "The Statue and the Bust"—*aba bcb cdc*, and so forth.

CHILDE ROLAND TO THE DARK TOWER CAME

In a letter written on January 31, 1904, Hardy stated that a scene in one of Edmund Gosse's books "takes a sad and curious hold upon the imagination, not unlike that of Childe Roland's Dark Tower."

EASTER-DAY

"How very hard it is to be a Christian!" Browning's thought that "the whole or chief of difficulties is belief" (lines 29-30) is echoed in Hardy's poem "The Impercipient."

KARSHISH

This poem about the Nazarene who

> "Perished in a tumult many years ago,
> Accused . . . of . . . rebellion"

is paralleled, both in subject matter and in the rationalizing manner and scientific tone of its presentation, by Hardy's "Panthera" with its story

"how at Nazareth long before . . .
He . . . waked sedition long among the Jews
With sundry other incitements to misrule."

THE WORST OF IT

This poem, or at least lines 3 and 4, Hardy knew by heart, and quoted them in a letter written to Miss Gilder on July 16, 1896.

TOO LATE

Line 100 is quoted in *Jude the Obscure* (3,4), and line 119 in a later chapter (6,1) of the same novel.

ABT VOGLER

The musician's conception, as expressed in lines 81-84:

"—what is our failure here but a triumph's evidence
For the fullness of the days? Have we withered or agonized? . . .
Why rushed the discords in but that harmony should be prized?"

is echoed in Part III of *The Dynasts*:

"Though seers do not as yet explain
Why Suffering sobs to Thee in vain,
We hold that Thy unscanted scope
Affords a food for final Hope."

The anapestic meter of "Abt Vogler," Browning's poem about an organist, is used by Hardy in *his* poem "The Chapel-Organist." On May 14, 1920, Hardy visited Exeter Cathedral, and after listening to the organ-playing, quoted lines 2-3 of Browning's poem.

RABBI BEN EZRA

This poem stood second only to "The Statue and the Bust" in the list of Hardy's favorites among Browning's poems.

In *Two on a Tower* (25) and again in *Tess of the D'Urbervilles* (49) Hardy paraphrased the lines (133-50)

"Not on the vulgar mass
Called 'work' must sentence pass,
Things done . . .
But . . .
All purposes unsure . . .
This, I was worth to God."

In a letter written on January 17, 1883, he similarly paraphrased lines 127-32, ending: "Whom shall my soul believe?" Hardy asked: "Which am I to believe?"

In a late poem "The Child and the Sage," he similarly refuses to accept the world's judgment. And just as Browning had declared that "The best is yet to be," so Hardy, in this poem, was always looking for and expecting something better than a world of pain. S. P. B. Mais declares: "This it is to be an optimist."

On the night before he died Hardy asked to have the whole of "Rabbi Ben Ezra" read aloud.

CALIBAN

The thought of lines 84-86 and the passage that follows them,

"If his leg snapped, brittle clay,
And he lay stupid-like,—why, I should laugh,"

is repeated in Hardy's early poem "Hap":

"Know that thy sorrow is my ecstasy,
That thy love's loss is my hate's profiting."

EPILOGUE TO ASOLANDO

On January 16, 1918, Hardy recorded in his notebook his belief that Browning's line "Never dreamed though right were worsted wrong would triumph" indicated "a lucky dreamlessness" on Browning's part.

The material here presented must not be taken to indicate that in all of his poetic activity or even in much of it Hardy was always a conscious imitator of Browning. What it does indicate is that for sixty-five years, from 1863 to 1928, Hardy was a serious reader of Browning. Not only did lines from the elder poet lodge in the retentive memory of the younger, but the unconscious imitation of sounds, rhythms, themes, and attitudes was thereby made possible.

11. HARDY'S NAPOLEONIC LIBRARY

Among the works in English are Archibald Alison's *History of Europe, 1789-1815*, E. P. Brenton's *Naval History of Great Britain*, William Siborne's *The Waterloo Campaign*, W. F. P. Napier's history of the Peninsula War, Beatty's narrative of the death of Nelson, Stanhope's *Life of William Pitt*, Elliott's *Life of Wellington*, Fitzgerald's *Life of George IV*, and J. S. Memes's *Memoirs of the Empress Josephine*.

Among the French books acquired by Hardy were A. Thiers's *Histoire du Consulat et de l'Empire*, together with an English translation of this work by D. Forbes Campbell, M. Capefigue's *L'Europe pendant le Consulat et l'Empire*, Lanfrey's *Histoire de Napoleon*, Coquelle's *Napoleon et l'Angleterre*, De Bourrienne's *Memoires de Napoleon*, and Mery's *Trafalgar*.

12. THE HARDY PLAYS

Following is a list of the Hardy Plays given, usually in November, by the Dorchester Debating and Dramatic Society. Most of the plays were adapted from the Wessex Novels by A. H. Evans, but the last two on the list were Hardy's own work.

1908 "The Trumpet-Major," November 18-19
1909 "Far from the Madding Crowd," November 17-18
1910 "The Mellstock Quire" (from *Under the Greenwood Tree*), November 16-17
1911 "The Three Wayfarers" and "The Distracted Preacher," November 15-16
1912 "The Trumpet-Major," November 27-28
1913 "The Woodlanders," November 19-20
1916 Wessex Scenes from *The Dynasts*, December 6-7
1918 "The Mellstock Quire," January 31
1920 "The Return of the Native," November 17-18
1922 "A Desperate Remedy," November 15-17
1923 "The Famous Tragedy of the Queen of Cornwall," November 28-30
1924 "Tess of the D'Urbervilles," November 26-29

13. HARDY'S MANUSCRIPTS

Some of Hardy's manuscripts were destroyed. The whereabouts of others are not known. The following chronological list is fairly complete.

Manuscript	*Present Possessor*
1. Under the Greenwood Tree	Dorset County Museum, Dorchester
2. A Pair of Blue Eyes	Howard Bliss
3. Far from the Madding Crowd	A. Edward Newton
4. The Hand of Ethelberta	Dorset County Museum
5. The Return of the Native	University College Library, Dublin, Ireland
6. The Trumpet-Major	Windsor Castle Library

Manuscript	*Present Possessor*
7. The Romantic Adventures of a Milkmaid	Pierpont Morgan Library, New York
8. The Mayor of Casterbridge	Dorset County Museum
9. The Three Strangers	Sir Sydney Cockerell
10. The Woodlanders	Dorset County Museum
11. A Tragedy of Two Ambitions	John Rylands Library, Manchester
12. The Melancholy Hussar	Huntington Library, California
13. Emmeline	Pierpont Morgan Library
14. A Group of Noble Dames	Library of Congress, Washington
15. The Doctor's Legend	Howard Bliss
16. Tess of the D'Urbervilles	British Museum, London
17. A Committee Man of "The Terror"	Huntington Library
18. Jude the Obscure	Fitzwilliam Museum, Cambridge
19. Wessex Poems	Birmingham Art Gallery, Birmingham, England
20. Poems of the Past and the Present	Bodleian Library, Oxford
21. A Sunday Morning Tragedy	Huntington Library
22. The Tramp's Tragedy	Howard Bliss
23. The Dynasts	British Museum
24. The Duke's Reappearance	Edward Clodd
25. Time's Laughingstocks	Fitzwilliam Museum
26. Night in a Suburb	Howard Bliss
27. The Abbey Mason	Pierpont Morgan Library
28. Satires . . . Lyrics and Reveries	Dorset County Museum
29. Moments of Vision	Magdalene College Library, Cambridge, England
30. At a House in Hampstead	British Museum
31. And There Was a Great Calm	British Museum
32. Late Lyrics and Earlier	Dorset County Museum
33. Waiting Both	Paul Lemperly estate
34. The Queen of Cornwall	Dorset County Museum
35. Human Shows	Yale University Library, New Haven, Conn.
36. Winter Words	Queen's College Library, Oxford, England

INDEX

INDEX

174; perception of social disparity between himself and wife, 158; wanted children, 160; religious and philosophical views make intellectual sympathy with wife impossible, 163; society belles mere portraits, 165; crisis presented by *Jude*, 166 f.; visit to Windsor Castle, 169; genuine affection, 172; after death of wife, 172, 220; memorial tablet to her, *text*, 174; happiness in his marriage to Florence Dugdale, 218, 221, 225; her services before their marriage, 219; volume of verse inscribed to second wife, 221

—— the novelist: specific with regard to geography and topography, 26, 45, 65, 109, 176; expert knowledge of painters, 26, 236; annoying habit of referring to them, 27; plays and dramatizations of his works, 27, 82, 88, 195 ff., 206, 222 ff., 277; drawings by, 27, 86, 186, 222; tendency to quote, 29, 65, 188; debt to Shakespeare, 30, 187, 193, 246-257; descriptions of himself at end of London life, 32, 33; autobiographical material in writings, 33, 43, 87, 167 ff., 207, 209; transferred much of self into character of Springrove, 33, 43; turns to fiction, 34; never wanted to write novels, 34, 131, 146, 152; first novels, 32-46, 52-59; method of teaching himself how to write, 36-38; satire on London society, 38, 58; first novel published, 44; anonymous publications, 44, 52, 56, 60; chronological precision, time charts, 45, 63, 72, 109, 125; never objected to repetition, 46; power of description, 46, 59, 66; heroines, 46, 53, 54, 64, 74, 75, 82, 86, 96, 112, 132; rustic characters, 46, 52, 58, 64, 65, 178; relations with, and indebtedness to, Browning, 50, 187-193, 194, 205, 216, 269-76; never again had to seek out publisher, 52; compared with George Eliot, 52, 60; undertone of bitterness in writings, 53, 65; begins the practice of writing for magazines, 55; gives up architecture for authorship, 56; first use of his name on novels, 56; works published in America, 56, 61, 73, 74, 81, 86, 95, 104, 131, 134, 135,

148; use of his courtship experiences, 57; overemphasis upon accident and coincidence, 57, 62; characterization, 58, 63, 64, 68, 74, 95, 101, 131; end of anonymous publication, 60; first great success, 60-66; tones down novels for benefit of magazine readers, 61, 73, 146; having learned how to construct plot uses device over and over, 62; troubled by denunciations of his writings, 63, 92, 131, 148, 153; compared favorably with Shakespeare, 64, 76, 184; first use of "Wessex," terminology for, 65; after shifting of residence settles down in Dorchester, 67, 98; sensitiveness to criticism, 68, 105, 148, 152; need for philosophical motif leads to artistic formula, 70; preparation of Wessex map, 71, 176, 181; his most nearly perfect work of art, 73; praise of Egdon Heath most magnificent piece of prose writing, 74, 228; most powerful climax, 75; service as antiquarian and historian, 77, 201; short stories, 78-84, 115, 116, 129, 135, 176, 177, 227, 265-68; success as a writer of short stories, 80; compared with Poe and Maupassant, 84; works about Napoleonic era, 84 ff., 195 ff.; copies description from Gifford's *History*, resulting difficulties, 85, 86, 92; novel dictated during long illness his poorest, 87; controversy over coincidences between Pinero's play and his, 89 ff.; writes astronomical novel, 94; melancholy, 96, 170, 230; philosophy, 96, 163, 203, 209, 213; interest in ancient landmarks, 99; importance of leisure and careful revision, 99; minor literary activities, essays and articles, 99, 236; first novel to deal with townspeople and center drama in one person, 100; most powerful piece of portraiture, 101, 131; had warranty in real life for all of his characters, 102; extreme sensitiveness to criticism, 105; revolt against fundamental conditions of existence frankly expressed in novels, 109; bitter quarrel with society for its attitude toward sex relationships, 109; writes novel on Fridays, considers it his best, 111; editors

ADDENDA AND CORRIGENDA

Page 3, line 1: for Roland, read Rowland

Page 14, line 20: for Hick's, read Hicks's

Page 55, line 23: for *Tinsley's*, read *Tinsleys'*

Page 95, lines 7-11: for "he had the manuscript . . . magazine", read:

he had the first installment of *Two on a Tower* ready to mail across the ocean by February 1882, and in the May number of the *Atlantic Monthly* this astronomical story began its eight-months' run.
   (Omit the sentence beginning "It was the first . . .")

Page 130, 5th line from bottom: for Humphrey, read Humphry

Page 140, line 1: for to, read of

Page 163, line 21: for Frederick, read Frederic

Page 188, line 8: for man-, read maw-

Page 212, line 10: for anniversity, read anniversary

Page 220, line 26: for 1896, read 1893

Page 223, line 13: cancel the paragraph beginning "The possibilities . . ."
         to the bottom of the page, and substitute:

   On January 2, 1896, Hardy wrote to William Archer, "I have finished the *Tess* play," and to Henry Arthur Jones he wrote: "Fancy me getting up a play!" Hardy eventually gave Forbes-Robinson permission to produce the work, with Mrs. Patrick Campbell in the role of Tess, provided the production took place within a limited time. But when Forbes-Robertson dilly-dallied and raised questions about a revision of the text, Hardy (in August 1896) withdrew his permission. After this collapse of his plans for a London performance, Hardy gave his New York publishers, the Harpers, permission to arrange for an independent American dramatic adaptation of the novel. As a result, Lorimer Stoddard, the thirty-two-year-old son of Richard Henry Stoddard, wrote a play in five days—one that opened at the Fifth Avenue Theatre in New York on March 2, 1897, with Mrs. Minnie Maddern Fiske as Tess. To protect his copyright in this version, Hardy himself was called to finance what he called a "copyright performance" at the St. James Theatre in London. There the Stoddard play was read on the same day as the American opening. "It is a farce," Hardy wryly told his wife, "which will cost me more than twenty pounds," and on March 15, 1897, he again wrote to Henry Arthur Jones: "I am in a hopeless fog on the matter." Thus, once again, the divinity that shapes our ends seemed determined to frustrate Hardy's theatrical plans. His own dramatization of *Tess* had been

Page 225, seven lines from the bottom: for "in an LL.D gown", read "with an LL.D. hood."

Page 242, line 10: for Aeniad, read Aeneid

Page 243, line 14: for "the apocryphal Gospels", read *The Apocryphal Gospels* by Benjamin Harris Cowper

Page 246, line 20: for Humphrey, read Humphry

Page 258, line 4: for *Tinsley's*, read *Tinsleys'*

Page 258, line 16: for Jan. 31, 1873, read Jan. 31, 1874.

Page 278, item No. 9: for Sir S. Cockerell, read New York Public Library (Berg Collection)

Page 281: for Aeniad, read Aeneid

Page 291: for Hill, Sir Roland, read Hill, Sir Rowland

INDIAN RIVER JUNIOR COLLEGE LIBRARY
FORT PIERCE, FLORIDA